THE MEDIEVAL MOON

THE
MEDIEVAL MOON

A History of Haunting and Blessing

AYOUSH LAZIKANI

YALE UNIVERSITY PRESS
NEW HAVEN AND LONDON

For information about this and other Yale University Press publications, please contact:
U.S. Office: sales.press@yale.edu yalebooks.com
Europe Office: sales@yaleup.co.uk yalebooks.co.uk

Set in Adobe Caslon Pro by IDSUK (DataConnection) Ltd

Printed and bound in the UK using 100% renewable electricity at CPI Group (UK) Ltd

Library of Congress Control Number: 2025939085
A catalogue record for this book is available from the British Library.
Authorized Representative in the EU: Easy Access System Europe, Mustamäe tee 50, 10621 Tallinn, Estonia, gpsr.requests@easproject.com

ISBN 978-0-300-27828-6

10 9 8 7 6 5 4 3 2 1

• • •

CONTENTS

CONTENTS

CONTENTS

Excerpts from *The Book of Hippocrates* • Excerpts from
The True Knowledge of Astrology • Excerpts from
The Moon of Ptolemy • Excerpts from 'He Who Will
Harken of Wit' • Excerpts from John Metham's
(*c.* 1400–1500) *Book of Destiny* • Excerpts from
'Aries, prima mansio' • Excerpts from 'For
Journeying' • Al-Shushtarī's 'Moon Song I' •
Al-Shushtarī's 'Moon Song II' • Ibn ʿArabī's
'Moon Girl'

NOTE ON QUOTATIONS, IMAGES, AND DATES

With the exception of quotations of Middle English (the English language from approximately 1100 to 1500) and Early Modern English (English from approximately 1500 to 1700), quotations are generally given in translation. This is to allow accessibility for a range of readers. The endnotes do nonetheless provide references to the texts in the original language for readers interested in exploring these further. The system of romanisation used for words from languages that do not use the Roman alphabet is that specified by the Library of Congress: https://www.loc.gov/catdir/cpso/roman.html.

Wherever possible, for images not included in the book, I have directed readers to places where the images are freely available online. There are cases where this has not been possible, however.

For ease of use for English-language readers, I use the dating system of the Gregorian calendar.

· · ·

ACKNOWLEDGEMENTS

There are so many people who inspired and helped the development of this book. I am deeply grateful and indebted to each person, and I will thank each individually. At times in this book, I have mentioned with thanks people who have given me specific information or directed me to particular resources. I am also immensely grateful to the anonymous reviewers of the book manuscript, whose detailed and rigorous feedback was truly invaluable.

Here I will just mention two deeply beloved people without whom this book would not have been possible: my father, Muhydin, and my partner, Will.

INTRODUCTION

We begin this story with two people, from many centuries ago, gazing at the moon (Plates 1 & 2). The first image is from a twelfth-century English manuscript: it shows a scholar inspecting the moon above, hand outstretched as he examines the celestial body. The second image is of a scroll from fifteenth - to sixteenth-century China, during the Ming dynasty, which also depicts a scholar viewing the moon. The scholar is seated in a pavilion as he gazes raptly at the moon. Like these two medieval scholars from different parts of the world, we will contemplate the moon in order to tell its story: or rather, to tell multiple stories. For there is no single medieval 'moon'; we find instead medieval *moons*.

Moons That Haunt and Bless

In the medieval world, moons both haunted and blessed. When they gazed on the moon in the sky, like our two scholars mentioned above, medieval people around the globe saw an object that was at once powerful, fragile, distant, intimate, threatening, tender, unknowable, readable – and sometimes, all this at once. Medieval people had a vast range of ideas about and attitudes towards the moon, which could at various times be a 'she', a 'he', or an 'it'. We can see this complexity everywhere as we read the writings, or look upon the paintings and artefacts, left to us by medieval people. The moon could be all about love, beauty, and gentleness; yet the moon could also be about pain, hatred, and violence. Around the globe, the moon played a vital role in how people made sense of their world, providing a space for handling intricate ideas and intense emotions. The medieval world offers a rich canvas of stories of the moon across languages and cultures in the time spanning the years 700–1600 CE, and this book tells these glimmering tales. We find stories of the moon from many angles: riddles, mysteries, travels, adventures, prophecies, signs, illnesses, cures, sorrows, illusions, loves, embraces, worlds, and tales – and so much more.

As distant as it may have seemed, the moon provided people with opportunities for enriched reflection on earth and life within it. After all, the moon was believed to deeply influence life on earth – from the growth of trees and the movement of seas, to the health and working of human bodies. Additionally, the moon had particular affinities with the 'imagination', as embodied and celebrated in forms of literary and artistic expression. The moon's connection with the literary imagination is a strong and abiding one. As put by Edgar Williams, 'virtually every well-known writer has something to say about the Moon or has used its characteristics to set the scene, whether it is a romantic moonlit situation, a ghostly dark Moonless night or a supernatural full Moon'.[1] Poet Carol Ann Duffy has curated a whole anthology of poems about the moon, asserting that 'the moon has always been, and always will be, the supremely prized image for poets'.[2] As we will see, the moon itself could be considered a kind of riddle. It is an object that invites itself to be deciphered, inspiring a range of complex and at times conflicting responses across cultures.

This Book of Medieval Moons

In this book of moons,[3] I am writing for people for whom the medieval world and its literatures and arts may be unfamiliar. I hope that in telling the stories of medieval moons, I also introduce these readers to the wonderful, mesmerising realm of medieval texts and images. But I also hope that this book may be useful to those with greater famil-iarity with medieval languages, literatures, and arts. I will speak about medieval moons through examining a wide range of international sources – writings alongside visual art. These sources will come from an expansive global range: from Arabic, Chinese, English, French, German, Indian, Italian, Japanese, Korean, Latin, Mayan, Norse, Persian, Polynesian, and Welsh traditions, among others. All these sources together reveal the complex ways people around the world who lived from *c.* 700 to 1600 interpreted and interacted with the moon.

There are many excellent books that provide general histories of the moon, but these do not focus on the medieval period; a deep focus on medieval centuries is a need this book seeks to meet.[4] The reasons for such a gap in existing scholarship are complex. There remains a tendency to overlook the medieval period, seeing it as an irrelevance to later, more modern histories. The now outdated and problematic term 'Dark Ages' also still lingers in approaches to the medieval European world, with the sense that the Renaissance and then the Enlightenment brought much-needed illumination to a dismal and dreary time. But as this book seeks to show, the medieval world was far from unen-lightened; it was a period of immensely rich cultural and intellectual achievements. This book seeks to show this by taking a global perspec-tive. The hope is for this book to acknowledge and celebrate a range of regions, cultures, and traditions that formed the medieval world, not remaining confined to Europe or 'the West'.

Let us outline the journey of this book. This introduction discusses the definitions and methodologies that are at the heart of the following chapters. Chapter 1 then gives an overview of the ways that different medieval people across the world saw the moon. It argues that the moon can be approached as a medieval riddle in a number of ways: it does not have a clearly defined meaning; it is an object that inspires playful approaches to it; and it is associated powerfully with the imagination. Chapter 2 turns to medieval travels to and adventures on the moon. It argues that stories of imagined travel and adventure to and from the moon allowed reflection on the blurred boundaries between 'self' and 'other' across cultures, and that medieval people used these stories as a way to engage with socio-political critique and ideas of exile. Chapter 3 focuses on how the moon was believed to provide prophecies, indicate future occurrences, or act as a sign of divine truth. It argues that the moon played a vital role in how medieval people read hidden meanings in their world. Chapter 4 reflects on the moon's association with illness and healing in medical and spiritual contexts. It argues that the moon was understood to have very visceral connections with human bodies and minds across cultures, and that this in turn richly informed healing practices. Chapter 5 considers how the moon could be a sign of sadness, weakness, and changeability for many medieval people. It argues that medieval people used the moon to reflect on and negotiate painful experiences on earth. Chapter 6 looks at how medieval people associated the moon with love. It argues that the moon provided a vehicle for expressing love and imagining the one who is beloved across cultures, and that this idea is reclaimed by mystics to express divine love. Chapter 7, the epilogue, ends with three further sources that show how medieval people harnessed the moon's imaginative powers to tell stories and create new worlds. This final chapter is followed by an appendix with translations of 'moonbooks' and Sufi poetry, which will be discussed in Chapters 3, 4, and 6.

An Alchemical Reaction with the Past

Of course, surviving writing can also only tell us so much about medieval people, especially given that illiteracy – if narrowly defined as the absence of the skills to read and write text – was much more widespread globally than it is today. In the early medieval British Isles, for example, the production of manuscripts was often the province of monks and nuns. Later medieval centuries in those regions saw an expansion of literacy with the rise of universities and wider manuscript ownership, but texts can still not be seen as a reflection of all segments of the medieval population.[5] There are problems too if we expect art or artefacts to be a mere 'mirror' on the medieval world. Some of the surviving art and artefacts are very luxurious, and cannot be seen as representative of all segments of a given society. There can also be a tendency to simplify the complexity of a 'medieval world'. Just as today there are so many different beliefs and ways of seeing and being, we can find no one sole representative of what everyone of the time thought or felt. What is more, any approach to the medieval period is necessarily partial and limited; we look back to the Middle Ages through the shadows and unclear light caused by the surviving information being fragmentary, biased, or simply lost.

We might playfully say, though, that such limitations are not out of place in a book on the moon. We look back to the Middle Ages as though through moonlight – a light that is imperfect, and meaningfully so. In the words of James Attlee, moonlight is 'alchemical', for 'moonlight does not *reveal*, in the straight-ahead, visual sense; it transforms, changing colours and contours in its shape-shifting light'.[6] An explorer of the past perhaps does the same. With every attempt to reach the long-dead people of previous ages, we are not simply shedding light on them. Rather, we are engaged in a subtle, alchemical interchange with these historical people, each moment of connection creating new colours, new meaning, depending on its participants. The story of this book is just that: an alchemical reaction with the particular sources available to us.

'Medieval' Moons?

The term 'medieval' is used in this book as a shorthand, but it is not without its problems. For a start, it is used here to cover many centuries (700–1600) – a vast length of time. Over nine centuries, it is not surprising to think that profound changes took place, in all aspects of life. It must also be remembered that 'medieval' indicates different periods depending on the region and culture. In Western Europe and in Islamic regions, 'medieval' generally refers to 500–1500 CE. 'Old Russian' or medieval Russian literature stretches from the eleventh to seventeenth centuries. 'Medieval' in a Chinese context starts after the fall of the Han Empire in 220 CE and continues to the fall of the Yuan dynasty in 1368 CE.[7] The time span I have chosen – 700–1600 – allows for a range of different 'medieval' cultures to be brought into contact, while not adhering to strict period boundaries. With an endpoint in 1600, it deliberately pushes into what is more commonly known as the 'early modern' period, in order to challenge the artificial distinction between medieval and modern.

The term 'medieval' itself is Latin for 'Middle Age', and both 'medieval' and 'Middle Ages' betray their own strangeness in this way: they refer to the midpoint between the ancient world and the Renaissance. But this is a demeaning way to look at a period of history, to see it as just a 'midpoint' between two other periods. It degrades those centuries, which had an immense richness of culture and sophistication of thought and development.[8] This then brings us to another crucial problem with the term 'medieval': it is primarily used to describe European cultures, and attempting to apply it unthinkingly to other cultures studied here – Japanese, Chinese, 'Indian', 'Polynesian', Mesoamerican, among others – is very problematic. We should try to listen to each culture with sensitivity, and use terminology generated and born from particular cultures. But I also follow Jonathan Hsy in actively 'disassociating the term "medieval" from an exclusively European framework'.[9] In short, although the term 'medieval' is used in this book, we should remain mindful of the difficulties this nomenclature carries.

Within this broad span of centuries, c. 700–1600, our minds might immediately be drawn towards the end of this period, traditionally defined as the early modern period – to Galileo Galilei (1564–1642) and William Shakespeare (1564–1616). Their role in lunar histories can certainly not be overlooked. Galileo's contributions to scientific understandings of the moon were truly foundational.[10] Shakespeare's plays are replete with moon references and significances, most prominently the moonlit world of *A Midsummer Night's Dream*, which has at least fifty-two mentions of the moon and even has a character called 'Moonshine' in the play-within-the-play (see Act V, scene i). From the very start, Theseus draws attention to the moon ('how slow / This old moon wanes!'), and Hippolyta responds that 'the moon, like to a silver bow / New-bent in heaven, shall behold the night / Of our solemnities' (Act I, scene i). The moon is found aplenty in Shakespeare's other works too. Othello refers to moon-madness: 'It is the very error of the moon; / She comes more nearer earth than she was wont, / And makes men mad' (Act V, scene ii). The witches from *Macbeth* brew a potion 'silver'd in the moon's eclipse' (Act IV, scene i). In *The Tempest*, Caliban is a 'mooncalf', a creature whose birth was impacted by the moon; and Stephano refers to the myth of the 'man in the moon' (Act II, scene i). In *Richard II*, the moon is part of the foreboding prophecy in the skies: 'meteors fright the fixed stars of heaven; / The pale-faced moon looks bloody on the Earth' (Act I, scene iv).[11] But part of the goal of this book is to give attention to lesser-known works in this period of 700–1600 – for the Bard is not the only contributor to moon lore across the centuries. So although Galileo and Shakespeare must be acknowledged, for they are two great contributors to traditions on the moon, they will not form a focal point in this work.

A Global Middle Ages

I am concerned in this book with what has come to be known as the 'Global Middle Ages', a term coined by Geraldine Heng.[12] I have been inspired to look outwards, which for me means beyond the British Isles. There are inevitable problems with this approach. Any attempt to look 'outwards' from Europe places 'the West' and Europe as the centre or the 'norm'. I am also using English to discuss texts from a range of languages and regions, which brings with it its own limitations – not only does the use of English risk homogenising these distinct traditions, but it is also a language with a painful colonialist history. The coverage in this book is certainly not perfect: some traditions receive more attention than others, due to the sources available, and some, such as the Gaelic Irish and Slavonic traditions (to name just two), are not covered.

In taking a global approach, we can highlight two methodologies: an 'avian' perspective and the 'multi-glance'. I have outlined the idea of the 'avian' perspective elsewhere:

> As a bird shifts across multiple regions, a comparative study seeks to become a kind of flight, a cyclical movement that is sensitive to the rhythms of the surrounding environment. It embraces similarity as well as difference; it moves from one to the other with the same flight, but with subtle modulations depending on the region it traverses.[13]

In this model for comparative work, the comparative reader becomes like a bird, gently and sensitively shifting from region to region. I developed this idea for thinking about religious texts in the twelfth and thirteenth centuries, in the Christian and Islamic traditions, but the concept of an 'avian' perspective might be applied to any global approach to the medieval world.

The idea of a dual glance or shift of focus has been developed by Hans Belting. In his work on Renaissance Florence and Baghdad, Belting talks of a *Blickwechsel*:

> Viewing Western pictorial culture through the lens of a different culture remains a daring undertaking, but it may result in seeing both in a better light. My sole aim in taking up this twofold topic and discussing Renaissance and Arab cultures in one and the same context has been to achieve such a *Blickwechsel*, a word that can mean both a 'shift of focus' and an 'exchange of glances'.[14]

As he expands:

> My intention was to place both cultures side by side and on the same level, so that neither would be overvalued or undervalued. This is the only way to limit or contain the inevitable Eurocentrism that long characterized Western views of other cultures.[15]

So a *Blickwechsel*, a shift of focus or exchange of glances, leads to a scholarly gaze that puts distinct traditions on an equal footing, not leading to a focus on one culture at the expense of another. In this book on medieval moons, I am expanding the idea of a dual glance or exchange of glances to a 'multi-glance': a look across many regions, traditions, and cultures – a look across many moons.[16] This is the principal methodology that will inform the coming chapters.

Such a multi-glance is not always about 'influence' – and 'influence' itself can be employed in a problematically Eurocentric way.[17] On the one hand, it is true that some of these cultures are related and influenced one another, including those which we may not think had contact. It is now well acknowledged that Arabic literature and culture had an influence on the West, thanks to the work of Peter Dronke, María Rose Menocal, Karla Mallette, Suzanne Conklin Akbari, and Shazia Jagot, among many others.[18] There was a large-scale translation project that saw the rendition of much Arabic learning on Greek texts into Latin. This included major commentaries on Aristotle (384–322 BCE). Especially significant authors of Arabic who influenced the Latin West include Averroes/Ibn Rushd (d. 1198), Avicenna/Ibn Sīnā (d. 1037), and Abu Nasr al-Fārābī (d. 950).[19] The influence of Arabic texts also crucially impacted astrology and astronomy. The authors from the Islamicate world writing in Arabic who informed and interacted with Latin traditions on astronomy and astrology include the Persian and Jewish Masha'allah (c. 740–815), known as Messahala in Europe; Abu Ma'shar al-Balkhi (787–886); Ahmet Abu Ja'far, known as Abugafarus (writing in the 900s); and Ḥasan ibn al-Haytham, known as Alhazen (c. 965–c. 1040). Also relevant are the Emerald Tablet, originating as part of the *Kitāb Sirr al-Asrār* (*Book of the Secret of Secrets*), adapted as the *Secreta Secretorum* (tenth century onwards), and the Andalusian text *Ghāyat al-Ḥakīm* (*Aim of the Wise*), translated by Alfonso the Wise in 1256.[20] But on the other hand, many other traditions explored in this book did not necessarily directly 'influence' one another, and it is important to say that influence is not a mechanism through which I am approaching a Global Middle Ages – and certainly not the only approach through which a Global Middle Ages can be embraced and studied. This will become clear as our stories of medieval moons unfold.

1

• • •

THE MOON OF RIDDLES
AND MYSTERIES

The Riddle of the Moon

In the Introduction, I suggested that the moon may be considered a kind of riddle in itself. It is perhaps thus very fitting that the moon is the subject or solution of riddles written in the very earliest English that survives ('Old English', the English language from *c.* 410–1066). As we travel to tenth-century England, where the Anglo-Saxons lived, we find that like many of us today, the Anglo-Saxons loved riddles; we have many riddles surviving in a large manuscript of poetry known as the Exeter Book (950–1000), now kept at Exeter Cathedral library. One of these riddles reads as follows:

I saw a creature wondrously
carrying plunder between its horns,
luminous air-container, decorated skilfully,
plunder from the battle-journey to home:

It wanted to build for itself a living-place in the castle,
skilfully set it, if it could.
Then a wondrous creature came over the wall's roof:
it is known to all earth-inhabitants;
it set free then the plunder and drove the
stranger to its home against its will; it departed west from there,
Travelling in enmity, it hastened forth.
Dust rose to the heavens, dew fell on the earth,
night departed forth. Afterwards nobody
knew the journey of that creature.[1]

One possible solution to this riddle – usually labelled as riddle number 29 or riddle number 27 – is believed to be 'moon and sun'; the moon is chased away by the sun, causing day to overtake the night. The 'horns' refer to the shape of the crescent moon. This riddle brings to the surface the baffling complexity of the moon. The moon is powerful yet also vulnerable; it carries its spoils as a mighty warrior but it is finally defeated. The moon remains a stranger, and it retains its many mysteries: the moon acts in a wondrous way ('wundorlice') in how it carries its freight of light, and its movements are unknown once the night has passed. The moon has a will of its own in this riddle. It has the strong desire to build a dwelling place of its own, and it is then driven away against its will. Yet its creativity is of a particular kind. The word used to describe the moon's creativity is 'searu', which is associated with treachery and slyness.[2] It is important too that the light it carries has been taken, even stolen, from the sun – there is the emphasis on the moon as a mere reflection of the sun, as incapable of generating or owning its own light, an idea that keeps recurring in the medieval world. Despite all the moon's skill and power, the composers and audiences of this riddle clearly still saw some negativity and weakness when they considered the moon.[3]

Let us now look at another Old English riddle, riddle number 39, one that has baffled readers and inspired a host of interpretations:

Writings say that the creature is
among humankind much of the time
clear and visible. She has a unique skill,
much greater, when humans know it.
She will seek separately each
of the life-bearers, departs again to travel away.
She is never there another night,
but she must widely travel exile paths,
homeless for a long time; she is not humbled by this.
She has neither foot nor hand, never touches the earth,
does not have either of two eyes,
nor does she have a mouth with which to speak with humanity,
nor has a mind, but writings say
that she is the most wretched of all creatures
that were conceived naturally.
She has neither soul nor life, but she must suffer travels
widely throughout this wonder-world.
She has no blood nor bone; however, she is
a comfort throughout this middle earth to many children.
She has never touched heaven, nor may she travel to Hell,
but she must for a long time dwell in the teachings
of the glory-king. It is long to tell
how her condition of life goes afterwards,
the crooked shape of fates; that is a wondrous thing
to see. True is each
of that which is betokened with words about this creature.
She has no limb, but lives even so.
If you may say the solution straight away,
with true words, say what she is called.

Unlike riddle 29, where 'moon and sun' is an accepted solution, the answer of 'moon' to riddle 39 has been less popular. If we do take one of the solutions of riddle 39 to be 'moon', however, we find the moon presented in arresting ways. First, a number of features of the moon are conveyed in this riddle. The moon is clearly visible, with unique skill ('sundorcræft'). She comes to see life-bearers (humans) but also travels away. She is not present a second night – one of the details that could disprove the solution of the moon, though this could be explained by the moon's changing forms, never to be the same each night. The moon is in exile, but exists in this state proudly. The moon has no recognisable anatomical features, does not make contact with the earth, does not speak, and does not have a mind. Yet she is the most wretched ('earmost') of all creatures created naturally. She does not have a soul nor life but continues to travel. She has not touched heaven – indicative of the moon's liminal position between the earthly and 'spiritual' realms. Her paths would take long to describe, a detail reminiscent of her unknown paths in riddle 29.

In this riddle, the moon's many paradoxes are again evoked. The moon is in a state of sadness, in an exiled state; here again is the sense that the moon is vulnerable. Despite the suggestion that it has no soul or mind, the moon's emotion is made palpable. There is a clear sense that though it may not have human anatomical features, the moon shares human affect and is in many ways human. This recalls riddle 29, with the moon a powerful warrior who is wilful: full of will to build and to create. The moon becomes a surface on which is projected human desire and feeling. The moon is also clearly in a liminal position in riddle 39, touching neither earth nor heaven. This seems a clear gesture towards the idea that the moon exists in the borderland between earthly and celestial realms, and acts as a border-marker between these realms. The verb used is 'hrinan' – it does not touch, or reach, or strike the earth; it shimmers between heaven and earth but remains disengaged somewhat from both, never quite reaching either realm.[4] The moon provides comfort for humanity; it has a level of intimacy with people. But it remains ungraspable, the routes it takes an utter mystery. Beyond these two riddles that reveal the complexity of the moon to medieval audiences, there are other Old English riddles we could consider. Neville Mogford argues that riddle 22 may also be about the moon and tide. Mogford specifically suggests the solution of 'full moon' for the riddle, explaining this through the science of medieval computus.[5] But for now, with the methodology of the multi-glance that looks across cultures and traditions, our focus shifts to another language that explores the moon through riddles.

Old Norse is the language of medieval Iceland and Scandinavia, and it is closely related to Old English. The Norse deity Thor plays an important role in a collection of Old Norse poems known as the *Poetic Edda* from the 1200s. One of these poems, the *Alvíssmál* (*All-Wise's Sayings*), tells the story of Thor intercepting a dwarf (a supernatural creature from Germanic legend) who intends to marry Thor's daughter. Thor engages the dwarf in many games, sneakily wanting to keep him occupied until the sun comes out and turns him into stone. One of the questions Thor asks is 'what is the moon called?':

> Tell me this, All-Wise – I think that
> you know, dwarf, all the history of living things:
> what is the moon, which men see,
> called in each world.[6]

The dwarf replies as follows:

> 'Moon' it's called by humanity,
> and 'Ball' it's called by the gods.
> It's called the 'Wheel' in Hell,

It's called the 'Goer' by the giants,
it's called the 'Shiner' by the dwarfs,
it's called by the elves the 'Counter of Years'.[7]

Each of these names for the moon is a mini-riddle: if we were just told the 'Wheel', we would not know immediately what it is referring to. In the dwarf's mini-riddles, we get a glimpse of the complexity of the moon when seen from different angles, being granted a different name depending on the viewer. Its physical form and movement are revealed in these words, as well as its functions and values: for instance, in providing light or measuring time. So the moon is a central solution to various Old English and Old Norse riddles – a very apt medium given how much of a riddle the moon itself is. Let us now consider further how various medieval people from around the world understood the moon.

The Moon as Planet

Everywhere in medieval literature, authors and scribes emphasise our riddlic moon as a glistening part of the cosmos. In a thirteenth-century *Life* of St Margaret in English, the saint imagines the whole of the Creation, with the moon as a fundamental part of it. As she says in a prayer to God:

The sunne reccheth hire rune withuten euch reste; the mone ant te steorren the walketh bi the lufte ne stutteth ne ne studegith, ah sturieth áá mare, ne nohwider of the wei thet Tu havest iwraht ham ne wrencheth ha neavre.

(The sun goes on her course without any rest; the moon and the stars which move through the air neither stay nor stop, but stir evermore, nor do they ever turn away anywhere from the way that You have wrought for them.)[8]

In both the Christian West and the Islamicate regions, the moon was understood to be a planet. It was the closest planet to the earth, followed by Mercury, Venus, the sun, Mars, Jupiter, and Saturn.[9] The 'planet' of the moon was said to move through a concentric sphere around the earth. In his now classic work *The Discarded Image*, C.S. Lewis (of Narnia fame) describes the universe in the medieval imagination:

> The central (and spherical) Earth is surrounded by a series of hollow and transparent globes, one above the other, and each of course larger than the one below. These are the 'spheres', 'heavens', or (sometimes) 'elements'. Fixed in each of the first seven spheres is one luminous body. Starting from Earth, the order is the Moon, Mercury, Venus, the Sun, Mars, Jupiter and Saturn; the 'seven planets'. Beyond the sphere of Saturn is the *Stellatum*, to which belong all those stars that we still call 'fixed' because their positions relative to one another are, unlike those of the planets, invariable. Beyond the *Stellatum* there is a sphere called the First Movable or *Primum Mobile*. This, since it carries no luminous body, gives no evidence of itself to our senses; its existence was inferred to account for the motions of all the others.[10]

This is a helpful summary of how medieval people imagined the universe. Such an understanding of the universe came especially from second-century Alexandrine scholar Ptolemy. The works of Ptolemy had an unparalleled influence on medieval astronomy in the Christian and Islamicate world, particularly his *Almagest* and *Tetrabiblos*. The *Tetrabiblos* was translated into Latin from Arabic by Plato of Tivoli in 1138, and the *Almagest* was translated into Latin from Arabic by Gerard of Cremona in 1176.[11] The spheres are shown in diagrams by scholar John of Sacrobosco (*c.* 1195–1256); we will return to John of Sacrobosco in Chapter 5.[12] We can also see an illustration of the moon as a planet in a bowl from Iran, dating to the late twelfth to early thirteenth centuries (Plate 3). It shows the sun encircled by all the planets, including the moon, personified as deities.

The Moon's Appearance and Qualities

For many medieval minds, the moon was a planet. But what did it look like, what was it made from, and what qualities was it associated with? There was a great deal of interest in why the moon looks the way it does. The French text *Romance of the Rose* is a complex allegorical tale about love, court, and desire. It was started by Guillaume de Lorris (*c.* 1200–*c.* 1240), and continued by Jean de Meun (*c.* 1240–*c.* 1305). The text was translated into English, and part of this translation may have been by poet Geoffrey Chaucer (*c.* 1343–1400). In the continuation of the French text by Jean de Meun, there is this reflection on the moon's appearance:

> People think that the moon is not quite clean and pure, because it looks dark in places, but it is because of its double nature that it sometimes looks dense and murky: one part of it shines but not the other, because it is both clear and opaque. Its light is extinguished because the clear part of its substance cannot reflect the rays of the sun that shine upon it; instead they pass straight through it. But the opaque part is luminous, because it is resistant to the rays and thus takes its light from them.[13]

The author then continues to explain this through optical mechanics; this consideration of the moon's appearance is informed by astronomical, astrological, and optical learning. The passage also presents the moon as inherently double-natured. In being both luminous and dark, the moon is both known and unknown, reachable and unreachable; the moon is at once lucid and obscured in mystery.

Medieval people often wondered if they saw some kind of wondrous creature in the moon. As *The Romance of the Rose* says on the 'dark part of the moon':

> Now the dark part of the moon represents the figure of a most marvellous beast: it is that of a serpent whose head is always bent towards the west, while its tail points to the east. On its back it bears a standing tree, which spreads its branches towards the east but inverts them as it does so. On the underside of the branches is a man, leaning on his arms, who has pointed both his feet and his thighs towards the west: this is what their appearance suggests.[14]

This description of the creature is based on Albertus Magnus' (*c.* 1193–1280) *De celo et mundo* (*On the Heavens and the World*, ii. 3, 8).[15] In another text known as *Meteorologica*, the creature is a lion.[16] Such a detailed account of the appearance of the moon adds to its unknowability and unreachability, yet it also suggests a creature that can be dissected cognitively – a creature that can be described and known.

A description of the moon's dark spots might also be found in Dante Alighieri's (*c.* 1265–1321) *Paradiso*. Dante's Paradise has several spheres, of which the moon is the outermost. Dante and Beatrice are in the Heaven of the Moon in Canto 2 of the *Paradiso*. He alludes to humans believing the dark spots of the moon to be Cain, the first murderer in history:

> Tell me what those dark signs are that mark
> the body of the moon? Down there on earth
> some folk are led by these to speak of Cain.[17]

Dante first explains the dark spots as coming from density or rarity of parts of the moon. This is a subject also addressed in his treatise known as the *Convivio* (2.13.9): and it is an idea stemming ultimately from Andalusian thinker Averroes.[18] But Beatrice in the *Paradiso* corrects this reading, emphasising that in fact the dark spots of the moon are not caused by difference in material.

The moon was also associated with moistness and cold. We find this witnessed in so many texts across languages, including one in Welsh – a Welsh rendition of *The Compost of Ptholomeus, Prynce of Astronomye* (1532), where the moon is distinguished from the planet Jupiter:

> When you see that the Moon is in a conjunction with the planet Jupiter within the sign of Aries (the planet being warm and damp, and the sign being warm and dry, and the Moon being cold and wet), in this conjunction the sign prevails over the planet: because of the planet's warmth which of its own nature has the dampness of the air. And the warmth of the sign, which is of the quality of fire, that warmth heats up the Moon's coldness, and makes the Moon's liquid dry and makes the dampness of the planet dry, and in this manner Aries prevails.[19]

Further information about the moon and its qualities may be found in the work of Baccio Baldini (*c.* 1436–1487), an Italian craftsman. In one image, he shows us a busy picture with the moon at the top represented as a woman in a chariot, ruling over all. The Italian text then tells us that the moon is a feminine planet in the first heaven, and that the moon is cold, moist, and phlegmatic. The text also tells us that the moon has friendship with Jupiter but enmity with Mars, and that her house is the sign of Cancer.[20]

There are also medieval cases of unique and astonishing sightings of the moon. Gervase of Canterbury (*c.* 1141–*c.* 1210) describes a strange appearance of the moon in the year 1178:

For the new moon was bright, [and] in accordance with its newness, had its horns projecting towards the east; and behold, suddenly the upper horn divided into two. From the middle of this division sprang a burning torch, throwing out flames, embers, and sparks. Meanwhile the body of the moon, which was lower, twisted up as though in anxiety, and to use the words of those who reported this to me, what they saw with their own eyes, the moon trembled like a stricken snake.[21]

Gervase expands on this startling wriggling and writhing of the moon:

After this it returned to its proper state. This fluctuation repeated twelve times or more, that is to say, that the fire kept up various projections as mentioned above and returned once more to its former state. After these fluctuations, from horn to horn, that is to say along its length, it became therefore semi-dark.[22]

Scholars Giles E.M. Gasper and Brian K. Tanner suggest that this striking movement of the moon is indicative of 'atmospheric turbulence'.[23] Beyond the scientific explanation, I am interested both in how the moon here has a compelling visual impact on the onlookers – invading their lives and marking them indelibly with itself – and in how it takes on emotional qualities. The body of the moon 'twisted up as though in anxiety': the moon is given the capacity to feel anxiety, the capacity indeed to feel. There is a shared anxiety, here, between the startled onlookers and the moon's own anxious shaking.

Influencing Earth

The moon was not seen as a passive object wandering aimlessly in the sky. It was believed to exert a tremendous influence on earth. Perhaps for medieval people it was not quite the 'shepherd' it is in Sumerian tradition, but it was certainly understood to affect and nurture the earth to a profound degree.[24] There are many sources that attest to this emphasis on the moon's influence, including the work of Ælfric of Eynsham (b. c. 955). Ælfric was an Anglo-Saxon monk. He wrote many texts, including lives of saints and sermons or homilies, in both Latin and English. The moon is a prominent subject in his work. In his collection of sermons known as the *Catholic Homilies*, he reflects on how the moon is in harmony with the entirety of Creation:

> It is [. . .] natural that in created things, each physical creatur which the earth brings forth is fuller and stronger in the full moon than in the waning. So also trees if they are hewn in the full moon are harder and more long-lasting for building and strongest if they are worked on while without sap. This is not divination but is a natural thing through creation. So also the sea wondrously agrees with the circuit of the moon; just as they are companions in growth and in waning, and just as the moon arises four points [of an hour] later daily, so the sea always flows four points later.[25]

Ælfric opposes the use of divination through the moon, which is why he wants to make clear that his comments do not pertain to divination.[26] Instead, in this passage, he demonstrates clearly the ways in which the moon impacts the natural world, especially the tides and the trees. Ælfric is drawing here from the work of the Venerable Bede (c. 672–735), another English monk and scholar, who was also in turn drawing on other authors.[27] Bede traces many influences of the moon on earth. The moon is above all moisturising:

> The Moon herself is said to abound in dew. Consequently, they say that when the night is clear and the Moon full, a greater quantity of dew bathes the lilies. Many who sleep in the open air claim that the more moonlight there is, the more dampness collects upon their head.[28]

The moon also causes oysters to be larger, and impacts the insides of trees:

> One should take particular note that the trees from which sailing ships are to be fashioned, or any public works to be constructed, be felled between the fifteenth day of the Moon and the twenty-second. For timber felled during these eight days will remain immune from rot, but wood felled on the other days will turn to dust within a year, consumed from within by the destructive action of worms.[29]

Bede goes on to describe 'the great fellowship that exists between the ocean and the course of the Moon':[30]

> The sea reflects the course of the Moon not only by sharing its comings and goings, but also by a certain augmenting and diminishing of its size, so that the tide recurs not only at a later time than it did yesterday, but also to a greater or lesser extent.[31]

The influence of the moon on earth is further testified in the bestiary tradition. Bestiaries were compendia of various animals, plants, and stones, with each entry accompanied by a description and at times an allegorical interpretation.[32] In the Aberdeen Bestiary (Aberdeen University Library MS 24) dated to *c.* 1200, for example, apes are happy at the new moon but sad at the moon's waning.[33] Echoing Bede, the compiler says that enclosed sea creatures and shellfish grow when the moon is waxing.[34] And we are also told that the livers of mice grow bigger in the waxing moon, a phenomenon compared to the rhythms of the tide according to the moon's changing phases.[35]

Moving forward in history, we find another text that argues for the influence of the moon on earth and the people within it. This is the fantastical travel narrative from the fourteenth century known as *The Book of John Mandeville*, which has a highly complex textual history: it is, in the words of editors Tamarah Kohanski and C. David Benson, a 'thoroughly unstable work'.[36] For a start, it exists in multiple languages. There are three traditions from the original French location. And then each tradition has numerous manuscripts which can be collected into different subgroups. But in a number of versions of *The Book of John Mandeville*, the narrator highlights a distinction between those that live under the influence of Saturn and those that live under the influence of the moon.

Those in 'India' – though Mandeville's conception of India is not an accurate reflection of India as known today – live under the influence of the planet Saturn. As put in a fifteenth-century English version of the text:

they dwelleth under a planete that men clepith Saturne, and that planete maketh his torn by the 12 signes in a monthe.

(they dwell under a planet that men call Saturn, and that planet makes its orbit through the twelve signs in a month.)

Such slow movement means that those that live under Saturn's influence are not very active, according to Mandeville:

for Saturne is of so late steryng, therefore men that dwelleth under hym and that clymate haveth no good wyll to mech styryng aboute.

(because Saturn is of so slow stirring, [therefore] men that dwell under it and that climate have no good will to much stirring about.)

This is all different in 'our country', says the Mandeville-speaker. In 'Mandeville's' country, people are under the influence of the moon:

we beth in a clymate that is of the mone and of leyght styryng, and
that is the planete of way.

(we are in a climate that is of the moon and of nimble movement, and that is the planet of travel.)

As such, the people of Mandeville's country are inclined to much
movement and desire for travel:

therefore hit gyveth us wyll to be moch steryng and to go into
diverse contreis of the worlde, for hit passeth aboute the worlde
more leyghtlych than another planete.

(therefore it gives us the will to move much more and go into
diverse countries in the world, for it passes around the world more
nimbly than any other planet.)

So the moon, explains Mandeville, has a quicker orbit than any other
planet, and this impacts people's capacity for movement. Two elements
in particular might be highlighted here. First is the clear influence that
the moon is said to have on the temperament and activity of those on
earth. Second, the moon causes in particular an impulse to move and
stir. It does not invite stillness; its influence is all about progress and
transformation.

The moon's role in influencing earth is attested further through the
wealth of surviving medieval equipment that was used to pinpoint the
exact position of the moon, vital for all sorts of scientific endeavours.
This equipment included the astronomical instrument known as the
astrolabe. The word derived from French and Latin, ultimately from
Greek, with the meaning of 'star-catching' or 'star-catcher'.[37] An
astrolabe showed the position of heavenly bodies and allowed the user
to make a number of astronomical calculations. Chaucer himself wrote
a treatise for his son, 'little Lewis', on how to use astrolabes. He had

clearly gifted the boy an astrolabe and provided the treatise as a companion for this new present:

> Lyte Lowys my sone, I aperceyve wel by certeyne evydences thyn abilite to lerne sciences touching nombres and proporciouns; and as wel considre I thy besy praier in special to lerne the tretys of the Astrelabie. [. . .] therefore have I yeven the a suffisant astrolabie as for our orizonte, compowned after the latitude of Oxenforde; upon which, by mediacioun of this litel tretys, I purpose to teche the a certein nombre of conclusions aperteynyng to the same instrument. [. . .] This tretis, divided in 5 parties, wol I shewe the under full light reules and naked words in Englissh, for Latyn canst thou yit but small, my litel sone.[38]
>
> (Little Lewis my son, I perceive well by certain evidences your ability to learn sciences relating to numbers and proportions; and as well consider I your intent desire in particular to learn the treatise of the Astrolabe. [. . .] Therefore I have given you a sufficient astrolabe for our horizon, computed according to the latitude of Oxford. Through which, by means of this little treatise, I aim to teach you a certain number of conclusions pertaining to the same instrument. [. . .] This treatise, divided in five parts, will I show you with very light rules and clear words in English, for you know still a small amount of Latin, my little son.)[39]

Another important instrument was the volvelle, a word which comes from the Latin *volvere*, to turn.[40] A volvelle is a tool with moving discs for ascertaining the position of the moon and the sun. The Ashmolean Museum at Oxford houses a lunar volvelle, found along with sundials and a clock-watch, from Munich, *c.* 1580.[41] One is furthermore found on fol. 25r of a manuscript housed at the Bodleian Library, Oxford: MS Ashmole 370.[42] The National Library of Wales also houses a manuscript containing a lunar volvelle, dating to 1488–9.[43] This manuscript seems to have been written by Gutyn Owain, and also contains a calendar, a treatise on urine, a *Life* of St Martin, and a history from Adam to 'Asclopitotus'. This demonstrates how astronomical and astrological learning existed alongside medical and biblical learning, all discourses interflowing.

When thinking about the influence of the moon on earth, there is also the question of alchemy, because the moon played an important role in the symbolism of alchemy: the turning of base metals into gold. As observed by Johannes Fabricius, alchemical and astrological symbolisms go hand in hand.[44] In alchemical models, the moon was associated with silver – we may remember here *Macbeth*'s witches' potion – while the sun was associated with gold.[45] That is why *The Canon's Yeoman's Tale*, one of Chaucer's *Canterbury Tales* which focuses on alchemy, has this adage:[46]

Sol gold is, and Luna silver we insist,
Mars iren, Mercurie quyksilver we clepe,
Saturnus leed, and Juppiter is tyn,
And Venus coper, by my fader kyn!
(Sun gold is, and the Moon silver we insist,
Mars iron, Mercury quicksilver we call,
Saturn lead, and Jupiter is tin,
And Venus copper, by my father's kin!)

Deities

We have asked *what* the moon is, but perhaps a more pertinent question would be *who* the moon is – for the moon is frequently imagined by medieval people as a deity, or a human being who has ascended to the heavens. An illustration in Oxford, Bodleian Library, MS Bodley 614, the manuscript we witnessed above with a scholar observing the moon, depicts the sun and moon as pagan gods, each in their chariot. The sun is on a red background at the top of the page, wearing a crown and in a chariot drawn by horses. The moon is on the bottom half of the page, on a blue background, in a chariot drawn by oxen and holding a lunar orb (fol. 17v). Another illustration in this manuscript shows the sun in the centre surrounded by planets, each in a roundel of its own. All are personified as pagan gods and goddesses. The sun in the central roundel is the largest, on a blue background, holding two flaming torches and wearing a crown. At the top of the page are Mars, Saturn, and Jupiter; at the bottom are Venus, Luna (the moon), and Mercury. The image of Luna shows her wearing a crescent moon on top of her head (fol. 23r).

The moon is at times invoked in medieval texts to denote such a pagan deity. In an early-thirteenth-century version of the story of the *Life* of St Katherine/Catherine, linked to the *Life* of St Margaret mentioned above, there is this mention of the moon:

The feont (the findeth euch uvel), bimong alle hise crokinde creftes, with neaver an ne kecheth he creftiluker cang men, ne leadeth to unbileave then thet he maketh men – thet ahten to wite wel thet ha beoth biyetene ant iborene ant ibroht forth thurh the heovenliche Feader – to makie swucche maumez of treo other of stan other (thurh mare meadschipe) of gold other of seolver, ant yeoven ham misliche nomen, of sunne other of mone, of wind ant wude ant weattres, ant hersumeth ant wurthgith as thah ha godes weren.[47]

(The fiend, who invented every evil, among all his crooked crafts, with none does he ever craftily catch foolish men, nor leads them to unbelief, than that he makes men – who ought to know well that they are begotten and born and brought forth through the heavenly father – to make such idols of tree or of stone or (through more absurdity) of gold or of silver, and give them various names, of sun or of moon, of wind and wood and waters, and praise and worship them as though they were gods.)[48]

In this passage from the *Life* of St Katherine/Catherine, 'moon' is one of the names given to the idols prayed to as though they were gods. As a Christian saint's life, this text views the non-Christian gods as mere 'idols' which are false, and dismisses all who believe in the idols as absurd and foolish. A 'moon god' is one such example of foolishness in the view of the anonymous author of this text.

But there are much more positive, celebratory identifications of the moon with a deity. In the Old Norse *Prose Edda*, it is the deity Mani who controls the moon's movements and phases.[49] This account is given of Mani's origins: a man named Mundilfari had two children; the son was named Moon (Mani) and the daughter Sun (Sol). Enraged by what they perceived as arrogance, the gods took up the children and positioned them in the skies.[50] In Polynesian traditions, there is the god Hinauri.[51] In traditions of South Asia there is Chandra, the god of the moon. As one artistic example, we find Chandra depicted in a painting on a cloth mandala from Nepal in the late fourteenth and early fifteenth centuries, with the moon god seated regally.[52] This is now housed at the Metropolitan Museum of Art.

Then there is the moon deity in the Mayan text *Popol Vuh*, an important epic associated with the K'iche' people (one Mayan group), first written down in the sixteenth century. In this story, the two hero twins, Hunahpu and Xbalanque, become the sun and the moon: 'And then the two boys ascended straight on into the sky, and the sun belongs to one and the moon to the other. When it became light within the sky, on the face of the earth, they were there in the sky.'[53]

The moon was also profoundly important to the Inca: it was the pinnacle of the 'female side of the Inca cosmos'.[54] She had immense power, and was named a 'queen':

The Moon was the sister and wife of the Sun, and Ilia Tecce [Viracocha] has given her part of his divinity, and made her mistress over the sea and winds, over the queens and princesses, and over the process in which women give birth; and she is queen of the sky. They called the Moon 'Coya', which means queen.[55]

The moon was fashioned like a woman in Inca statues,[56] and was further associated with the tools used by women; there was the threat that spindles and looms would turn into snakes, bears, and tigers during an eclipse.[57]

In the Greco-Roman tradition, a goddess associated with the moon is known as Diana (Roman) or Artemis (Greek). She also has a myriad of other names or associated deities, including Cynthia, Latone, Lucina, Luna, Phoebe, Proserpina, and Selene.[58] Diana is depicted countless times in medieval European art, literature, and music. She is a central presence in, for example, Chaucer's *Knight's Tale*, and Jacqueline de Weever suggests three dimensions to Diana present for Chaucer in this poem: Diana of the grove (Diana Nemorensis), goddess of childbirth (Diana Lucina), and the chaste hunter.[59]

In *The Knight's Tale*, we are treated to a detailed view of Diana's temple. Painted on the walls are scenes of Diana's terrible power and vengeance: she turns Callisto into a bear and then the North Star, she punishes Actaeon by turning him into a hart, and she releases the Calydonian boar to ravage the land in punishment; this latter story is of significance to Chaucer's *Troilus and Criseyde* as well.[60] We are given a close-up portrayal of the goddess:

This goddesse on an hert ful hye seet,
With smale houndes al aboute hir feet,
And undernethe hir feet she hadde a moone –
Wexynge it was and sholde wanye soone.

In gaude grene hir statue clothed was,
With bowe in honde and arwes in a cas.
Hir eyen caste she ful lowe adoun
Ther Pluto hath his derke regioun.[61]
(This goddess sat very high on a hart,
With small hounds all about her feet,
And underneath her feet she had a moon –
It was waxing and should wane soon.
In yellowish green her statue was clothed,
With bow in hand and arrows in a quiver.
She cast her eyes down full low
Where Pluto has his dark region.)

This is a multidimensional portrayal of the goddess. She is a hunter and associated with the woods, with the hart, hounds, bow, and arrows; she is also associated with Proserpina of the underworld, for she looks down to Pluto's gloomy realm below. Crucially for us, we see her with a waxing moon beneath her feet (lines 2077–8), perhaps echoic of the biblical verse Revelation 12:1, which we will encounter in Chapter 5. Earlier portrayals of Selene depicted her with a crescent moon adorning her head, and the moon beneath the feet is almost an inversion of such an image.[62] It is also notable that the moon beneath the feet of Chaucer's Diana is waxing and soon to be waning – we see the moon in transition, in its shifting state, hinting at inconstancy and change. The goddess herself later appears when the young girl Emelye prays to her (line 2296 onwards), but the goddess cruelly ignores her prayer and offers her no comfort. Diana is a goddess of harshness but also fecundity – in *The Knight's Tale* we see a pregnant woman pray to her – and immense power.

Such is Diana in *The Knight's Tale*. But there is another powerful moon goddess to rival her, and that is the Chinese figure of Chang'e, who we will encounter again in the following chapter. Chang'e is said to have drunk an elixir of immortality, but was doomed to remain separated from her husband forever. Her husband was the archer who shot down nine of the ten suns.[63] In one hanging scroll (ink and colour on paper), now found at the Metropolitan Museum of Art, we have an image of Chang'e radiating strength and grace. It dates to the Ming dynasty (1368–1644).[64] She is wearing a flowing dress and appears almost to levitate in her lightness and powerful beauty. We also see her with leaves around her person. The colours are soft blues and soft reds, with black lining to her garment. Her hair is tied up with a red ribbon. The image was perhaps painted by Tang Yin (1470–1524); the scroll also includes a poem by him, reading as follows:

> She was long ago a resident of the Moon Palace,
> Where phoenixes and cranes gathered and embroidered
> banners fluttered in heavenly fragrance.
> Chang'e, in love with the gifted scholar,
> Breaks off [for him] the topmost branch of the cassia tree.[65]

We witness Chang'e here among symbolically potent phoenixes and cranes, both associated with immortality.[66] The poetic act of removing the top branch of the cassia tree is also suggestive of the moon's potent, far-reaching luminescence. In fact, cassia trees appear frequently in Chinese moon scenes.[67] Another depiction of Chang'e may be seen in a statue made of bronze and gold plating, also dating to the Ming dynasty (c. 1600). Here she is again seen with a flowing dress and hair tied up, and she holds a rabbit or hare – the latter being a perennial inhabitant of the moon.[68]

A painting on a fan also shows Chang'e; this painting dates to 1350–1400 and is housed at the Art Institute of Chicago.[69] It uses ink and colour on silk material, with soft pinks and blue-greens (Plate 4). The fan shows Chang'e standing on rocky ground, poised beneath a tree. The tree gently bows down and almost embraces her as she stands. To Chang'e's left is a full moon, replete among the clouds. We see Chang'e again as an epitome of feminine strength and beauty, commanding the landscape that holds her.

• • •

And so we come to the end of the first chapter in this alchemical encounter with the past. The moon is its own riddle, full of enigmas to be decoded, and it is very apt that it is the solution to riddles in Old English and Old Norse. These riddles reveal the full complexity of the moon, replete as it is with contradictions and paradoxes: powerful yet vulnerable; near yet distant; unknowable yet emotionally charged. We have also begun to trace medieval understandings of the moon: for many it was believed to be a planet, associated with coldness, moistness, and the phlegmatic humour. It was a planet that was perceived to have extraordinary influence on the earth below it. We have also dwelt with two key deities personifying the moon, among many others throughout the medieval world: the Greco-Roman Diana and the Chinese Chang'e. Now this book turns to the moon of travels and adventures.

2
· · ·
THE MOON OF TRAVELS AND ADVENTURES

'Skirts of Rainbow, Feather Coats' (*Nichang yuyi*) is a traditional piece of Chinese music and dance from the Tang dynasty (618–907). The legend goes that Emperor Xuanzong (r. 712–756) travelled to the moon after an order from the Chinese goddess Chang'e, and there received his inspiration to compose this piece. Encountering the music on the moon, he wrote it down from memory when he awoke.[1] Nathaniel Isaacson even calls the dance a 'lunarian serenade'.[2] We encountered Chang'e at the end of Chapter 1: she was once a mortal woman, but she drank an elixir of immortality.

The legend of Emperor Xuanzong's journey to the moon forms an apt beginning to this second chapter in many ways. It shows that the moon is a realm of creation, where imagination and inspiration swirl together. Intimately associated as it is with the imagination, the moon engenders poetry, music, and dance. The moon is not only an object pausing inertly as creators gaze upon it; the moon itself also contributes to the creative process. In Chapter 1, we saw that Dante, that great supernatural traveller, visits the moon. But he and Xuanzong are certainly not the only ones. Throughout the broad medieval period, there were moon-people who came down to earthlings, as well as human beings who flew to the moon – whether to stay or just to visit. Edgar Williams observes a 'split' in 'science fiction' tales through the ages, between 'those where the Moon is seen as a harsh colonial outpost where strange things happen, such as alien encounters, and those where the Moon provides an environment for the founding of new utopian societies'.[3] I would add to this that in the medieval world, the moon's otherness and familiarity might be found within a single text – the 'foreign' and the domestic, the other and the self, might coexist and struggle within a single work. Even though, or sometimes because, it seems an icy wasteland, the moon offers rich opportunity for travel, adventure, and discovery.

With all the moon's wondrous creative potential, in this chapter we focus on journeys to and from the moon, using the 'multi-glance' outlined in the Introduction: a perspective that shifts across cultures and treats them with equal weight. We will begin, though, not with a journey to the moon itself, but with a journey shaped and supported by moon-light: the diary of Japanese woman Abutsu (c. 1225–1283). We will then turn to the legend of a 'man in the moon', attested in English, German, and Dutch sources, and we will dwell in particular on a comical English poem in which a helpful human tries to aid the woebegone man in the moon, but soon grows weary when the moon-man does not reply. Then we will fly with a knight to the moon in the sixteenth-century Italian epic *Orlando furioso*. Finally, we will look at the Japanese *Tale of the Bamboo Cutter*, where the journey is the other way – we have a radiant and special moon-dweller come to live on earth for a time, transforming her human carers and friends forever. In all these stories, the moon is both home and foreign territory. It is also a place of miraculous discovery and creation.

A Brief Interlude: Lucian of Samosata

Before we turn to the medieval stories, it is important to note that medieval people were not the first to imagine travelling to the moon. An early model is that of the ancient Greek and Syrian author Lucian of Samosata (b. *c.* 125). Travelling to the moon forms a key storyline in Lucian's *True Story* (160 CE). In this narrative, Greek explorers find themselves on the moon after a storm in which they are blown upwards. On the moon, they discover beings called Moonites. These Moonites are at war with the Sunites, the inhabitants of the Sun – they are warring over who will own the morning star. The Sunites force the Moonites into a peace treaty after effecting a kind of eclipse of the moon. Endymion, the king of the moon, invites the Greek explorers to stay, but they decide to leave. This is a story that deals with the search for truth and epistemological certainty. It grapples with the attempts to ascertain what is reality and what is fiction while using our own limited frameworks of perception and knowledge. This text also raises compelling questions about gender performance and gender roles, for on the moon there are no women: the role of 'wife' is taken on by young men, who procreate through their calf muscles. The moon becomes a site on which to explore these pressing questions of identity and truth. Lucian has provided us with an intriguing pre-medieval model for travelling to the moon, but now we turn to the medieval centuries.[4]

A Japanese Woman's Diary

Abutsu was a Japanese author and nun. Her works include the *Utatane* (*Fitful Slumbers*), which describes the end of a relationship between a woman and a man of higher status, and the woman's subsequent escape to a nunnery, and *Izayoi nikki* (*Diary of the Sixteenth-Night Moon/Diary of the Waning Moon*), which describes her journey from present-day Kyoto to Kamakura.[5] Abutsu was born into the nobility, belonging with courtiers of a high status who lived in present-day Kyoto, and she married a highly regarded poet. Abutsu worked in the court of Princess Ankamon-in. As Christina Laffin affirms, 'Compared with many medieval women, she led a privileged life, yet she also suffered through hardships, including self-imposed exile at a nunnery and destitution as a single mother.'[6]

Izayoi nikki is the work by Abutsu with which we are concerned. The name *izayoi* is a poetic label for the night of the sixteenth moon and that day. The *Diary of the Sixteenth-Night Moon/Diary of the Waning Moon* tells of Abutsu's travels and encounters. Abutsu says that she was encouraged to go on her trip through the waning moon (*izayou tsuki*); here she is playing with a literary idea or tradition.[7] The text is divided into four parts. The first part explains why Abutsu travelled from Kyoto to Kamakura; the second gives details of her travels; the third relays Abutsu's correspondence; and the fourth is a *chōka* or *nagauta*, a long poem.[8] The *Izayoi nikki* provides information about Abutsu's life, though much of this may be a literary construct.[9] For Laffin, *Izayoi nikki* shows Abutsu as a powerful legal interlocutor, as so much of the text is concerned with legalistic issues.[10] James A. Wren, in reference to the sociohistorical factors that shape the work, also views Abutsu as a strong and 'angry' woman.[11] We will focus here not on the legal complexities of the text but rather on what role the moon plays in Abutsu's travel diary.

Izayoi nikki is full of powerful vignettes of the moon and its appearance during this medieval woman's travels. Abutsu describes the beginning of her journey as follows: 'I decided to forget my countless fears, abandon all thought of myself, and go forth abruptly, enticed by the waning moon' (305–6).[12] On the seventeenth night, she recounts: 'The moon came out, and the pine trees, standing in rows on the mountain tops, were to be seen each separately [silhouetted]. It was most delightful' (313). Then, on the twenty-second dawn, she says she travels 'in the light of the moon of dawn' (323), using the word *ariake*, meaning 'the moon still shining at dawn during the second half of the lunar month' (323 n. 171). Her journey continues to be punctuated with sights of the moon, as when she says: 'At dawn when I awoke and looked forth, [I saw that] the moon had come out' (328). The moon accompanies her at every turn; it supports each step of her journey. The moon also serves a key chronometric function for Abutsu. She measures her trip through the moon ('About the beginning of the fourth moon', 353; 'not heard a cuckoo by the fifth moon', 354; 'the end of the fourth moon came', 355; 'On the twentieth of the eighth moon', 358–9).

But most potent of all, Abutsu even recalls poems as she travels, and they are full of the moon and its light: 'The moonlight which, weeping, weeping, I left behind me' (330–1). This is a poem by Fujiwara no Sadaie (1162–1241) (331 n. 201). Here there is a close emotional bond between moon and viewer: the seeping moonlight is like flooding tears. Another poem she recalls shows a less clear moon touching her life: 'Though the hazy moon is [that of] the sky of the capital, / Waves I have never heard before keep rolling in night after night' (348). And then there is this poem: 'Let us compare them – the spring moon in the mists / And my beclouded heart are similar rights' (351). This again demonstrates emotional closeness between moon and viewer: there is a stark comparison between the 'spring moon' and the 'beclouded heart'. At a later point in the diary she says, 'Alone I have gazed simply at the moon all night through', and recites this poem: 'The moonlight, clouded over by my tears of longing' (362). Again, moonlight and tears become joined: drops of emotion in brine and in light; the human and the lunar weeping together. Her gazing at the moon throughout the night demonstrates the moon's importance to her as well as the intimacy they share.

In Abutsu's text, the moon appears as an intimate companion. The moon accompanies Abutsu on these long travels and in her potent reflections on the events and relationships of her life. The moon-as-companion is a powerful image; it conjures up the sense of a human being travelling with the moon, step by step, with the moon as a kind of partner in the journeys we have to undertake in this life. Throughout *Diary of the Waning Moon*, a close emotional bond is formed between the moon and the humans who gaze upon it. Abutsu is enthralled when gazing at it, and her heart and her weeping are forever entwined with the moonlight. Abutsu's writing brings the moon that bit closer, rendering it psychologically much more present, and emotionally much more relatable to us.

Abutsu is of course not alone among medieval people in calling on the moon as an intimate companion. In the next chapter, we will witness Chaucer's character Troilus pouring out his anguish to the listening moon. Chinese poet Du Fu (712–770) imagines his wife watching the moon alone and conceptualises a time when they will be together in the caressing moonlight.[13] This is true also for Chinese poet Su Tung-P'o (1037–1101): he longs for the moon to accept him and declares that since he has wine, moon, and flowers he needs nobody else to accompany him while drinking.[14] Like Troilus and these earlier Chinese poets, the Japanese Abutsu reaches to the moon as companion, partner, and intimate fellow traveller.

Man in the Moon: A European Folktale

Now we turn from the guiding moonlight to travels to and from the moon itself. Medieval people throughout Europe insisted that they saw a man in the moon, particularly one carrying thorns. In apparent frustration, the author and thinker Albert of Saxony (*c.* 1320–1390) says he cannot see this man no matter how hard he tries – which suggests that many others could:

I do not know what that figure may be, for I have looked at the moon many times and I have certainly seen a black spot there, but in no way could I see there such a figure as some people say is apparent there, namely, the figure of a man having a load of thorns on his back.[15]

English, German, and Dutch traditions have a story of a man who was banished to the moon. This seems to have been inspired by a verse in the Bible (Numbers 15:32–6) about a man who works on the sabbath and then is killed:[16]

> And it came to pass, when the children of Israel were in the wilderness, and had found a man gathering sticks on the sabbath day, That they brought him to Moses and Aaron and the whole multitude. And they put him into prison, not knowing what they should do with him. And the Lord said to Moses: Let that man die, let all the multitude stone him without the camp. And when they had brought him out, they stoned him, and he died as the Lord had commanded.[17]

In various medieval stories inspired by this biblical narrative, the wretched individual is not killed – they are instead exiled to the moon. There are many versions of the story in German and Dutch traditions, recorded in the nineteenth century and purportedly from the Middle Ages. In one, the man was guilty of working on a Sunday as in the biblical version. In another, there was a man and a woman. The man was exiled to the moon because he placed thorns on the way to church to prevent people from going to Sunday Mass. The woman was exiled because she made butter on a Sunday. In a further version, a man stole cabbages, and in yet another he stole sheep. There is also a Dutch version in which he is a vegetable stealer.[18] And there was a further version that said the exile is actually Cain of the Bible. Cain was forever cursed for having committed the first murder, killing his brother Abel, as detailed in Genesis 4:1–16. As mentioned above, this is alluded to in Dante's *Paradiso*.[19]

The story of an individual exiled to the moon for committing a crime is also found in an alliterative English poem from the 1300s, now known as 'The Man in the Moon'. Although this text dates to the thirteenth or fourteenth century, alliteration in poetry has much deeper roots, from the time of Old English. It reminds us that rhyming was not always the standard for poetry: alliteration used to be paramount. Here is a full translation of the poem:

The man in the moon stands and strides;
on his forked stick he bears his burden [of thorns].
It's a great wonder that he doesn't fall –
For fear lest he fall, he shudders and meanders.
When the frost freezes, he endures much chill.
The thorns are sharp; they tear his clothes.
There is nobody in the world who knows where he sits,
Nor (unless it be the hedge) what clothes he wears.

Which way do you think this man has taken his path?
He has set one foot in front of the other;
for whatever effort one takes, one never sees him move.

He is the slowest man that was ever born!
Where he is in the field driving in stakes,
For hope of closing his doors with thorns,
he must with his twibill [two-edged axe] make a bundle [of
    brushwood],
or all his day's work there is lost.

This same man on high, whenever he appears,
there on the moon where he was born and raised,

he leans on his fork like a grey friar –
This hunched idler, he is sorely frightened!
It's many days ago that he was here;
I know he's not succeeded in his errand.
He's hewn somewhere a burden of briars;
therefore some hayward has taken his pledge.

If your pledge is taken, bring home the brushwood!
Set forth your other foot! Stride over the path!
We shall ask the hayward home to our house,
And put him at ease, most comfortably,
Drink to him affectionately with a very stiff drink,
and our sweet wife shall sit by him.
When he is as drunk as a drowned mouse,
then we shall take the pledge from the bailiff.

This man hears me not, though I cry out to him!
I think the churl is deaf! The devil tear him apart!
Though I shout up high, he will not hurry;
The spiritless lad knows nothing of the law.
Hop forth, Hubert, magpie in stockings!
I think you are bewildered into the maw.
Though I am so angry with him that my teeth grind,
the churl won't come down before the day dawns![20]

This poem is found in a famous collection of lyrics known as the Harley manuscript (London, British Library, MS Harley 2253). Matti Rissanen suggests it may have been recited as part of a performance.[21] In this version of the story, the man in the moon is guilty of stealing thorns to make a hedge (in order to keep livestock from roaming). The speaker of the poem is viewing the man in the moon and trying to help him. This poem even tells us the name of this man in the moon:

Hubert. The cunning plan to help Hubert is that the speaker and his wife will distract the 'hayward' (a legal official) in order to take the pledge (the penalty for the man in the moon's crime) and thus release Hubert from his lunar prison. But when the man in the moon does not seem to hear him, the speaker grows frustrated with the fellow, cursing him: 'May the Devil pull him apart!' ('The Del hym todrawe!', 34).[22]

The first stanza gives us a glimpse into the miserable life of the man on the moon. He is afraid of falling off and he 'shoddreth and shereth' (trembles and meanders). He experiences terrible cold and must bear his burden of thorns which continuously prick him:

When the forst freseth, muche chele he byd.
The thornes beth kene, is hattren totereth.
(When the frost freezes, he endures much cold.
The thorns are sharp, [they] tear up his clothes.)

The speaker wonders how this man in the moon does not fall off, and considers how nobody knows where he rests or what he wears. The man in the moon is clearly suffering a terrible exile. The second stanza shows how he is condemned to continual labour:

He mot myd is twybyl other trous make,
Other al is dayes werk ther were yloren.
(He must make with his two-edged axe a bundle,
Or all his day's work is lost.)

The third stanza suggests he was born and raised on the moon, which seems to go against the typical story that he was exiled there – but the man in the moon does seem entirely trapped. In this third stanza, the speaker describes the man as a worn-out and burdened figure:

He leneth on is forke ase a grey frere –
This crokede caynard, sore he is adred!
(He leans on his fork as a grey friar –
This crooked sluggard, greatly is he afraid!)

'Grey friar' refers to members of the Franciscan order, who stressed poverty and came to England around 1224. In the fourth stanza, the speaker details the cunning plan to release the man in the moon. When the legal official in control of his exile is as 'dronke ase a dreynt mous' (drunk as a drowned mouse, 31), the speaker and the wife will take the pledge and the man will be free.

But the fifth stanza suggests that even as the speaker is calling out to the man with this plan for securing his freedom, the lunar exile cannot hear him: 'This mon hereth me nout, thah Ich to hym crye!' (This man hears me not, though I cry out to him!) The speaker fires out in frustration: 'Ichot the cherl is def!' (I think the churl is deaf!). The speaker is very annoyed with Hubert to say the least, and we end with the speaker failing to communicate with Hubert, that wretched man in the moon.

The Harley manuscript comprises texts in English, French, and Latin; it contains love lyrics alongside religious lyrics and poems with a sharp political and even satirical edge. The manuscript is made up of seven individual booklets. 'The Man in the Moon' poem appears in the sixth booklet. This booklet contains a range of Anglo-Norman texts with a humorous bent, including 'Le chevalier qui fist les cons parler' ('The Knight Who Made Vaginas Talk'). Yet it also contains devotional texts, including a saint's life. Editor Susanna Fein Green posits that the audience for booklet six may have comprised not only young male students but also 'mixed-gender social settings at which comic entertainments could be read aloud, and perhaps enacted, for enjoyment and discussion'.[23] 'The Man in the Moon' is found between two French poems, 'Talent me prent de rymer e de geste fere' ('Survival Makes Me Rhyme and Create a Story', a political poem) and 'Le chevalier e la corbaylle' ('The Knight and the Basket', a comic poem about lovers). The former speaks to the 'Man in the Moon' in compelling ways, for there too we have an exiled speaker – not unlike the man exiled cruelly to the moon. The exiled speaker of this poem, though, roams in more hospitable terrain:

> That is why I will stay in the woods under the pretty shade,
> Where there is neither treachery nor any bad law.
> In the woods of Belgrave, where the jay bird flies,
> And the nightingale always sings without pause.[24]

So the English poem is in dialogue with other texts in this manuscript that deal with exile. On one level, the poem could be seen as pure comedy – it is an example of classist 'humour' from the Middle Ages. The poem is perhaps an example of a higher-class audience laughing at people of a lower class. These man-in-the-moon stories primarily circle around this central idea of a labourer being exiled. Who was enjoying these stories? Were they nobility or gentry laughing at the expense of the lower classes? Or it is about Cain – the ultimate social reject of history? The poem also plays with the ideas of how the earth and the moon might connect. The thwarted communication between speaker and lunar man is clear: try as the speaker might, he cannot be heard by Hubert up in his moon-prison. As hard as we try to reach the moon, there remains a barrier. The speaker shifts between referring to the man in the moon in the third person and the second person – *he* versus *you* – which suggests on the one hand an observation of him, yet on the other a direct address to, a direct connection with, the man in the moon.

In these man-in-the-moon stories, like the English poem and the German and Dutch narratives, the moon is a place of harsh exile. It is where the rejects of a society are thrown out; the terrain is inhospitable, full of cold and harshness and fear. Perhaps we all, like the speaker of the English poem, have a desire to save the man (or woman) in the moon, seeing ourselves in their fate, imagining the horrors both of living in such a cruel terrain and of social rejection. But perhaps the exiles, whether named Hubert or something else, are always condemned to never hear us as we call out.

Lost Sanity: An Italian Epic

Hubert in the English poem 'The Man in the Moon' is trapped in a lunar prison, but there are cases in the broad medieval period of characters actively wanting to travel to the moon. One such case is found in a poem known as *Orlando furioso* (*The Frenzy of Orlando*), an Italian epic by Lodovico Ariosto (1474–1533). It tells the story of noblemen and their adventures. They are knights of King Charlemagne, and the backdrop is formed by the ongoing war with the Saracens, an outdated term for a Muslim or Arab, often used in the medieval period to describe any non-Christian. One of the noblemen is Astolfo, who is a cousin to the titular Orlando. Orlando has 'lost his mind' because his lover, Angelica, has been unfaithful to him. His wits can only be found on the moon, and so Astolfo has to travel there. He meets St John the Evangelist in the 'earthly paradise' (a liminal realm between heaven and earth) and in canto 34 they embark together on the journey to the moon, travelling on a flaming chariot. This journey is depicted arrestingly in an engraving by the French printmaker and illustrator Gustave Doré (1832–1883) (Plate 5). This is an intriguing passage, because it tells us so much both about the moon itself and about what the moon means and might represent to the author Ariosto and his audience.

Ariosto describes the moon in detail. It looks like 'spotless steel' (verse 70).[25] Astolfo is surprised by the size, for it is the same size as the earth according to this text, and yet seems so small from the earthly perspective (verses 70–1). And we are now in a place where we cannot see the earth clearly (verse 71). We are then treated to a tour of the moon:

> There, other lakes and rivers, other rills
> From ours down here on earth are to be found,
> And other plains and valleys, other hills.
> Cities and castles on the moon abound;
> The size of houses with amazement fills
> The paladin; extending all around
> Are deep and solitary forests where
> Diana's huntress-nymphs pursue the deer.   (verse 72)

But for all its vastness and grandeur, the moon is a waste-body. All that has been discarded from earth finds its way to the moon. The moon carries not only physical objects that have been disposed of, but also abstract entities such as fame, broken promises, and the tears and sighs of lovers (verse 75). Ancient royal crowns, for all their potent glory and symbolism, have become nothing but a mount of tumid bladders (verse 76).

Yet the moon serves a much more powerful role than simply being a waste-body. It is a mirror image of earth and its people, with all their limitations and frailties. Thieves and counterfeiters are represented as snakes up in the moon; kindness and charity delayed until the point of death become a deluge of used soup bowls (verse 80). There is also a stab of antifeminism, describing snares on the moon as being women's charms (verse 81). The one thing that cannot be found on the moon is foolishness or madness, for that remains in plenteous quantity here on earth (verse 81).

In this dizzying wasteland, Astolfo must remember his mission: to find Orlando's 'wit' (his 'reason' or 'sense') that has departed from him. The senses of all those poor souls on earth who have lost their wits find their place in the waste-body of the moon, in a large mountainous heap (verse 82). The heap of people's reason is much larger than all the other mounds found on the moon (verse 82), for so many people on earth have lost their reason that it is found in near-suffocating abundance up on the wasteland of the moon. People's reason is found in the form of thin, subtle liquid preserved in flasks:

> A liquid, thin and clear, Astolfo sees,
> Distilled in many vases, large and small,
> Which must (so volatile the fluid is)
> Be tightly corked; the largest of them all
> Contains the greatest of those essences:
> The mind of mad Anglante, of whose fall
> You are aware and of his frenzied fits.
> And on it the duke read: 'Orlando's wits'.   (verse 83)

So Astolfo finds Orlando's lost reason as liquid corked in a flask or vase. Astolfo then finds many other names on the bottles, including, much to Astolfo's surprise, his own. He smells the contents of the bottle which bears his name, and his portion of lost reason returns to him (verse 84). Astolfo wonders how so many people on earth have lost their reason:

> Some lose their wits for love, some for reward
> Of fame, still others scour the seas for gain;

Another hopes for favours from his lord;
Others in futile magic trust in vain;
Some paintings treasure, others jewels hoard;
All for their hearts' desire have gone insane:
Astrologers and sophists by the score
Have lost their reason, poets too, still more.   (verse 85)

With Orlando's reason in hand – a heavy flask – Astolfo has completed his mission on the moon and is ready to return to earth.

In an essay on this part of the poem, Ita Mac Carthy suggests that the moon is a very special kind of reflection, in that it shows the true essence of everything on earth. As Mac Carthy argues, the moon 'offers something other than a mirror image of reality', for it 'reflects back an altered version of it, one that highlights the essential rather than the outward qualities of the objects placed before it'. The moon might even, then, be 'an allegory for the literary text'.[26] Jeffrey T. Schnapp argues that Ariosto is also putting pressure on the idea that poetry can offer a secure repository for memory; there is always a struggle to account for details, to keep secure inventories, to hold onto matter that always flies from our grasp. As Schnapp argues, Ariosto 'hints that the exponential growth of things lost and forgotten with respect to those remembered and found will forever thwart human efforts at storage and retrieval, not to mention ordering'.[27] Daniel Leisawitz argues that the moon is an ironic landscape, an 'ironic mirror image of the earth'.[28] Ladina Bezzola Lambert reads the moon as a space of metaphor, a landscape where metaphors proliferate, but suggests that Astolfo struggles to read the moon in new ways – he is trapped by earthly perception.[29]

With all these interpretations in mind, I am struck by the level of intimacy between the moon and the earth. Although the moon is in many ways an 'otherworld' in this poem, it is also deeply connected with the earth and its population, inextricably tied with human ways of thinking and being. The moon is linked with all the needs and desires that seethe in the world, with all its flaws. It may reveal the true essence of life on earth, throwing into sharp relief the cognitive, emotional, and moral limitations of humanity. So much of what pours out of human hearts and human hands ends up in this lunar realm, bonding the earth and the moon in a shared enterprise of understanding human endeavour. In order to reach the moon, we need St John the Evangelist's chariot: a form of transport beyond the ability of most of us. But once we arrive, precious, lost reason can be retrieved from there. Our sense – what makes us who we are, according to Ariosto – shimmers so near and yet so far.

Princess in the Moon: The Earliest Japanese Fiction

We have travelled with the knight Astolfo to the moon. But just as important as earthlings travelling to the moon are those moon-people who might try to travel the other way. This very thing happens in a Japanese story from the late ninth or early tenth century, during the Heian period: a story known as *Taketori Monogatari* (*The Tale of the Bamboo Cutter*), which has been famously adapted into a Studio Ghibli animation, *The Tale of Princess Kaguya*. The medieval story on which this film is based may be the earliest work of fiction in Japanese of which we know. It is the earliest surviving example of the *monogatari* ('tale', 'romance', 'novel').[30] In this story, a moon-princess comes to earth, is raised and nurtured by human hands, but must in the end leave and return to her moon-dwelling. The girl is in a sense exiled in the opposite direction when compared with the man in the moon we encountered earlier: she belongs to the moon, but is exiled on earth for a time. This story brings us close to the moon while also reminding us of our distance from it. Reading *The Tale of the Bamboo Cutter*, it is as though a piece of the moon comes to sit with us for a while, only to suddenly disappear again. H. Richard Okada suggests a parallel between the style of narration and theatrical performance.[31] This vivifies the presence of the moon and renders the sense of a moon-princess visiting the earth all the more palpable.

An old man, while cutting bamboo, finds a tiny, three-inch-tall girl bathed in light. He takes her home, and he and his wife nurture her tenderly, even placing her in a cradle. A late-seventeenth-century illustration now housed at the Metropolitan Museum of Art shows the young girl in a basket, being watched and cared for by her parents (Plate 6). She grows up remarkably quickly under the care of her adoptive parents, bringing them great joy. The girl has a palliative effect on those around her: 'When the old man felt in poor spirits and was in pain, just to look at the child would make the pain stop, and his anger too would melt away.'[32] The man continues to find gold when cutting bamboo, and becomes increasingly wealthy. They bring a diviner to grant her a name, and she is called 'Nayotake no Kaguya-hime' (Shining Princess of the Young Bamboo).

Many men begin to desire Kaguya-hime, but she does not wish to be married, part of a broader critique in the text of both objectification of women and court politics. Under pressure from her father, she says that if she must marry, she desires sincerity in her husband. She sets five suitors particular tasks: Prince Ishizukuri must acquire the stone begging bowl of the Buddha; Prince Kuramochi must bring a branch of a tree that grows in the mountain of the Eastern Sea, which has silver roots, a gold trunk, and fruits of white jewels; Abe no Mimuraji must bring a robe made from Chinese fire-rat fur; Ōtomo no Miyuki must bring a jewel from a dragon's head; and Isonokami must bring 'a swallow's easy-delivery charm' (333). Most of the suitors fail but attempt to deceive Kaguya-hime, who nonetheless remains undeceived. Isonokami dies in the quest. Through all these adventures, the emperor has heard of Kaguya-hime and summons her, but Kaguya-hime refuses the summons. Nevertheless, she and the emperor strike up a tender friendship and correspond with one another.

Three years pass, and we are told that Kaguya-hime keeps looking at the moon in downcast spirits, weeping. Those around her become increasingly concerned for her wellbeing:

> At the time of the full moon of the seventh month, she sat outside seemingly immersed in thought. Her maidservants informed the bamboo cutter: 'Kaguya-hime has always looked sadly at the moon, but her preoccupation of late has not been normal. There must be something which is deeply worrying her. Please watch her carefully.' (350)

When her father asks Kaguya-hime what is wrong, she answers: 'When I look at the moon the world seems lonely and sad. What else should worry me?' The old man tells her not to gaze at the moon, but she replies: 'How could I live without gazing at the moon?' (350). Her sadness continues every time she sees the moon, until she finally reveals what it is that affects her so deeply when she looks at the moon:

> I am not a creature of this world; I come from the Palace of the Moon. I visited this world because of an obligation from the past. Now the time has come for me to return, and on the night of the next full moon people from my old country will come for me. (350)

Her father is devastated, and father and daughter sob uncontrollably; the old man even says he will try to prevent the moon-people from taking her away. But Kaguya-hime explains further:

I have a father and a mother in the Palace of the Moon. When I came here from my country I said it would be for just a little while, but I have already spent many years in this land. I have long dallied here, without thinking of my parents on the Moon. I feel no joy now that I am about to return, but only a terrible sadness. (350)

The fateful day of the full moon comes (the fifteenth), and Kaguya-hime's adoptive parents and the emperor decide to resist the troop coming from the moon, though Kaguya-hime tells them that all resistance would be futile. The emperor even sends troops for the purpose, feeling sympathy for her parents. Kaguya-hime then tells her father more about the moon-people, and how desperate she feels. She says, weeping:

When I used to go and sit outside I would always beg for just one more year with you, but my wish was not granted. That was what made me so unhappy. It breaks my heart to upset you so and then to leave you. The people of the Moon are very beautiful and do not grow old. They have no worries either. And yet it does not make me happy to be going there. Instead, I am torn by longing because I shall not be able to look after you when you are old and decrepit. (352)

Kaguya-hime has developed a real, profound attachment to her earthly parents, and we the audience become moved by the terrible separation that is to come. At last, a magnificent moon-troop, with a chariot canopied in silk, comes to take her away:

About midnight the area of the house was suddenly illuminated by a light brighter than noon, as bright as ten full moons, so bright that one could see the pores of a man's skin. Then down from the heavens came men riding on clouds, who ranged themselves at a height of about five feet from the ground.

All attempts to resist this troop fail, and Kaguya-hime must be taken. The king of this moon-troop calls to Kaguya-hime, asking her, 'Why have you lingered so long in such a filthy place?' Kaguya-hime is forced to leave the 'filthy' earth she loves and return to the moon. The moon-people bring with them a box with a feather-robe and an elixir of immortality. Once she wears the feather-robe, she will forget her temporary home among loving people on this earth. The elixir she gives as a gift to the emperor, who, broken-hearted, does not want to take it. Having sent this gift and written a letter to her parents, she wears the robe of feathers, and forgets her earthly attachments (354). She no longer remembers them, but her parents and the emperor continue to grieve her.

Scholars have made many links between the story and historical and religious contexts.[33] Joshua S. Mostow observes parallels between *The Tale of the Bamboo Cutter* and other sources; as he explains:

Elements of the *Taketori* resemble some of the tales or myths found in the *Nihon shoki* (or *Nihongi*; Chronicles of Japan, 720), and the *fudoki*, or local gazetteers, originally ordered from each province by Empress Genmei in 713. Each province was to provide accounts of its topographical and other natural features, along with legends concerning local sites of significance. *Tango fudoki* includes the legend of Nagu Shrine, which is similar to the basic *Taketori* story, being a version of the 'swan-maiden' tale that is found throughout East Asia, in which a heavenly maiden is robbed of her feather-robe and married to a mortal or raised by a mortal couple.[34]

And as observed by Jonathan Stockdale: 'In the items that the princess requests from her suitors, the story offers a rich mixture of religious symbolism, from the begging bowl of the Buddha to the branch of a tree from a Daoist mountain of immortality.'[35] As mentioned, the narrative critiques male desire and court politics, challenging the Heian court and its values. It is a powerful social commentary, even as it deals with the fantastical subjects of moon-creatures and immortality. Stockdale suggests that the text is profoundly concerned with the concept of exile: Kaguya-hime is exiled from the moon, and this 'provides a context by which the other characters are finally able to "place" Kaguyahime, whose beauty and radiance "unlike anything of this world", together with her utter contempt for royal commands, had alternately enthralled and unsettled everyone around her'.[36]

I would like to add to Stockdale's reading by considering whether the human beings on earth, too, are suffering from a form of exile and might be happier on the moon. Human beings received a radiant, immensely special princess, and these humans subjected her to the strictures and pettiness of political and social rules. She is then taken from them, as though humanity did not deserve her on this planet, that 'filthy place' as the moon-king called it. Perhaps this also suggests, though, the beauty that can be possible on earth – if only at times, and only in fragments. Kaguya-hime's light might be a curative taste of how amazing the world can be. *The Tale of the Bamboo Cutter* is not only about the beauty and splendour and enticing wonders of the moon; it is also about the beauty and joys and tenderness and love to be found on earth, in all its limited and broken forms.

• • •

For both Abutsu and Ariosto, the moon is a creative space, bound with the act of composition and creative action. As we have continuously seen from Chapter 1, the moon is forever intimately bound with the human imagination. In both *Orlando furioso* and *Taketori Monogatari* (*The Tale of the Bamboo Cutter*), journeys to and from the moon offer the opportunity for scathing socio-political critique. 'The Man in the Moon' also has a rich socio-political subtext, with the English poem perhaps a form of classist humour. Both 'The Man on the Moon' and *The Tale of the Bamboo Cutter* grapple with questions of exile – whether from the earth or from the moon itself; the moon is at once a home and a terrain of exile in these works. Ariosto in *Orlando furioso* also reflects on the sense of the moon as a waste-body, a place where all that is lost, forgotten, and broken on earth is cast away.

While the moon is 'Other' in all these texts, there are also moments of deep familiarity, where the moon is not a magical realm, distant and fantastical, but something much more like home. In fact, in each text we see a constant pull between the alien and the familiar, each jostling against the other to claim the moon. Abutsu's moon remains at a remove from her, but still acts as a kind of intimate companion on her journey. The moon is a place of exile for the man in the moon, and yet we can see him here from earth – the homeland still calls out to him, quite literally in the English poem. In *Orlando furioso*, the moon is an 'Other' place and yet it is bound inextricably to earth, just as metaphor and allegory and mirror images are bound with 'reality' as they try to create and express it. And of course, in *The Tale of the Bamboo Cutter*, we have a moon-dweller living with us here on earth, forming profoundly intimate bonds with human beings; and although she leaves, her moon-imprint on this world, and on human hearts, never fades.

3

···

THE MOON OF PROPHECIES
AND SIGNS

In a tale from the 700s, a pregnant woman has a vision: a waxing moon is before her. The moon grows and grows, and when it reaches the size of a full moon, it tumbles through her lips and her chest becomes aglow with light. This is the mother of Willibrord, a man who will become a saint; the dream is thus prophetic. As a priest explains to her, the moon represents her saintly son: he will remove darkness through his light, and he will be like the full moon in his perfection.[1] This powerful image portends the coming of a special infant, represented in the fullness of the growing moon. The image speaks to a deep link between the moon and fertility across cultures. But more broadly, it also tells us that the moon could be a very meaningful sign: it indicated momentous events to come, and was involved in all forms of prophecy. This is our focus in the coming chapter, which deals with how the moon often has a symbolic or 'semiological' role – linking as it does so to events on earth and to other celestial bodies.[2]

In order to explore the moon's role in prophecies and signs through a multi-glance, this chapter is divided into two halves. The first half is concerned with the moon foretelling the future: we will consider the moon as a sign of tragedy in Chaucer's *Troilus and Criseyde*, before turning to models of prognostication in traditions in medieval England and Polynesia. This will be followed by a consideration of the moon's role in the act of prophecy in medieval European literature. The second half is concerned with the moon's various meanings as a sign in religious contexts, specifically medieval Islamic and Christian traditions: we will examine medieval conceptions of an important Islamic miracle concerning the moon, before turning to Christianity, investigating the moon as a sign of God, and its representational role in major Christian doctrines, figures, and events.

PART I: FORETELLING THE FUTURE

Sign of Tragedy: Chaucer's *Troilus and Criseyde*

We saw in the Introduction that the moon makes important appearances in much of Chaucer's work.[3] The moon has an especially profound role in Chaucer's epic and tragic poem, *Troilus and Criseyde*, set against the backdrop of the Trojan War. Chaucer's main source for this poem was *Il filostrato* (*The One Made Prostrate in Love*) by his Italian near-contemporary, Giovanni Boccaccio (1313–1375). In *Troilus and Criseyde*, we see Pandarus – the mediator between the two lovers, Troilus and Criseyde – making calculations to determine whether the moon is in a good position for his undertaking (Book II, lines 74–5).[4] Lunar prognostics became especially popular in the mid-fifteenth century, but were employed before this period, and from the end of the fourteenth century they had widespread use.[5] Pandarus also refers to the moon's role in shaping dreams and how they should be interpreted, as seen in the following lines:

thorugh impressiouns,

As if a wight hath faste a thyng in mynde,

That therof cometh swiche auysiouns;

And other seyn, as they in bokes fynde,

That after tymes of the yer, by kynde

Men dreme, and that th'effect goth by the moone.

(Book V, lines 372–8)

(Through impressions,

as when a person has a fixed thing in mind,

some dreams [or visions] come.

And others say, as they in books find,

that through nature, by the seasons of the year,

men dream, and that the effect occurs according to the moon.)

Pandarus refers here to the moon actually impacting dreams, differently from those dreams that are inspired by images or impressions in the mind.

Even beyond Pandarus' moon-calculations and moon-dreams, there is an intimate link between celestial events and the experiences of those on earth throughout *Troilus and Criseyde*. Criseyde is frequently associated with the moon; this is a troubling association because of the moon's link with capriciousness. Unfortunately, Criseyde naively swears by the moon in Book IV (lines 1590–6), as though to announce her own inconstancy and to prefigure her eventual shift in loyalties and affections, for, under duress, she will abandon Troilus for the Greek warrior Diomede. Leona O'Desky has even suggested that we should see the moon as associated with the Trojans and the sun associated with the Greeks. As the sun overtakes the moon, the Trojan war finds its reflection in the celestial realm, the Greeks overcoming the Trojans. The sun's dominance signals the fall of Troy and the dissolution of Troilus and Criseyde's relationship.[6]

In the final and fifth book of the poem, we see, in M. Stokes's words, 'the narrator's marked tendency [...] to retreat to the sky'.[7] Again and again, the narrator returns to celestial occurrences. Something peculiar happens in Book V that concerns the moon and portends the oncoming tragedy. We are told that the moon moves out of the star sign Leo:

> And Cynthea hire char-hors overraughte
> To whirle out of the Leoun if she myghte;
> And Signifer hise candels sheweth brighte
> Whan that Criseyde unto hire bedde wente
> Inwith hire fadres faire brighte tente,
> Retornyng in hire soule ay up and down
> The wordes of this sodeyn Diomede,
> His grete estat, and perel of the town,
> And that she was allone and hadde nede
> Of frendes help; and thus bygan to brede
> The cause whi, the sothe for to telle,
> That she took fully purpos for to dwelle.
>
> (Book V, lines 1016–29)

> (And Cynthia, her chariot-horse reached over
> to whirl out of Leo if she could;
> And the Zodiac showed his bright candles
> when Criseyde went to her bed
> inside her father's bright, handsome tent,
> always revolving in her soul, up and down
> the words of this fiery Diomede,
> his high status, and the danger of the city,
> and that she was alone and had need
> of friends' help; and thus began to breed,

to tell the truth, the reason why
she decided fully to stay.)

Criseyde had promised to come back before the moon passed Leo – but this has not ended up being the case. The moon, here personified as the deity Cynthia, leans over her chariot horses to try to urge them to shift out of Leo just as Criseyde reflects in her father's tent that, in her lonely state, she has no choice but to stay with the Greeks and forsake Troilus. Chaucer adds this to Boccaccio's poem. This decision of Chaucer's emphasises the intimate dance between the celestial and the earthly. The moon moves out of Leo at the precise moment Criseyde tries to remove herself from Troilus' heart.

The moon has many other significant appearances in *Troilus and Criseyde*. For example, one night Criseyde is forced to stay at Pandarus' house because of a storm that suddenly comes on. The storm is caused by the crescent moon, Saturn, and Jupiter all being in conjunction in the sign of Cancer:

The bente moone with hire hornes pale,
Saturne, and Jove, in Cancro joyned were,
That swych a reyn from heven gan auale,
That every maner womman that was there
Hadde of that smoky reyn a verray feere.

(Book III, lines 624–8)

(The bent moon with her pale horns,
Saturn and Jupiter in Cancer were joined,
That such a rain from heaven began to fall
That every manner of woman that was there
Had a true fear of that smoky rain.)

63

This conjunction actually happened, on 9 or 10 June 1385, and Chaucer may have witnessed it or at least read about it.[8] Again, events in the sky directly impact the love story on earth, the moon becoming ever more associated with the tragedy that is to come.

Repeatedly, the moon shows the passing of time, and the terrible coming of pain and loss:

> On heuene yet the sterres weren seene,
> Although ful pale ywoxen was the moone,
> And whiten gan the orisonte shene
> Al estward, as it wont is to doone;
> And Phebus with his rosy carte soone
> Gan after that to dresse hym up to fare
> Whan Troilus hath sent after Pandare.
>
> (Book V, lines 274–80)

> (In heaven still were the stars seen,
> Although the moon had grown very pale,
> And the bright horizon began to whiten
> All eastwards as it is wont to do.
> And Phoebus [the sun] with his rosy chariot soon
> Began after that to prepare to travel upwards
> When Troilus had sent for Pandarus.)

As mentioned in the previous chapter, Troilus in sorrow speaks to the moon while he pines for his beloved:

> And every nyght, as was his wone to doone,
> He stood the brighte moone to byholde,
> And al his sorwe he to the moone tolde
>
> (Book V, lines 647–59)

(And every night, as was his custom to do,
He stood to behold the bright moon,
And all his sorrow he told to the moon)

The moon plays a narrative, representational, and affective role in *Troilus and Criseyde*. It is deeply linked with events on earth, even acting in unison with and as an influencer on decisions made by human beings. But it is also part of this poem's abandonment of earth. When the narrator looks up, more and more intently as Stokes notes, he is further abandoning the world below. As we gaze all the more intensely on the moon, says Chaucer in this epic poem, we are leaving more and more of the world behind.

Prognostication in England

We have witnessed Pandarus make moon-calculations to predict and plan events. Planning activities by the moon was a well-worn and meaningful practice for many: there are abundant examples of lunar prognostication around the world from 700 to 1600. Anglo-Saxon England had examples of 'lunar hemerologies' or 'lunaria'.[9] As seen in the Introduction, Ælfric of Eynsham, a monk and abbot who wrote in English and Latin, talks about the moon's influence on all of creation. His scientific interest in the moon, however, does not mean he approves of using the moon to make decisions or calculations. As he says slightly earlier in the same sermon quoted above ('Octabas et Circumcisio Domini', 'The Octaves and Circumcision of Our Lord'):

There are also many who are caught in such great error that they plan by the moon their travels, and their deeds by the day, and will not let blood on Monday because it is the beginning of the week. But Monday is not the first day of the week, but the second. Sunday is the first in Creation and in order and in honour.[10]

Ælfric might not approve, but this did not change the fact that lunar prognostication did take place in Anglo-Saxon England; it was perhaps used by the clergy or others with high levels of education. One Old English text, for example, predicts the fate of those born on days of particular ages of the moon. Someone born when the moon is one night old, for instance, will have a long and prosperous life; but on two nights old, the person will always suffer from illness. And on the thirteenth and fourteenth nights, one will be 'devout and righteous' (p. 202).[11]

A further Anglo-Saxon text, also in Old English, goes into detail about what to do on each day depending on the age of the moon. When the moon is one night old, it is a good time to ask the king for something, as it will be granted; on the second night of the moon, one can buy land owned by one's ancestors. The third night of the moon is good for many things: the land will be managed well; friends will be joyful for you; and it is a good time for fishing. On the fourth night, it is a good time for enemies to make peace, and a good time for the ploughman, the miller, and the merchant to engage in their labours. On the fifth night, one can steal without being caught. On the sixth, it is a good time to put hay in the bed, which will prevent the usual pains; this is also a good day for building churches and to begin building ships (p. 190). The seventh night is good for fishing; the eighth to travel to another land and bring back a wife. On the ninth, one can ask something of the king's petitioner; the tenth night is good for asking whatever one wants. On the eleventh, one can go to any part of the world one wishes and will remain unharmed (p. 192). The twelfth night is good for sea travel and for taking a wife. On the thirteenth, there is profit in milking (p. 192). The fourteenth night is good for any labour and for nuns to begin their profession and take up their habit. The fifteenth night is good for fishing and hunting harts and wild boars. On the sixteenth night, it is a good time to find friends over the sea and establish a minster. The text breaks off as it describes the seventeenth night, in the midst of something about building a house.

A similar text has predictions for what will happen if the new moon falls on particular days. On a Sunday, there will be rain, wind, calm, barren cattle, but healthy people. On a Monday, there will be sorrow for those born on the day and the heads of young men will be painful. On a Tuesday, there will be joy for men but mourning for the young. On a Wednesday, peaceful men will be with good friends; on Thursday, kings will be healthy and cured; on Friday, there will be good hunting during that month; on Saturday, it is particularly dramatic: there will be 'struggle, and bloodshed, and whoever begins with the south wind will have victory' (p. 198). As one final example, a further text predicts the weather based on the colour of the moon. A reddish or golden moon indicates winds; a clear moon indicates calm weather; a spotted moon indicates rain. A reddish moon in the evening means a sunny day tomorrow.[12]

There was also a great deal of interest in what a moon signifies in dreams. In a Latin text from the Anglo-Saxon period, the following proclamations are made: if one dreams of being girded with the moon, it signifies protection; to lose the moon in one's dream signifies that faith will lessen; to be girded with a golden moon signifies envy; to be girded with a divided moon means strength. When seeing a clear moon in one's dream, this means envy. If one sees two moons in one's dream, this too indicates envy. A bloody moon signifies harm; a moon rising or falling signifies struggle; a white moon signifies wealth; a moon with colours signifies harm (pp. 100, 102). Seeing the sun or moon in a dream means happiness in judgement (p. 112); two moons mean joy and happiness (p. 118), an idea repeated in another text in English (p. 208).

Lunar prognostication persisted in England in later centuries, and a selection of these texts from late medieval England is available in translation in the appendix of this book. These texts are in Middle English, a later stage of the language than Old English (Middle English spans from approximately 1100 to 1500), with these texts dating mainly to the mid-fifteenth century.[13] Their contents suggest they were used by wealthy secular people of high status. Laurel Means identifies two types: those that work according to the 'day' or 'mansion' of the moon, functioning with the moon's position and amount of light within a twenty-eight-to-thirty-day cycle; and those that work according to 'month', or the ascendant zodiacal sign of the moon.[14] We will look at some of these texts in detail in Chapter 4, but we will glance at some of them now. A Middle English poem, going day by day, says what is good to do on each day of the moon, linked to biblical events. On day 1, it is good to buy and sell, for example. On day 14, all things are good to do, whereas on day 27, all activity will turn out badly (p. 139).[15] The text declares that we must follow it – or else:

Whanne ȝe seen wythoute mysse,
What tyme of þe mone hyt ys,
Wher he be olde oþer newe,
Go to þys story agayn,
And do ryȝt as hyt schal ȝow seyn,
Or ells hyt schal ȝow rew.

(p. 142)

(When you see clearly
What time of the moon it is,
Whether the moon is old or new,
Go to this story again,

And do right as it will say to you,
Or else you will rue it.)

Another poem works in a similar way: it links biblical events to all that is good or not good on each day, and likewise the fate of children born on particular days of the moon (p. 154). To take day 18, for example: a child born on that day, 'A brauler he shall be, parfay, / Full of wordys and of stryfe, / Prude and stoute and of short lyfe' ('A brawler he shall be, indeed, / Full of words and of strife, / Pride and stout and of short life', p. 165).

There is also advice to be found for those of us embarking on a journey. One text advises: 'Whanne though wolt done any thinge or begynne any thing, loke in what signe the monke makithe his cours' ('When you will do anything or begin anything, look in what sign the moon makes its circuit', p. 201). If in Aries, for example, all will be well; but if in Taurus, one will suffer harm (p. 201). Another text goes month by month, explaining that we need to know where the moon is in each month in order to tell if it is a good time to go from home. For example, if the moon is in Cancer in June, one can go securely and not fear, for all will be joyful and well (p. 203). A further text says when or where we should go depending on the moon's compass and zodiacal position. If the journey is into the east, we should go where the moon is in the west and an air or wind sign. If in the west, we should go when the moon is in the east and in a fiery sign. If the journey is into the north, the moon should be in the south and a dry sign; if the journey is to the south, the moon must be in the north and in a watery sign (p. 204).

For those suffering imprisonment, the moon has something to say, too. There is a Middle English text advising on the state of someone imprisoned depending on the moon. If someone is imprisoned when the moon is in Aries, for example, they will soon be free. If in Taurus, it will be long before one comes out. If in Gemini, one will be out in a certain number of days or will die. In Leo, it will be long but one will have a good release. In Virgo, one will go out easily. In Libra, one will eventually be released. In Sagittarius, one will go out in peace. In Pisces, though, one shall never be released (p. 209).

Prognostication in Polynesia

It is important to remember that prognostication was not limited to Western regions, for we have evidence of prognostication practices globally, including in Polynesia during the years 900–1600. 'Polynesia', as Madi Williams shows, 'is itself a Western label and an artificial construct.'[16] I will use this label as a shorthand, while acknowledging the significant problems with the term itself. Polynesian travellers used a variety of methods in nature to navigate, including the moon, alongside the sun, stars, waves, and birds.[17] The moon was also crucial for cultivators of the land, with the *maramataka* or moon calendar used by medieval people of Polynesia.[18] As observed by Daniel Hikuroa, the word *marama* signifies both the moon and the lunar month.[19] The *maramataka* formed a crucial tool or framework that was strong and rigorous:

The maramataka is a framework to mark time, based upon the moon's orbit around the Earth and is structured to respond to the natural rhythms and variations of the lunar cycle. Centuries of detailed observations built up evidence, and hypotheses and predictions were made, tested and critically analysed. Inductive reasoning was employed with results and conclusions subjected to verification and testing.[20]

In the words of a number of collaborative scholars: 'Underpinned by the lunar cycle, from new moon to new moon, the maramataka was used to inform the best time to plant and harvest certain crops, collect shellfish, and direct the course of ocean bound vessels.'[21] And as remarked by Williams:

A specific example of a maramataka is that of the Ngāti Kahungunu tribe in the North Island of Aotearoa New Zealand. In this tradition, it is said that the phase after the new moon known as Hoata is the time for fishing and planting.[22]

As also observed by Mere Roberts, Frank Weko, and Liliana Clarke:

Oceanic peoples such as the Polynesians were thoroughly conversant with the moon and other planets and stars in the night sky, upon which their voyaging and navigational skills were dependent. They would also have observed that the moon regulates the tides and together these would have contributed to their time keeping skills. Horticultural and fishing activities also required the ability to predict the right times to plant and harvest, and to know when migratory species were present or absent.[23]

There are a number of names for each phase of the moon. These include: Whiro (when the moon is invisible or becomes visible); Tirea (a very small moon); Hoata (a visible moon); Huna (a hidden moon); Turu (a filled-out moon); and Rakaumatohi (a waning moon).[24]

Given the rigorousness of the *maramataka*, it follows that the moon calendar was an important system of knowledge. Hikuroa identifies the *maramataka* as a system for 'codifying knowledge', including it among many other such systems:

After their arrival in Aotearoa and Te Wai Pounamu many centuries ago, Māori developed various forms of codifying knowledge – many based upon oral delivery. Some narrative forms include moteatea (chants, poems), whaikorero (oratory, speechmaking), maramataka (calendar), waiata (songs), pepeha (quotations), whakataukī/ whakatauāki (proverbs), whakapapa (genealogies) and pūrākau (stories) – each with its own categories, style, complex patterns and characteristics.[25]

Hikuroa particularly connects the *maramataka* with *pūrākau* (stories), suggesting that the *maramataka* may be paralleled with narrative frameworks especially:

Pūrākau and maramataka are frameworks by which Māori under-stand and comprehend Te Taiao – the universe, the natural world (including us) – add to and test that knowledge, share it within generations, and pass it down through the generations.[26]

Considering that the *maramataka* is 'dynamic' rather than 'fixed and static', knowledge of it was transmitted through a combination of teaching and 'experiential learning'.[27] It is also important to keep in mind that the *maramataka* served an important communal function:

it [*maramataka*] formed the basis of the cultural life of the commu-nity, acting as an indicator of appropriate times for the onset or cessation of various activities. Foremost among these was their ability to foretell appropriate and inappropriate times for food gathering such as the planting and harvesting of crops and the catching of fish.[28]

The *maramataka* thus served as vital roles in communities, bringing people together and acting as a firm and respected system of knowl-edge among the medieval people of Polynesia.

Merlin's Prophecies

Across the medieval world, the moon was also central to prophecy. The moon has a prominent position in Geoffrey of Monmouth's (d. *c.* 1155) great work, *History of the Kings of Britain*. First, it should be noted that Geoffrey describes incubus demons – part-human part-angels who simulate the form of humans and have sex with women – living between the moon and the earth.[29] These incubus demons, hovering malevolently, draw attention to the liminal space of transit to the moon. That space is filled with the unknown, and potentially full of danger. With its ominous associations, the moon is also central to prophetic activity.

Geoffrey explains the name of a mythical king, father to the illustrious King Arthur: Uther Pendragon. The name Uther Pendragon is explained as meaning *caput draconis*, 'head of the dragon'.[30] As Geoffrey remarks, Uther Pendragon was so named because Utherpendragon means 'a dragon's head' in the British language, and it was through a dragon that the famous sorcerer Merlin prophesised Uther becoming king.[31] The 'dragon's head' is terminology related to the lunar nodes. The lunar nodes are the two places where the moon passes the ecliptic plane.[32] As summed up by Elizabeth Bryan: 'Medieval Arabic astronomers employed "head of the dragon" and "tail of the dragon" as technical terms for the points in the moon's orbit that had been referred to by earlier Greek astronomers, like second-century Ptolemy, as lunar nodes.'[33] Laȝamon (late twelfth–early thirteenth century), who composed an English version of Wace's (b. *c.* 1100) Anglo-Norman version of Geoffrey, seems also to have been very cognisant of what 'head of the dragon' means.[34] The moon also appears as an important sign in another one of the prophecies of Merlin. As part of this prophecy cited in Geoffrey's work, Merlin says that there will be havoc in the skies: the moon's chariot will be out of control in the zodiac, and the Pleiades, the group of stars, will weep.[35]

The Trees of the Sun and the Moon

We have seen how the moon could signal important events for medieval people, and even form a part of a sorcerer's prophecy. We will now turn to thinking in more detail about how the moon could be implicated in the act of prophecy. In the same manuscript in which the epic poem *Beowulf* is found, there is a prose text about the famous emperor Alexander the Great and his exploits: *The Letter of Alexander to Aristotle*. This text includes the story of the 'trees of the sun and the moon', a very popular legend which survives in many versions. In addition to the Old English version discussed here, there is for example a later, Middle English reference in *The Book of John Mandeville*.[36] The episode of the trees of the sun and the moon is the climax of the Old English text, and differs from the Latin source. In the Latin, Alexander goes on to have many other adventures. But these have all been removed in the Old English.

In this legend, Alexander and his most intimate companions come to magical trees in India. When each tree is touched by sunlight or moonlight, it speaks a prophecy, telling Alexander of his fate. The trees' powers are dependent on the sun or moon – the prophesying power rests in the interaction of the celestial light with the sentient treetops; the moon-tree has its powers awoken by the touch of moonlight.[37] But the trees speak in a language which Alexander and his companions cannot understand, and which a priest of the trees must translate for him: 'I did not understand the meaning of the Indic words the tree has spoken to me; then the bishop explained it and told me' (p. 76).[38] Unfortunately for Alexander, the trees tell him of his doom. The moon-tree answers Alexander's thoughts to tell him of his coming death; this also happens with Alexander's most intimate companions. Kate Perillo and Brian McFadden have highlighted the role of translation in this episode of the *Letter*. McFadden observes that the tree episode is the first time in the text that translation has been required.[39] Perillo suggests that it is in this part of the text, nearing the end, 'when the text's translational self-consciousness reaches a climax in its acknowledgement of Alexander's own reliance on interpreters'.[40] I would add to this that the sun and moon themselves need to be translated: celestial light is rendered linguistically into tree language, relayed in human tongue, and translated into Alexander's own specific language.

The moon of this text works translationally and symbiotically with the sun to activate the prophesying powers of sentient trees: tree and sky work in cohesion. We can highlight three points in particular that tell us about medieval understandings of the moon. First, Alexander's conversation with the trees can be read as a contemplative or mystical encounter. It bears many of the hallmarks associated with contemplative activity. There is emphasis on privacy and intimacy: the trees are found in a grove amid other trees; the moon-tree is consulted by Alexander only with his most intimate companions (p. 78); and the trees impart secret knowledge which is subsequently shared only through translation by a priest. Virginity is required, too, along with a level of cleansing preparation (removal of shoes and clothes). Bloodshed is forbidden, and instead the voice of the trees is elicited through prayer: the bishop tells Alexander to pray (*beodan*) at the foot of the trees (p. 76). The prayer, the bidding for the trees to speak, occurs internally. The moon is implicated in this private, interior, contemplative process.

Second, we see the trees working in harmony, and thus the moon-tree allows a deeper prophetic encounter than if the sun-tree were to work alone. The tree of the moon's prophecy penetrates deeper than the first, sun-based prophecy. In the first stage, the tree of the sun tells Alexander he will not return to the country from which he departed. In the second stage, the tree of the moon confirms Alexander's death. As the moon-tree says, 'Alexander, you have lived your life to its full term, but you will die this coming year in Babylon in the month of

May, of what you least expect you will be deceived by.' In the third stage, after which the trees refuse to impart further information, the tree of the sun gives further details of the fate of Alexander, his mother, and his sisters. The moon, sun, and trees all work in unison, with the moon allowing deeper, more complete knowledge.

Third, what we see are 'affective' trees – trees that, in harmony with moonlight and sunlight, can feel and perform emotion. When there is an eclipse, Alexander's trees of the sun and moon weep and are also 'stirred' by 'much pain':

> Also the bishop said that when there was an eclipse, that is, failure of the sun or the moon, the sacred trees wept severely and were stirred with great pain, because they dreaded that they would be deprived of their divine power. (p. 76)

They show a tactile and affective receptivity; it is touch that awakens the prophesying power and voice of the trees. In this, the trees are in good company in Old English poetry. In the Old English poem known as *Christ III* or *Christ in Judgement*, there are trees that weep and bleed.[41] More famously, there is the highly sensitive Tree-Cross of *The Dream of the Rood*, which weeps, trembles, bleeds, and receives wounds.[42] The trees in the *Letter of Alexander* are sentient, and their tips seem to be like fingertips. The prophecy occurs through touch, a caress of sunlight and moonlight on the feeling tips of the trees. The moon here is an essential part of the affective receptivity of creation.

PART II: RELIGIOUS SIGNS

Muhammad and the Cleaving of the Moon

In the first half of this chapter, we saw how the moon is an important sign for medieval people of what is to come: it foretells future events, as epitomised in Alexander's moon-tree. In the remainder of the chapter, we will consider how the moon had an important function in the religious ideas of medieval people. The moon frequently represented important concepts and was conversant with religious symbolism in different traditions. We will focus especially on medieval Islam and medieval Christianity.

The moon is immensely important in Islamic teaching. There is a whole surah, or chapter, of the Qur'an entitled *'Al-Qamr'* ('The Moon'). The moon also has a vital chronometric function in Islam, underpinning the Hijri calendar. In the famous twelfth-century Islamic poem *The Conference of the Birds*, which we will return to in Chapter 6, the Prophet Muhammad is directly likened to the moon.[43] The moon's significance is further demonstrated in a sixteenth-century manuscript by Zakariyyā al-Qazwīnī's/Qazvini (1203–1238), *'Ajā'ib al-makhlūqāt wa gharā'ib al mawjūdāt* (*The Wonders of Creatures and the Marvels of Existence*), now housed at the Museum of Fine Arts, Boston. Qazvini was an Arab-Persian cosmographer.[44] In an illustration of his work, an archangel, possibly Israfil, holds a large full moon (Plate 7). According to the Qur'an (39:68) and *hadith* (teachings associated with the Prophet Muhammad), Israfil will blow the trumpet at the Last Judgment, and so this image links the moon with the eschatological doctrines of Islam.[45]

The moon is also the basis of an important miracle in Islam. The opening verses of the surah of the moon read as follows: 'The Hour draws near; the moon is split. Yet whenever the disbelievers see a sign, they turn away and say, "Same old sorcery!"' (54:1–2). This verse has been interpreted as referring to a miracle known as the splitting of the moon (*shaqq al-qamar*), often attributed to the Prophet Muhammad. The splitting of the moon has been the subject of much exegetical work, with differing interpretations. One reading is a historical or narratological one: that the people of Mecca asked for a sign, and Muhammad performed this miracle, only for them to continue to disbelieve. Alternative readings have been based on eschatology; in these readings, the splitting of the moon was a sign of the Last Day and the Hereafter. Questions have also been raised regarding the agent of the miracle: the Prophet Muhammad (acting through God's power), or solely God.[46]

A significant amount of this exegesis dates to the medieval period, including by the 'two Jalals', Jalāl al-Dīn al-Maḥallī (1389–1459) and Jalāl al-Dīn al-Suyūṭī (1445–1505). They explain the following: 'The Hour has approached means the Day of Judgement (al-Qiyāma) is near. The moon has split means that it has split into two halves.' They also say that the ones who see and reject the sign are 'the unbelievers of the Quraysh' (kuffār Quraysh), and that the sign itself is a mu'jiza, a miracle, by the Prophet's hand.[47] In his Revival of the Religious Sciences (Iḥya' 'Ulūm al-Dīn), the scholar Abū Ḥamid Muḥammad ibn Muḥammad al-Ṭūsiyy al-Ghazali (1058–1111) places this miracle as the first in a list, with the following words: 'God violently interrupted the natural order via Muhammad several times: [for example] when he split the moon for him in Mecca when Quraysh asked him for a miracle (āya).'[48]

A fifteenth-century poet, 'Abd ar-Rahmān Jāmī, explains the miracle numerically and graphemically, using gematria (the attribution of numerical values to letters). The full moon is the circular letter mīm, which has a value of forty. In the split moon, each half becomes an Arabic letter nūn, at a value of fifty.[49] Thus Muhammad increases the value of the moon through the miracle. This reading invests the moon with quantifiable value, multiplied by the Prophet's hand.

The Moon as a Sign of God

Moving now to medieval Christian contexts, it is clear that the moon could at times act on God's behalf. In a medieval French romance known as Cligés, written by Chrétien de Troyes (b. 1135), the moon emerges through God's hand to reveal treachery.[50] *Cligés* follows the story of the hero Cligés and his love for Fenice, as well as telling the story of Cligés' parents, Alexander and Soredamors. The moon shines its inescapable light on the acts of traitorous warriors, and it does so through God's actions:

> That night, neither stars nor moon had shown their rays in the sky; but before the soldiers had come to the tents, the moon began to rise. And I think that it was to grieve them that it rose earlier than usual, and that God illuminated the dark night because he wished to disadvantage them and had no care for them; rather, he hated them for the sin which had corrupted them, because God hates traitors and treason more than any other sin. So, he commanded the moon to shine, so that it would disadvantage them. The moon did disadvantage them by shining on their bright shields, and their helmets also disadvantaged them as they glittered in the moonlight.[51]

The warriors are thwarted by the moon's luminescence: the moon's light is as revealing as the sun's. In Chrétien de Troyes' romance, the moon acts as a sign of God's displeasure, and works to achieve God's will.

The moon could also signify important religious occurrences in Christian history, and we see this in an earlier text known as the *Old English Martyrology*, dating possibly to the ninth century. The *Old English Martyrology* is a collection of short excerpts: not only does it partly celebrate the lives of saints according to each of their feast days, but it also contains cosmological information. The moon is prominent throughout it, and we even have the detail that October is known as the month of 'Winterfylleth' (Winter Full Moon; pp. 194–5, 208–9).[52] The moon also emerges repeatedly as a powerful sign of events. The text tells us that on 25 December, the supposed birth date of Christ, people saw three suns and at another time three moons (p. 34). The moon here again has a portending function. On 30 August, dedicated to Felix of Thibiuca, there is said to have been a blood moon when Felix was beheaded (p. 173).

We are told that on 21 March, which was the fourth day of Creation, God placed the sun and moon: 'The sun was then seven times brighter than it is now, and the moon had the brightness that the sun now has' (p. 68). But when Adam and Eve committed the original sin, the light of the sun and moon was reduced, each body having only a seventh of its former brightness. On Doomsday, all will be restored – and in fact enhanced, for the moon will no longer wax and wane:

> The sun will then shine seven times brighter than it does now, and it will never set. And the moon will shine like the sun does now, and it will never after that wane and wax, but it will always remain in its position. (p. 68)

This leads onto a passage about the dance between moon and sun, the moon forever entwined with the fate of the sun:

> Always when the moon follows the sun, then its light grows; when the moon is before the sun, then its light wanes. And by as much as it is nearer the sun, so much is its light the less; and by as much as it is far from the sun, so is its light the greater; and, however, it is always illuminated by the sun. (p. 68)

The compiler of the *Old English Martyrology* here focuses on the natural order of the world, with the moon illuminated by the sun to varying degrees depending on the position of both; the compiler brings this natural order into dialogue with the powerful signification of these celestial bodies in the Creation of the world and in the Last Judgment. Medieval people were encouraged not only to observe the moon, but also to imagine how its light has changed throughout Christian history and all its momentous events.

The Moon as Christian Symbol

In addition to the 'real' moon changing according to the patterns of Christian history, there is also an emphasis in medieval thought on the moon as an important symbol for various Christian concepts. There was, for example, the idea of hierocracy: the dominance of the Church over the state. The moon as a reflection of the sun's light was understood and employed by Pope Innocent III in his promulgation of hierocracy. Whereas the pope is the sun, the generator of heat, the emperor is merely the moon reflecting it. The pope says exactly this in a letter to the prefect Acerbius and the nobles of Tuscany (dated to 1198).[53]

And yet, although in the words of Pope Innocent III, the papacy is the sun, the Church was also frequently represented by the moon in Christian medieval traditions – a subject we will return to in Chapter 5. This was the case in the *glossa ordinaria*, a compendium of biblical interpretations, and in many other sources. Authors who wrote about the church as the moon include Ambrose of Milan (d. 397), Augustine of Hippo (354–430), Isidore of Seville (d. 636), the Venerable Bede (c. 672–735), Rabanus Maurus (c. 784–856), Gerhoh of Reichersberg (c. 1092–1169), and Peter Lombard (c. 1110–1160), among many others.[54] Augustine, for example, puts forward two cosmic possibilities: that the moon generates its own light, or that it only reflects the light of the sun. In both of these scenarios, Augustine argues, the moon is a very suitable representation of the Church. If the moon does generate its own light, then it is like the Church in that it has both a 'light' and a 'dark' side – a spiritual and a carnal side. If the moon does not generate its own light, then it is like the Church in that it is illuminated by Christ.[55]

Furthermore, the moon also represented Jesus Christ. In one later medieval text, a sermon associated with John Wycliffe (d. 1384) and

his followers, Christ in his humanity is represented by the moon –
reflecting God as the sun:

Iericho is 'þe mone' or 'smellyng' þat men schulden haue, for eche
man in þis lif schulde smelle Crist and sewon hym; and riȝt as þe
Moone is principal planete aftyr þe sonne, so Cristis manhede is
pry[n]cipal after his godhede. And as fadres of þe oolde lawe smell-
iden Crist in þer deedis; so myche more we schulde now smelle
Crist in alle owre deedis; and þanne we schulden sewe þis|mone,
and ende sikerly þis weyȝe.[56]

(Jericho is the 'Moon' or the 'smelling' that men should have, for
each man in this life should smell Christ and see him; and just as
the Moon is the principal planet after the sun, so is Christ's
manhood the principal after his Godhead. And as fathers of old
law smelt Christ in their deeds, so much more should we now
smell Christ in all our deeds; and then we should see this Moon,
and end securely in this way.)

This is in the sermon for the Sunday before Lent ('Quinquagesima
Sunday'; Sermon 39). It plays on two meanings of 'Jericho' in Hebrew:
fragrance and the moon.[57] Just as the moon is the principal planet
after the sun, so is Christ's humanity principal after his divinity. In
this example, medieval readers or listeners are invited to imagine
Christ's humanity as the moon, bound with the sun of his divinity.
Given that the moon is such a potent symbol in medieval thought, it
follows that it also appears very frequently in Christian iconography
during this period.

Passion, Last Judgment, and Saints

Christian iconography in the medieval period deals with many themes
and biblical stories – two of the most widespread being scenes of the

Passion and the Last Judgment. The moon makes an appearance in many of these scenes, where it is often set against the sun. Together, the iconographical moon and sun had an important symbolic role for medieval Christian people. For example, in Last Judgment or 'Doom' scenes, the moon and sun could remind viewers of God as the ultimate Creator, an Author whose inscriptions are in every living thing; and in Crucifixion scenes they could show the cosmic significance of Christ's death.[58] Seeing the moon and sun in these scenes, medieval viewers from many walks of life could reflect on the awesome creative power of God, and on the depth and multilayered meaning of Christ's death, his sacrifice for the sake of humanity.

In manuscript illumination throughout the medieval centuries, we find the moon and sun are together grieving during the Crucifixion. *Sol* (sun) and *Luna* (moon) are seen veiled and weeping. Art historian Moshe Barasch even suggests that in pre-thirteenth-century depictions, *Luna* and *Sol* convey lamentation, while angels in this period do not.[59] We can find a wealth of examples of Passion scenes with the moon. One example is in a medieval psalter from thirteenth-century Flanders (Oxford, Bodleian Library, MS Douce 49, fol. 123v). As Christ's body is lowered from the Cross, the sun and moon shine above (Plate 8).

One particularly striking image of the moon and sun during the Passion shows each as a pagan god with their chariots.[60] This is an ivory panel (Reims, *c.* 870) that was eventually placed in the cover of a Book of Pericopes for King Henry II (before 1014). There are two scenes: a Crucifixion and the holy women at the sepulchre. At the top, there are the figures of the sun and the moon, each enclosed in a circle with a jagged leaf pattern. The figure of the moon has a crescent moon placed on the head.[61] Between them is the hand of God emerging from a cloud. The ivory panel has exquisite foliage borders, and it shows a riot of figures: it is a very busy scene. The moon with the sun reminds us of the celestial realm in which the events are located. Together they also offer a certain calm and stillness within the mass of movement below. We are compelled to draw connections, bringing the scene of the Crucifixion and the holy women at the sepulchre in unison with the skies, filling each scene with cosmic resonance. This reminds us of the many layers of any biblical event, and a cosmic, celestial layer at the core of every happening on earth. Another example of the moon in the Crucifixion is an image from King Henry II's sacramentary (a manuscript of liturgical texts made for the king): we see two figures at the top personifying the sun and the moon; the sun is clothed in light rose-gold sun rays with the word 'Sol'; on the opposite side is a figure cloaked in blue, with a crescent moon adorning the head, and the word 'Luna'.[62] The sun and moon figures clearly show emotion, with their cloaks held to their faces in signs of mourning and shock.

Beyond manuscripts, we can find Crucifixion moons in church wall paintings, for medieval churches were richly adorned with images of biblical stories and the narratives of the saints. An example is found at Dorchester Abbey in Dorchester-on-Thames, a village in Oxfordshire (Plate 9). It shows Christ crucified between Mary and St John the Evangelist, with the sun and the moon at the top of the scene. This is an example of restoration work in the nineteenth century of an originally fourteenth-century painting.[63]

Just as significant is the lunar presence in images of Doomsday; surviving images in England also show the moon and sun in various Last Judgment scenes. A church wall painting in the chancel of St Mary's Church in Kempley, Gloucestershire (c. 1120), depicts the risen Christ in Majesty. He sits in triumph and judgment on a rainbow, and above him glow images of the sun and the moon. These images show how he rules over all Creation, and all Creation bows down to him.[64] A church wall painting in St Mary the Virgin, Great Shelford,

Cambridgeshire (fifteenth century), again shows Christ in Majesty, seated on a rainbow, and above him are the sun and the moon. But this image also reminds us of his suffering, for he bleeds from his arms along with other signs of his Passion, like the instruments of torture. The sun and the moon here remind us that his triumph is tied with his anguish. They gaze above him in both states: his human, agonised state and his risen, celebratory state.[65] A wall painting at St Denys' in Rotherfield, East Sussex (fourteenth century), shows Christ in Majesty on a rainbow, this time with two orbs above him. These could represent the sun and the moon.[66] If they do, their abstract shapes mean they act as signifiers for all the cosmos, the Lord's Creation beside him as he sits in judgment.

As a final note, the moon also occurs in iconography related to God's saints, for the moon has symbolic function there too. As mentioned above, in the *Old English Martyrology*, for example, the blood moon signals St Felix's beheading. In a church wall painting depicting a scene from the *Life* of St Catherine (or Katherine) in St Mary of Sporle, Norfolk, an empress, who has been martyred after converting to Christianity, is buried by moonlight; the moon is very visible in this image (*c.* 1400).[67] On the simplest level, the moon here indicates to viewers that the empress is being buried under cover of night, away from the prying eyes of the violent emperor. But the moon in this image also has much more to say to the medieval viewer. It is an example of an outflow of God's light and love, shimmering on the empress's decapitated body after she was so cruelly abandoned by her husband – then claimed tenderly by Christian devotees. The moon glimmers to show the ultimate victory of the saint over the pagan torturers, the divine light overcoming violent rage and disbelief.

• • •

In the Aberdeen Bestiary – a compendium on various animals, plants, and stones that we encountered Chapter 1 – there is an entry on the stone chelonite. According to the wisdom relayed in this text, if one places chelonite under the tongue at the waxing of the moon, one will have the ability to see the future.[68] This encapsulates the moon's enduring association with the gift of prophecy. For the moon represented so much more than itself to medieval minds. This chapter was divided into two halves, and throughout it embraced a 'multi-glance' – even if this multi-glance was not perfect, with some traditions receiving more attention than others. In the first half, we studied the moon's role in foretelling the future. We dwelt with the tragic lovers Troilus and Criseyde, for whom the moon becomes a sign of the breakage of their relationship. Troilus' friend and Criseyde's uncle Pandarus is seen consulting a 'moonbook'; this reflects medieval practices of prognostication, and we also considered the moon's central role in prognostication in both medieval England and medieval Polynesia. This chapter then investigated the moon's part in the prophecies uttered by Merlin and by Alexander's trees of the sun and the moon. In the second half of the chapter, we turned to the moon's various meanings as a sign in medieval Islam and medieval Christianity. We encountered the tradition of the Prophet Muhammad's miraculous cleaving of the moon. In Christian contexts, we saw how the moon acts as a sign of God; how it emerges to represent the Church and Christ himself; and how it is used to explain the concept of the pope's supremacy over the king. We finally gazed at the moon's presence in various paintings of the Passion and Last Judgment, and in hagiographies. Everywhere in these writings and artworks, we encountered medieval people reading rich, at times hidden, meanings in the world around them. Throughout all these myriad texts and images, it is evident that the moon is fundamental to the stories medieval people told, the narratives they created about their lives, and how they imagined their unknown futures.

4

• • •

THE MOON OF ILLNESSES
AND CURES

A lunar eclipse was believed to have caused the Black Death – that terrible pandemic which aggressed Europe, Asia, and Africa and killed significant swathes of the population. On 18 March 1345, there was a lunar eclipse in Libra, alongside a conjunction of Mars, Jupiter, and Saturn in the sign Aquarius.[1] This eclipse and conjunction together were seen as the direct celestial cause of the traumatic pandemic that ensued. Such thinking is attested in the work of Geoffrey of Meaux, a French author and scientist (active 1310–48).[2] We see here how the moon plays a central role in beliefs about illness, even being linked to causing a devastating pandemic. For in the medieval period the moon did not have only an imaginary or metaphorical bond with human beings. It was also understood, throughout the period and around the globe, to have very physical, visceral impacts on human bodies and minds. As author Peter of Abano (c. 1250–1315) says in his translation of the *Libellus de medicorum astrologia* (*A Small Book on Medical Astrology*), also known as the *Astronomia*, a doctor must consider the moon. If it is full of light, this means it increases the blood and marrow of all human beings and animals, and causes the expansion of sea and everything on earth.[3] Astrological medicine was a major part of medieval life around the world, and it was common for physicians (in, for example, Europe and the Islamicate regions) to be trained in astrology. The moon was tremendously important in prognosis and regimes related to health and sickness. The moon's movements and phases were vital in medical contexts because it was believed that the precise positions of the moon affected the body and healing practices – and there has been an enduring connection between the moon and mental illness. There were even special 'moonbooks' designed to help the healer to assess and treat particular cases of physical and mental ill health.

Cornelius O'Boyle, who has written on astrological medicine in medieval England, explains that since the moon was closest to the earth of all the planets, 'its sphere gathered up the motions of the higher spheres and transferred this motion to the sublunary world'; and linked to this, 'the moon magnified the astrological influences of the zodiacal signs through which it passed'. The moon was also believed to have 'a special influence upon fluids in the bodies of living things, especially the blood'.[4] Medieval medicine followed humoral theory (the theory that health was impacted by various liquids in the body), and so, given that the moon was believed to have a significant impact on bodily fluids, it makes sense that it was so deeply tied to health and wellness.[5] The moon was particularly associated with the humour phlegm, and those with a phlegmatic disposition were associated with the element water, in turn impacted by the phases of the moon.[6] In this chapter, we will harness the multi-glance to consider the 'zodiac man'; the moon in the rich medical traditions of medieval Islam; moonbooks of medieval England; the importance of the moon in treatment and surgery; a story about the moon itself wasting away; the link between the moon and mental illness and epilepsy; and, in a very different context of healing, the invocation of the moon for resolving feuds.

The Zodiac Man

Diagrams of the zodiac man were quite widespread in Europe by the 1400s.[7] The 'zodiac man' refers to illustrations which show how each zodiac sign impacted a particular part of the body, according to melothesia: the idea that each bodily part was governed by a particular zodiacal sign. This is germane for us as much medicine linked to the moon was based on melothesia. We find examples of the zodiac man in the important astronomical works of two fourteenth-century English authors mentioned by Chaucer in his *Treatise on the Astrolabe*, Nicholas of Lynn (flourished 1386–1411) and John Somer (b. *c.* 1340), who both produced astronomical calendars, accompanied by a significant amount of medical information.[8]

There is a famous diagram of the 'zodiac man' in Nicholas of Lynn's calendar in the manuscript known as MS Ashmole 370, housed in Oxford's Bodleian Library (fol. 27v; Plate 10). As is clear, it shows a drawing of a male human body, imposed on a red background. Each personification of the zodiacal sign is placed on a particular part of the body: a ram sits on his head (Aries); a bull rests on his shoulders by his neck (Taurus); a crab is on his throat (Cancer); two twin figures grasp his arms (Gemini); a lion stands erect on his upper chest (Leo); a young woman in his midriff (Virgo); scales sit on his hips (Libra); and what appears to be a scorpion rests on his genitals (Scorpio). A centaur with a bow and arrow stands on his legs (Sagittarius), and a goat on his knees (Capricorn). Finally, a man holding jugs of water stands by his lower legs (Aquarius), and two fish lay crossed by his feet (Pisces). Around the image are reams of text, pinpointing particular zodiacal signs. This diagram has a clear educative purpose, demonstrating through images how the position of planets (especially the moon) in each star sign can impact the health of particular parts of the body.

John Somer's calendar in MS Ashmole 391(2) (c. 1440), again housed in Oxford's Bodleian Library, also has a zodiacal man (fol. 3r).[9] An image of the zodiacal man of John Somer's calendar in another manuscript (Oxford, Bodleian Library, MS Selden Supra 90) shows a very similar image: the zodiacal man with each zodiac sign governing a particular part of the body. In this case, Taurus is blue rather than orange-brown, perhaps simply a result of the colouring available (fol. 11v).[10] Further manuscripts linked to John Somer show a zodiacal man in an arrow-like position, with arms outstretched to form the point of the arrow, and text written around him. This is evident in a manuscript dating to c. 1433–8 (Oxford, Bodleian Library, MS Digby 48, fol. 15v).[11]

We also find zodiacal men available in a range of other sources. A Book of Hours (a luxurious manuscript of devotional texts and images), known as the Très Riches Heures du Duc de Berry (c. 1410–1416), shows a particularly exquisite example of the zodiac man, each zodiacal sign in a mandorla that encloses the man. One German print dating from 1484 tidily places each sign in a box down the margins and points to the respective part of the body.[12] A fifteenth-century Italian manuscript writes the names of the zodiac signs rather than figuring them through pictures (Oxford, Bodleian Library, MS Bodley 266, fol. 144v).[13] A further example of a zodiac man is found in the English fourteenth-century manuscript known as Oxford, Bodleian Library, MS Ashmole 210 (fol. 9r).[14] Another is found in a French collection of astronomical tables and diagrams from the third quarter of the fourteenth century, this with both an image and written name of the sign (Oxford, Bodleian Library, MS Canon Misc. 248, fol. 42r).[15] Additionally, there is an image of the zodiacal man found opposite an astronomical chart in a late-fourteenth-century English manuscript

(Oxford, Bodleian Library, MS Rawlinson D. 939, section 5 verso).[16] An astrological miscellany with texts in Latin and French dating to the fourteenth century (Paris, Bibliothèque Nationale, lat. 7351) shows another zodiacal man, each sign figured on the relevant part of his body, and the background covered with flowers (fol. 2b).[17]

The Moon in Medieval Islamic Medicine

Melothesia and other aspects of astrological medicine were present in medieval Islamic medical works, though astrological medical practices were less prevalent than in Western Europe.[18] For this reason, the present section on Islamic medicine is necessarily shorter than the following one on English moonbooks – and this is one example of how the global multi-glance across many moons is far from perfect. As summarised by Cyril Elgood with reference to Islamic medicine: 'Each organ of the body was believed to be connected with one of the signs of the zodiac. To let blood from a member during the sign of the moon governing that part was a perilous procedure.'[19]

A physician from Baghdad, Abū-Naṣr ʿAdnān ibn Naṣr al-Ayn-zarbī (d. 1153), who acted as the physician for the caliph aẓ-Ẓāfir bi-Amr-Allāh (d. 1154), wrote on melothesia.[20] In his treatise *Risāla fī-mā yaḥtāj aṭ-ṭabīb min ʿilm al-falak* (*Epistle on What the Physician Needs to Know of the Science of the Celestial Sphere*), he writes, for example, how bleeding of the neck is not a good idea when the moon is in Taurus, and it is not a good idea on the back when the sign is in Leo.[21] Earlier, in the ninth century, Yuhanna ibn aṣ-Ṣalt also wrote a book on astrological medicine, and an entire chapter of Ibn aṣ-Ṣalt's work is focused on the moon's role in illness and healing.[22]

Another physician from Baghdad, Bukhtīshūʿ ibn Jibrīl (d. 870), only prescribed an enema when the moon was in its descending node, and asserted that medications should be taken only when the moon was aligned with Venus.[23] A Persian physician, Muḥammad Ḥusaynī

Nurbakhshī Bahā'-ul-Doula (d. 1507), treated a child's rash by wiping it with a duster while exclaiming: 'O Moon, even as thou dost diminish, so make these spots to grow smaller.'[24] The moon appears in medieval Islamic paediatric medicine as well. An Andalusian physician, 'Arīb ibn-Sa'īd of Cordova (d. c. 980), mapped each stage of foetal development onto a particular planet. In the seventh month, the foetus is under the influence of the moon, associated with fast movement:

> In the seventh month the foetus stands under the sway of the moon whose attributes are swift movements. By now the child is fully formed and thrusts outwards. If it is actually born this month, it can live, and grow, because it has experienced the influences of the seven planets in their entirety.[25]

'Arīb ibn-Sa'īd also observes that in the first four years of life, a child is most impacted by the moon, resulting in the child being tender, unintelligent, and able to eat only a little.[26]

There were also those Islamic physicians who actively rejected astrologically informed medicine. One of the Bukhtīshū family of physicians (seventh–ninth centuries) rejected moon-informed practices 'by administering clysters [enemas] when the moon was in conjunction with an unfavourable planet and by giving draughts when the moon was in opposition to Venus'.[27] This reminds us that just as today, beliefs were not uniform across all people in the medieval world. While some Islamic physicians embraced astrological medicine, others were less keen.

Moonbooks of Medieval England

We saw in Chapters 1 and 3 that medieval European people (including Chaucer's fictional character Pandarus) used 'lunaries' or 'moonbooks' to determine when it would be best to carry out certain actions or pursue certain goals. 'Lunaries' and 'moonbooks' are not, strictly speaking, the same (nor are they unproblematic as terms), but for convenience I am using both terms interchangeably.[28] These moonbooks were very much used in medical contexts. One late medieval example tells us that all surgeons, physicians, barbers, administerers of medicine or laxatives should know about the sign and degree of the sun and moon in each day.[29] It was very important to make accurate calculations on the impact of particular days of the age of the moon. Day 7 is a good day for treatment, but the fourteenth day often causes problems for it 'initiates the beginning of decrease or wane and the moon's diminishing control over benefics', benefics meaning celestial bodies with favourable influence.[30] Many moonbooks employ learning according to melothesia. For example, as seen above, Aries was linked to the head, and Virgo to the womb and midriff. The moon's position in particular zodiacal signs could then reveal a lot about a person's health and potential effective cures. We will consider moonbooks first in Old English and then in Middle English.

An Early Moonbook: Old English

A 'medical lunarium' from the Anglo-Saxon period explains what will happen if someone is seized by illness on particular days of the moon.[31] The first day is very bad indeed: 'On a one-night old moon, if one is seized with illness, one will be dangerously unwell' (p. 194). The text then continues, day by day. On the seventh day, for example, one will travail a long time; on the twenty-fifth, the illness will be very grave; and on the thirtieth, 'he will recover without ease, but arise' (p. 194).

Middle English Moonbooks

Given the close links between the moon and human blood, moonbooks could tell people when it was or was not a good time to undertake bloodletting. Bloodletting was a widespread healing practice in the Middle Ages in Europe and Islamicate regions, but it had to be done at carefully chosen times. One Middle English moonbook explains that for knowing the best time for bloodletting, we need to know the condition and the days of the moon thoroughly. As the writer of this treatise remarks: 'The mone is a planet of the wiche planet man hathe moste kynde by reason' ('The moon is the planet with which humanity has most affinity by reason', p. 89). This text then goes through each day, one by one, giving information on whether it is a good day for bloodletting, and the fate of those who fall ill on any given day.

On the second day, for example, whoever falls sick will be healed (and bloodletting should be done at midday). On the seventh day, the person will be sick for a long time, but if they visit the physician, they will soon be well. The text also tells us that all kinds of healing are 'good and profitable' on this seventh day. On the fifteenth, it is a good time to bleed old men and women, both for removing bad blood and for putting in nourishing blood. This must be done at the 'onderne' (9 a.m.). On the sixteenth day, bloodletting can be done on the left arm or spleen, but nowhere else. On the nineteenth day: 'bleed on leggys with garsyng with a rasur, and that is good for the regge' ('bleed on the legs with scarification with a razor, and that is good for the back'). The twenty-fifth day is unfortunate, for the patient will suffer severely in the illness and will not recover.

'The True Knowledge of Astrology'

Another Middle English text, 'The Sothfast Kunnyng of Astrologie' ('The True Knowledge of Astrology'), also explains why the moon is so important in illness. It outlines that the moon:

is the nexte planete to the erthe and therffor he hathe more uertu and effecte þan anoþere planete to erthely thingys and more sewing to [the] creature of man. So þat be the mone and be the complexion off the syngne þat the mone ys inne, ye mowe knowe what ys good to doo or nowght, leue or take, begynne or reste. (p. 223)

(is the next planet to the earth and therefore has more strength and effect than any other planet [with regard to] earthly things and more linkage to the creature of humanity. So that by the moon and by the complexion of the sign that the moon is in, one may know what is good to do or not good to do, leave or take, begin or rest.)

The text then details the state of illness depending on the moon's position in the zodiac, according to melothesia. When the moon is in Taurus, for example: 'Yt ys not good to do medycynys to þe nekke ner throte, ffor yffe a man be horte in these parties, it is perell of dethe or offe mayme. Yt is not good to be lete bloode' ('It is not good to give medicines to the neck or throat, for if a human being is hurt in these parts, it is peril of death or of maiming. It is not good to have blood-letting done', p. 225). In Cancer, the breast should not be healed (p. 227). But 'Good it is to bathe or to stewe or to do al maner of þing þat longeth to the water' ('Good it is to bathe or to stew or to do all manner of things that relate to the water', p. 228). This is because Cancer 'gouernyth the brest and þe legges þat ben cold and moyst, off the kynde of the water' ('governs the breast and the legs that are cold and moist, of the nature of water', p. 228). When in Virgo, 'good it is to lete þe bloode and to take medicynys laxatyffe' ('it is good to let blood and to take laxative medicines', p. 230). When in Sagittarius, it is a good time to cut fingernails and toenails. As Sagittarius governs the thighs, one should not administer treatment to these parts (p. 234).

The Book of Hippocrates

Another Middle English source, called 'The Boke of Ypocras' (*The Book of Hippocrates*), matches signs with parts of the body and expands in depth on illness and health depending on the moon's position. In this text, the moon acts as a 'catalyst', instigating various effects according to the properties of the signs and the planets, and all is further influenced by Galenic humoral theory.[32] The text explains what to do based on which sign the moon is positioned in: 'wanne þou takest a cure, be it of [fysyke] or ellis of surgery, ta[ke] keep of þe mone and of þe time wan þe seknesse took and in w[h]at sygne it began' ('when you take a cure, whether of remedial treatment or else of surgery, take heed of the moon and of the time when the sickness took and in what sign it began', p. 245). Let us see a few examples in this source too.

Aries matches up to the head and chin, and it is a fiery, hot and dry sign, associated with the choleric humour. Taurus is of the earth, cold and dry: 'And i[f] a planete þat is callid Saturnus [be] with þe mone in þis sygne and Mars, þat is a planete be contrarie to þe mone, þis syknesse xal be of coldnesse and drinesse' ('And if a planet that is called Saturn is with the moon in this sign and Mars, that is a planet which is contrary to the moon, this sickness shall be of coldness and dryness', p. 246). Taurus, of course, matches up to the throat. On Cancer, the writer explains:

Cancer is a sygne þat is cold and moyst of kind of flewme. Wan þe mone is in þis sygne, he is in his propre hows. Yf a man falle syk atte þat tyme and þe syknesse be of flewme þat is cold and moyst as be dropsye, feuere cotidiane, and postemus þat ben in colore wythe and in felyng nessche, þei mow nowt be curyd or þat þe mone com in to a sygne þat hatte Leo. (p. 247)

(Cancer is a sign that is cold and moist, of the nature of phlegm. When the moon is in this sign, the moon is in its own house. If a person falls sick at that time and the sickness is of phlegm that is cold and moist as is dropsy, daily fever, and swelling or inflammation that is in colour white and in feeling soft, they may not be cured until the moon comes into a sign that is called Leo.)

If Saturn is with the moon and there is no other planet giving light, the person shall never recover but will die the next cold winter (p. 247).

Two Further Middle English Moonbooks

Yet another moonbook in both prose and verse remarks, as observed above, that all who dispense or provide treatments must know the sign and degree of the sun and moon in each day of the twelve signs. When in Aries, one must take special care of the head and should not consume any medicine or potion. When in Taurus, one must not draw blood in the neck. When in Gemini, one must not be bled in the arms. When in Cancer, if someone falls ill, there is a high chance of death. When in Leo, it is not a good time to take medicines. When in Virgo, one should not marry a maiden, because of infertility:

> Take þanne no mayden to þi wijf,
> Lest sche be bareyne alle hire life.
>
> (p. 216)
>
> (Take then no maiden to your wife,
> Lest she be barren all her life!)

When in Libra, it is a good time for bloodletting except in the genitals, and there is a similar message for Scorpio. When in Sagittarius, it is a good time to wash or bathe and shave the head. If someone is ill in Capricorn, they will soon recover. In Aquarius, there should be no medicine or incisions done to the leg. Pisces has a similar comment about the legs (pp. 210–22). And in one final moonbook I will mention, the author says that anyone who falls sick in any way on the twenty-sixth day of the moon is strongly advised to make their confession and penitence because they will not survive (p. 87).

Administering Medicines and Surgery

We have seen the immense significance of moonbooks in identifying a prognosis and for bloodletting. It was highly important to administer medicines and provide healing practices at certain times in medieval Europe and Islamicate regions, and we will now consider the significance of the moon in administering healing practices in European sources beyond the English moonbooks. The *Old English Herbarium* or *Old English Herbal*, a compendium of herbal remedies in English from the Anglo-Saxon period, frequently links healing practices with the moon. Herbs need to be plucked and prepared at certain ages of the moon. Take the following examples:

> If anyone is suffering from an infirmity in which he may be fastidious, you can free them from it. Take the plants that we call lion's foot, without their roots; simmer in water while the moon is waning, and wash them with it. (p. 82)[33]
>
> For epilepsy: take the berries of this plant that we call *asterion*: give them to eat when the moon is waning. (p. 166)
>
> So that you do not dread encountering any evil, pick this same plant, *cardum silfaticum*, at the break of day, when the sun first rises – and let it be when the moon is in Capricorn – and hold it with you. As long as you bear it on you, no evil will come to you. (p. 242)
>
> You must take it [greater periwinkle] when the moon is nine nights old, and eleven nights, and thirteen nights, and thirty nights, and when it is one night old. (p. 354)
>
> This plant [melilotus], you should pick when the moon is waning, in the month that one calls August. (p. 360)

Surgical practice was also influenced by the position of the moon. A Middle English translation of the Italian author Lanfranc's (*c.* 1250–1315) *Chirurgia parva* says that humoral categories are blended under the circle of the moon. As the author explains: 'A surgian muste knowe þat alle bodies þat ben medlid vndir þe sercle of þe moone, ben engendrid of foure symple bodies [...] þat is to seie: fier & water, erðe eir' ('A surgeon must know that all bodies that are blended under the circle of the moon are engendered of four simple bodies [...] that is to say: fire, water, earth, and air').[34]

John Arderne (b. 1307) was an English surgeon, and has even been hailed as 'a founder of modern surgery'.[35] In a work known as the *Treatises on Fistulo*, Arderne designed lunar tables to calculate the best times for undertaking surgical interventions; they are based on Toledan tables said to have been composed by Peter of Dacia (*c.* 1230–1289), a Swedish friar.[36] As Arderne says:

A cyrurgien ow noʒt for to kutte or brenne in any member of a mannes body, ne do fleobotomye whiles þe mone is in a signe gouernyng or tokenyng þat membre.[37]

(A surgeon ought not cut or burn any member of a person's body, nor do phlebotomy, while the moon is in a sign governing or betokening that member.)

Arderne specifies, for example:

It is best & most sikir þat he kutte noʒt in þe lure ne do no violence ne greuousnes to it in þe tyme þat þe mone is in Scorpion or Libra, or Sagittarius, for þan of astronomyeʒ is forbede þer kuttyng.[38]

(It is best and most certain that he does not cut in the anus nor do no violence nor grievousness to it in the time that the moon is in Scorpio or Libra, or Sagittarius, for astronomy then forbids to cut there.)

This is reinforced in the accompanying Latin text, with the explanation that each sign rules or signifies a bodily part, and that the surgeon must refrain from making an incision or undertaking a procedure on that particular body part when the moon is in 'its' sign.[39] There is also guidance for how to ascertain the position of the moon in order to undertake the surgery accurately. Such a procedure begins with using the almanac to establish where the moon is in conjunction with the sun and the day of the conjunction, followed by further complex calculations.[40] Ardene offers tables to help with these calculations.[41]

King Moon and the Wasting Disease

Links between the moon and health extend beyond Western and Islamicate spheres. In Ayurvedic medicine, there is a kind of health system known as *rasāyana* (rejuvenation therapy). *Rasāyana* is intimately in synch with the cosmos. While the sun 'drains the life from everything and dries up essential fluids', the moon 'cools, replenishes, and moisturizes'.[42] The moon is especially powerful in the winter monsoon.[43] 'Soma' is a name for the moon but also signifies the matter from which it is formed.[44] There is a South Asian tradition of a royal illness, a form of consumptive illness or wasting disease affecting the king. And it is said that the moon himself suffered from this illness.

The story seems to have developed from a hymn to Soma (the moon) and Sūryā, daughter of the sun. King Moon is married to twenty-seven or twenty-eight stars which form the *naksatras* (lunar mansions).[45] But King Moon neglects most of his wives, spending his time with one called Rohini. As a result of failing in his husbandly duties, King Moon is afflicted with a wasting illness which also diminishes his ability to light the night sky and to stop at and visit each lunar mansion. His bodily illness directly correlates with his lunar incapacitation. There are sexual connotations to his bodily infirmity, too. Dwelling too long with Rohini means all his 'semen' is used up, and this prevents him from illuminating the sky and from travelling through the other lunar mansions. In particular, as a result of his infatuation with Rohini, King Moon's *dharma* is disrupted. There is a link in Hindu teaching between the moon and this *dharma* – the essential reality and order of all that is. The moon is considered a 'witness' to whether or not the rules of *dharma* are followed.[46] Once King Moon is healed, he is able to fulfil his lunar and marital obligations again. Joseph S. Alter observes that King Moon himself is restored through *rasāyana*.[47] As explained by David Gordon White:

> In Hindu mythology, the prototypical king to suffer from royal consumption is the moon itself, the same moon that is responsible for revivifying a desiccated world at the end of each hot season, the same moon whose substance, whose fluid rasa, has been identified, since at least the time of the Taittirrya Samhitii (2.3.5.2) with semen.[48]

King Moon's story appears in a variety of other South Asian contexts. In particular, there is a medieval Tibetan text named after King Moon which deals with pulses. This text is known as *The Medicine of the Moon King* (eighth–twelfth century), or *Medical Method of the Lunar King* (*Sman dpyad zla ba'i rgyal po*; also called *Somarāja*). This has been discussed by a number of scholars, including William McGrath and Ronit Yoeli-Tlalim.[49]

There are many elements that emerge in this story of King Moon: links between the lunar and the bodily (here also with the sexual connotations), the moon and royalty and the moon and marriage; the close bond between earthly and cosmic activity; and the moon's links with social order and cohesion. King Moon's story brings together all these elements. Somatic activity is bound intimately with lunar capacity, and the moon brings with it a host of associations with social obligations and normality. What the moon should do is linked to what people 'should' do socially and communally. Medieval people familiar with this story would find the moon intimately linked with the human body and health, and with 'proper' social and communal behaviour.

Mental Illness and the Moon

So far, we have been concerned on the whole with physical illness. But there is a long and well-known association between the moon and so-called 'madness' – what we more sensitively today would call kinds of mental illness. One key influence in this regard is Origen (185–254), one of the Church Fathers. In his commentary on the Gospel of Matthew, Origen made a link between the moon and what he termed 'madness' as well as demonic possession.[50] Such association continued and is found in the writings of, for example, the important physician Paracelsus (1493–1541). His real name was Philippus Aureolus Theophrastus Bombastus von Hohenheim, and he came from Switzerland.[51] Paracelsus recognised that mental illnesses were diseases rather than a symptom of possession by the devil.[52] Paracelsus saw some people as particularly affected by the moon, with their 'sensitive spirit' susceptible to the moon's influence.[53] Although it is not considered a mental illness in modern medicine, epilepsy was linked with various mental illnesses and was also associated with the moon. Such an association was foregrounded as early as the work of the Roman author Pliny the Elder (c. 23–79): because the moon caused the brain to become overly moist, the result was mental illness and epilepsy.[54]

The association between the moon and mental illness is inscribed in the (now very outdated) English word 'lunatic', which comes from the Latin *luna*, the moon.[55] Its earliest recorded use in the English language is the year 1300, in a saint's life (the *South English Legendary* version of St Bartholomew), where it is used as an adjective. The story refers to a king who 'hadde ane douȝter þat was lunatyke' ('had a daughter who was lunatic').[56] From this early point in the word's usage, there is the clear sense that periods of mental illness vary according to the moon. The quote above from the *Life* of St Bartholomew in fuller form reads: 'He hadde ane douȝter þat was lunatyke [...] þe deuel [...] made hire witles euerech monthþe ase hit feol in þe stat of þe mone' ('He had a daughter who was lunatic [...] The devil [...] made her witless every month according to the state of the moon').[57]

Works by the English author John Trevisa (d. 1402) corroborate this usage of the word 'lunatic': 'lunaticus, þat is, mad in certayne tymes of þe mone' ('lunatic, that is, mad at certain times of the moon').[58] It is important to note that the word 'lunatic', from its early history, was also associated with epilepsy.[59] As Trevisa also says, the brain follows 'þe meuynge of þe mone' ('the moving of the moon'), 'And þat is I-seye in lunatik & epilentik men, þat bene most I-greued whanne þe mone is newe & also whanne he is olde' ('And that is seen in lunatic and epileptic men, who are most afflicted when the moon is new and also when it is old').[60] The word 'lunatic' is also used as a noun to refer to one who is 'lunatic'. A version of the Bible known as the Wycliffite Bible, associated with John Wycliffe (d. 1384) and his followers, refers to 'lunatikes and paralitykis' (lunatics and paralytics) being offered to Christ.[61] Lunacy was seen as a very particular, formally defined illness, and John Trevisa refers to it as the 'passioun lunatik' (the lunatic passion, or the lunatic affliction).[62]

It should also be noted that the term 'lunatic' could mean more generally varying with the moon, or having the inconstancy or changeability of the moon. This is expressed in a text by poet John Lydgate (*c.* 1370–*c.* 1451): 'Ther [women's] sect ys no thing lunatyke, / Nor of kynde they be nat lyke / To no monys that be wane' ('Women's sect is not lunatic [moon-changing, unstable], and in nature they are not like the waning moon'). This use of the word in Middle English is much less frequent than 'lunatic' as associated with mental illness, however.[63] Earlier in the history of the English language, there was also so-called 'moon-sickness': one who would later be termed 'lunatic' or 'epileptic' was 'mon-seoc'.[64] There is also 'monaðseoc', or month-sickness.[65] 'Moon-sick' is attested in the Rushworth Gospels, an early English version of the New Testament gospels. The word 'monað-seoc' is found in a range of texts, including Ælfric's *Homilies* and the *Lives of Saints* and a medical text known as *Bald's Leechbook*.[66]

Medieval people invested a lot of energy in curing 'lunacy' or 'moon-sickness'. The *Old English Herbarium* says the following about the herb clufwort:

For lunacy, take this herb and tie it with a red thread around the person's neck during a waning moon in the month called April and at the start of October. He will be healed immediately. (p. 86)[67]

Trevisa says the following about potential cures for lunacy, the gemstones topaz and celidonius:

Þe rede [stone celidonius] helpeþ aȝeins þe passioun lunatik [L *lunaticam passionem*] and aȝeins woodnes.

(The red stone celidonius helps against the lunatic passion and against madness.)

[The topaz] folweþ þe cours of þe moone and helpeþ aȝenst þe passioun lunatik..as þe moone is more ful oþe lesse so, his effecte is more oþer lasse.

(The topaz [stone] follows the course of the moon and helps against the lunatic passion . . . as the moon is more full or less so, its effect is more or less)[68]

Trevisa's words suggest lunacy is distinct from, but tied to, a generalised 'madness'. A number of other texts discuss potential cures for 'lunacy' among gemstones. In *The Book of John Mandeville*, it is said that a particular diamond 'heleth him þat is lunatyk & hem þat þe fend pursueth' ('heals him who is lunatic and those who are pursued by the devil').[69] A lapidary (a book which lists the properties of stones) found in a manuscript known as Peterborough, Dean and Chapter Library 33 says the following: 'Þe red [stone calidonie] is gode aȝens a malady þat men clepen lunatix, wherby he falleþ, & wherby he is foolych & wytles & falleþ þer-with long tyme' ('The red [stone calidone] is good against a malady that people call "lunacy", whereby one falls and whereby one is foolish and witless and falls [ill] with it a long time').[70] Paracelsus prescribed various cures for moon-time 'madness'. This included the 'lunar plants' Christmas rose (*Helleborus niger*) and thyme (*Thymus majoram*), magnets, and immersion in water.[71]

Healing Feuds

We will end with a gesture to the moon's healing in a very different context. The *Havamal* (*Sayings of the High One*) is a long poem in Old Norse, part of the *Poetic Edda* found in a thirteenth-century manuscript known as the Codex Regius. The poem is spoken by the Norse god Odin, who utters a series of gnomic statements or statements of wisdom. Carolyne Larrington refers to it as a 'conspectus of different types of wisdom'.[72] This includes statements regarding the power of runes and various magical spells. *Sayings of the High One* is in *ljodahattr* verse, an alliterative form commonly used for poems concerned with wisdom. In this poem, the moon is invoked among other remedies:

I advise you, Loddfafnir, to take this advice,
it will be profitable if you take it,
good for you if you get it:

where you drink ale, choose for yourself earth's power
for earth has power against ale, and fire against illness,
oak against constipation, an ear of corn against witchcraft.
The hall against household strife, for hatred should one invoke the moon,
Earthworm against inflammation, and runes against evil;
One must take earth for the flux [or flood].[73]

This invocation of the moon comes in a series of statements of wisdom uttered to someone called Loddfafnir.[74] So the moon's remedial power lies in healing hatred or feuds; it is in these cases that one should invoke the moon. The moon has a calming effect, dissipating the anger that fuels feuds. It is notable that it comes along with other natural portals of healing – earth, fire, oak, corn, the hall (meaning the place where the community would gather), earthworms, the runes themselves, and the land. As Larrington observes, 'the substances mentioned may be invoked or be incorporated into some kind of ritual'.[75] The moon here is a peaceful, unifying force, healing rifts, soothing friction, and mending ruptures.

• • •

In the medieval world, the moon was a major part of both illness and healing. Its position in the cosmos at any given point was believed to have an immense impact on one's health and wellbeing, and in Europe and Islamicate regions, for example, its position was essential for knowing when to undertake vital treatment programmes, such as bloodletting. In this chapter, we have considered various 'zodiac men' – the 'zodiac man' shows the link between certain zodiacal signs and different parts of the body; it was vital to know when a moon was in a particular sign because this would have a direct impact on prognosis and treatment. This was explored in more detail in Islamic medicine and so-called moonbooks, which expand on the health impacts of a particular day of the moon or its position in a particular sign. We subsequently encountered a South Asian story about the link between the moon and a royal wasting disease, and King Moon's own failing health due to his obsessive love for a particular star. We then turned to the intimate link between the moon and mental illness and epilepsy, as attested in a range of texts and with many cures employed to heal so-called 'lunacy' or 'moon-sickness'. We finally saw, with a different understanding of healing, how the moon is invoked to resolve feuds in Old Norse poetry. Throughout this chapter, the moon has revealed both benevolence and malevolence. It has the power to worsen our illnesses, even being involved in the onset of a pandemic. Yet it also has the very real potency to heal. The moon shows how close illness and healing can be – how health and ill-health accompany each other, perhaps embodied in the very form of the moon itself. Its sphere holds illness and wellness in its compass.

5

• • •

THE MOON OF SORROWS
AND ILLUSIONS

The moon is burdened throughout medieval texts and images with a range of negative, even sinister meanings – inconstancy, falsity, brokenness. It is the marker of an inferior world below, tantalisingly hinting at the secure heavens beyond. For medieval people, the moon could signify absence and confusion and sorrow; and at times, the moon itself becomes like a symbolic discard pile, onto which all the horrors of the world can be thrown. In the words of Sarah Harlan-Haughey, the moon is 'the most powerful sign of mutability next to the Wheel of Fortune' – the Wheel of Fortune being a symbol, inspired by Roman author and senator Boethius (d. 524), signifying the changing nature of human fortune in this world.[1] In the medieval Western and Islamicate world especially, the moon was understood to be the planet closest to earth. The earth is surrounded by spheres, and moving outwards are the Moon, Mercury, Venus, the Sun, Mars, Jupiter, and Saturn. The moon formed the borderland between the earth and the celestial realm beyond it. This meant that the moon could represent not only the borderland itself, but also the shifting, inconstant world beneath it. The moon became associated with the changes undergone in the world, and with the suffering people endure from the changeability of life on earth. There was an understanding of a 'sublunary' world: the world under the moon being subject to vacillation and painful change.

Through a multi-glance, we will begin this chapter by considering lunar and solar eclipses, subsequently turning to the Old Norse myth of the moon being swallowed by a wolf. We will then turn from this myth to see how, in a collection of animal tales known as *Kalīla and Dimna* and in works by the medieval authors Chaucer and Robert Henryson (Henryson having flourished later than Chaucer, in the fifteenth century), the moon is associated with illusion – what is artificial, easily dissolving when confronted with reality. After that, we will see how visions of the moon compelled one strong medieval woman to address a crucial absence she saw in her world. We will also uncover how, for other women, the moon was used to provoke feelings of shame, as echoed in an image of the Virgin Mary standing on a moon. And finally, we will pause on one poignant medieval poem in which a grieving father remains locked in this world beneath the moon, with all its anguish.

Eclipses

This chapter starts with eclipses: when the earth blocks the moon (lunar eclipse) and when the moon blocks the sun (solar eclipse). We are beginning with eclipses in a chapter entitled 'The Moon of Sorrows and Illusions' for a twofold reason. First, eclipses show the moon's susceptibility to disappearing, hinting at a potential vulnerability. Second, this susceptibility or vulnerability coexists alongside an awesome, unnerving power – the moon has the capacity to cause the sun itself to vanish. Medieval thinkers developed potent theories about eclipses, in terms of both how they work and how they might impact the earth. As observed in the previous chapter, a lunar eclipse was thought to have caused the Black Death – and eclipses were also seen as instigators of storms and wars.[2] Therefore, calculating when eclipses would occur was a very important activity. A manuscript known as MS Douce 18 (now in the Bodleian Library) has a table of the eclipses of the sun and the moon (fols 49r–51r). Many such tables exist throughout medieval sources.

One key theorist on eclipses was John of Sacrobosco, who flourished around the years 1220–50. John of Sacrobosco was likely born in England; he seems to have studied at Oxford and taught at the University of Paris. He is especially famous for his treatise *De sphaera mundi* (*On the Sphere of the World*), in which he describes the spheres of the universe.[3] John of Sacrobosco describes the causes of both kinds of eclipse in exacting detail. On lunar eclipses, he writes:

Since the sun is larger than the earth, it is necessary that half the sphere of earth be always illuminated by the sun and that the shadow of the earth, extended into the air like a cone, diminish in circumference until it ends in the plane of the circle of the signs inseparable from the nadir of the sun. The nadir is a point in the firmament directly opposite to the sun. Hence, when the moon, at full is in the head or tail of the dragon beneath the nadir of the sun, then the earth is interposed between sun and moon, and the cone of the earth's shadow falls on the body of the moon. Wherefore, since the moon has no light except from the sun, it actually is deprived of light and there is a general eclipse, if it is in the head or tail of the dragon directly but partial if it is almost within the bounds determined for eclipse. And it always happens at full moon or thereabouts. But, since in every opposition – that is, at full moon – the moon is not in the head or tail of the dragon or beneath the nadir of the sun, it is not necessary that the moon suffer eclipse at every full moon.[4]

This detailed description of the workings of the lunar eclipse is accompanied by other scientific knowledge – that the moon receives its light from the sun, for example. We will also return to this striking image of the dragon, which we encountered in Chapter 3 with Geoffrey of Monmouth.

On solar eclipses, John of Sacrobosco writes:

When the moon is in the head or tail of the dragon or nearly within the limits and in conjunction with the sun, then the body of the moon is interposed between our sight and the body of the sun. Hence it will obscure the brightness of the sun for us, and so the sun will suffer eclipse – not that it ceases to shine but that it fails us because of the interposition of the moon between our sight and the sun. From these it is clear that a solar eclipse should always occur at the time of conjunction or new moon. And it is to be noted that when there is an eclipse of the moon, it is visible everywhere on earth. But when there is an eclipse of the sun, that is by no means so. Nay, it may be visible in one clime and not in another, which happens because of the different point of view in different climes.[5]

Again, John of Sacrobosco gives detailed information on how an eclipse happens, the conditions under which it happens, and the timings. And again, there is this image of the dragon. As seen in Chapter 3, Geoffrey of Monmouth explained Uther Pendragon's name as meaning 'head of the dragon', and this image of the dragon is influenced by Arab astronomy: the head and tail of the dragon denote the lunar nodes. The image of the dragon-impacted moon is central to Persian poetry too, as in these images from the epic *Layla and Majnun* by Nezāmi Ganjavi (1141–1209), a text we will return to in Chapter 6: 'To place the moon within the dragon's jaws' (p. 100); 'Tell me the pale moon will break free at last / From the fell dragon that has held her fast' (p. 160); and 'A jewel that's like the moon in an eclipse / Confined within the dragon's slavering lips' (p. 208).[6] This is a frequent way of describing a lunar eclipse in this poem.

John of Sacrobosco also mentions the eclipse that is said to have happened during Christ's Passion and observes that this was miraculous rather than natural:

> From the aforesaid it is also evident that, when the sun was eclipsed during the Passion and the same Passion occurred at full moon, that eclipse was not natural – nay, it was miraculous and contrary to nature, since a solar eclipse ought to occur at new moon or thereabouts.[7]

As witnessed in Chapter 3, the moon can act as a potent sign or prophecy of what is to come – even when that is contrary to natural laws.

Beyond John of Sacrobosco, there is this observation in the Italian text *Cronaca Fiorentina* about planetary conjunctions causing the darkening of the sun and then the moon:

> In this same year in May [1384], there was a conjunction of Jupiter and Saturn at the beginning of Cancer [. . .] The Sun darkened the first day of January between the sixth and the third, and if it were not because it was cloudy, you would almost have seen the whole body of the Sun darken because it almost obscured ¾ of it [. . .] The Moon then darkened that month beyond the 13th of that month, coming the 16th, approximately for two hours.[8]

Many accounts of lunar and solar eclipses that actually happened survive from the medieval period.[9] Abraham Zacut (1452–c. 1515), a scholar in Salamanca, wrote *De los eclipses del sol y la luna* (*On the*

Eclipses of the Sun and the Moon).[10] Giovanni Battista Capuano (flourished fifteenth–sixteenth century) says he saw a lunar eclipse on 15 August 1505.[11] A much earlier sermon by Maximus of Turin (*c.* 380–465) criticises those who cry out at an eclipse, and asks them to think of their own flaws as those of the changing moon. Using the biblical verse Ecclesiasticus 27:12 ('A holy man continueth in wisdom as the sun: but a fool is changed as the moon'), he suggests that the moon is associated with foolishness. For Maximus, it is specifically the waning moon that is associated with deficiency; the full moon can signify perfection. He uses Psalm 88:38 in reaching this conclusion ('And his throne as the sun before me: and as the moon perfect for ever, and a faithful witness in heaven'). We will return to these ideas of a waning moon signifying deficiency.

Islamicate astronomers also wrote about annular eclipses: when a ring is left around the moon.[12] It was important for Muslim astronomers to calculate eclipses because Islam has an 'Eclipse Prayer'.[13] In one account from 867 CE, it is said that the moon 'was eclipsed and all of it was drowned (*gharaqa*) or most of it disappeared'.[14] In the year 1309: 'In the month *Rabi' al-Awwal* [August], the whole body of the moon was eclipsed.'[15] In 1460: 'In the month of Ramadan, the moon's body was completely eclipsed.'[16] And in 1462: 'In the month of Ramadan, the moon's body was eclipsed and the earth became dark. It continued like that until near the rise of *Fajr* (dawn).'[17] Furthermore, medieval sources attributed colours to eclipses. This was a practice that started with the Babylonians and is in clear evidence in medieval Jewish and Islamic sources.[18]

The Chasing Wolf

Such is the medieval teaching on eclipses, where the moon demonstrates a dual vulnerability and power, reminding us of the Old English riddle (number 29) encountered in Chapter 1. The moon's vulnerability is also very much in evidence in the Old Norse legend of the *Prose Edda*, written in Iceland in the 1200s. The *Prose Edda* is formed of prose and excerpts of verse, and it is a rich source for Old Norse mythology. It has a named author or compiler – Snorri Sturluson. The text is attributed to him, for example, in one early fourteenth-century manuscript known as the *Codex Upsaliensis*.[19] In the *Prose Edda*, the moon is chased and consumed by a wolf. There are two wolves: Skoll (mockery), who chases the sun, and Hati (hater) Hrodvitnisson or Mánagarmr (moon dog), who chases the moon.[20] These dogs were born from a female ogre who had many sons in the form of wolves, but the chaser of the moon is particularly strong. The text states directly that the most powerful of her sons is Mánagarmr, who will swallow the moon and fill the sky with blood.[21] This is reinforced in *The Sibyl's Prophecy* quoted in the *Prose Edda*.[22] The wolves will succeed in swallowing the celestial bodies when the cataclysmic event of Ragnarok comes; at that time, one wolf will swallow the sun and the other the moon, and the stars will vanish from the skies.[23] The moon, along with the sun, is rendered vulnerable, able to be chased and consumed by these monstrous wolves, who leave splattered blood and disappearing light in their wake. In its compendium of different stories, the *Prose Edda* makes us think about how the cosmos itself is susceptible to destruction, with the moon highlighted as a central part of this story of the universe's annihilation.

Tricking the Elephant

The moon may be vulnerable in this Old Norse tale, but it is also the source of powerful illusions, deceiving humans and animals alike. This is very clear in a collection of animal fables that exists across languages known as *Kalīla and Dimna*, which travelled widely in the medieval centuries. The Old Spanish version known as *Calila e Dimna* was a translation of the eighth-century Arabic *Kalīla wa-Dimna* by Ibn al-Muqaffa', who was basing his work on a Persian text, which was in turn based on the fourth-century Sanskrit *Panchatantra*.[24] *Kalīla and Dimna* is thus an example of rich cross-cultural and cross-lingual contact in the medieval centuries, given its multilayered history and the many contexts in which it was adopted. As observed by Bettina Krönung, *Kalīla and Dimna* 'circulated not only in every oriental language, but also in all the languages of the European Middle Ages as well as in Byzantium, where it had the Greek title *Stephanites kai Ichnilates*'.[25]

Here we will focus on a Persian version of Ibn al-Muqaffa''s Arabic work. The frame narrative of *Kalīla and Dimna* is of two jackals, Kalīla and Dimna, in dialogue; within this framing narrative are many different tales on a range of subjects, one of which is called 'The Rabbit that Made Himself a Messenger of the Moon'. In this story, elephants suffering a drought find a spring called the Spring of the Moon, located in the land of the rabbits. This causes mayhem for the rabbits, who are trampled by the elephants. The rabbits decide that action must be taken, and one of the cleverest, named Piroz, goes to see the elephants. He claims that he is a messenger of the moon and that the moon has announced the following:

> You, who think yourselves superior to other animals, have fallen prey to a great deception. You have gone so far as to bring your troops to a spring sacred to me and muddied its water. I give you fair warning with this message. If you stay in your own place and cease what you are doing, well and good. Otherwise I will come, pluck your eyes out, and put you to death in the most horrible fashion. If you have any doubt of this message, come now and see me in the spring.[26]

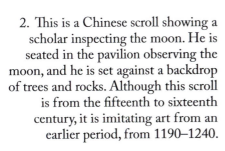

1. This illustration is from a twelfth-century English manuscript and shows a scholar studying the moon. He is seated comfortably but also grandly as he observes the moon with his hand outstretched; the moon is depicted in crescent form. Below him on the manuscript page is a scholar studying the sun.

2. This is a Chinese scroll showing a scholar inspecting the moon. He is seated in the pavilion observing the moon, and he is set against a backdrop of trees and rocks. Although this scroll is from the fifteenth to sixteenth century, it is imitating art from an earlier period, from 1190–1240.

3. This bowl, from central or northern Iran in the late twelfth/early thirteenth century, shows the 'planets', including the moon, surrounding the sun. The planets clockwise from the top inner circle are Mars, Mercury, Venus, the moon, Saturn, and Jupiter.

4. This silk fan shows the Chinese moon goddess, Chang'e, and dates to 1350–1400. Chang'e rests her hand on the tree which bows down towards her as if in an embrace. The full moon itself can be seen nearby in the skyscape.

5. This striking engraving by Gustave Doré (1832–1883) shows St John and Astolfo travelling to the moon. The moon's immensity contrasts with the small figures in the chariot as they ascend to the moon's realm.

6. This is a late-seventeenth-century illustration of *The Tale of the Bamboo Cutter*, showing the baby moon-princess cared for by her adoptive earthly parents. She is placed tenderly in a basket as they watch over her in their home.

7. An Islamic archangel, possibly Israfil, holds a full moon in this sixteenth-century illustration of Zakariyyā al-Qazvini's *The Wonders of Creatures and the Marvels of Existence*. The archangel clasps the moon to him as he flies in a sky full of ornate clouds.

8. This decorated initial in a thirteenth-century manuscript from Flanders depicts the Descent from the Cross, with the sun and moon radiating in the sky. The Virgin Mary holds Christ's hand, Joseph of Arimathea grasps Christ's body, and Nicodemus removes the nail from his feet.

9. This church wall painting in Dorchester Abbey in Dorchester-on-Thames, Oxfordshire, is from the fourteenth century but was restored in the nineteenth century. We can see Christ crucified between the Virgin Mary and John the Evangelist, a common pairing in medieval European art. The moon and sun can be seen in the background.

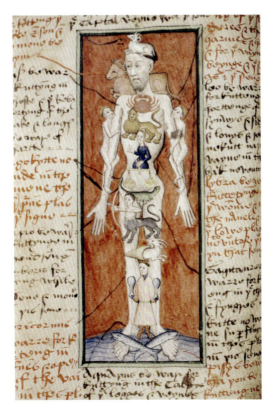

10. A 'zodiac man' from c. 1424, showing which zodiac sign impacts which part of the body. Each zodiac sign is illustrated in colour: for example, we can see Aries, the ram, on the head, and Pisces, the fishes, at the feet. Medicine related to the moon was often based on 'melothesia': the concept that particular zodiac signs were linked to specific parts of the human body.

11. Francisco de Zurbarán (1598–1664), *Immaculate Conception*. Mary, cloaked in precious blue cloth, stands on the full moon in a colourful sky. Beneath her at the lower corners of the painting are Faith (whose eyes are covered) and Hope (who holds an anchor).

12. In this sculpture from mid-fifteenth-century Tuscany, a crescent moon seems to hold the Virgin Mary and the infant Christ gently. The infant embraces the mother and their heads touch in an intimate gesture.

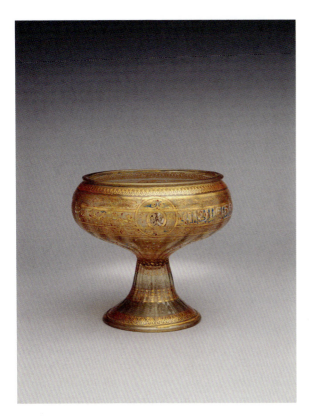

13. This glass *tazza* (or footed bowl) from thirteenth-century Syria is inscribed with *naskh* script (a kind of Islamic calligraphy); the inscription tells of a person who is as beautiful as the moon. A loved-one being as 'beautiful as the moon' is a common image in medieval Arabic and Persian poetry.

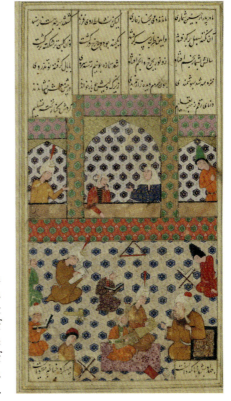

14. In this illustration from Iran in 1529, we see the famous lovers Layla and Majnun falling in love while at school. Many other such images of the two lovers while at school survive in other manuscripts. The story of Layla and Majnun itself exists in a wealth of versions.

15. At the bottom right of these pages from a twelfth-century manuscript from England, there is an illustration of 'the land of the sun and the land of the moon'. This story is found in the text *The Marvels of the East* or *The Wonders of the East*, which survives in English and Latin versions and tells many wondrous tales.

16. This is a fresco in the parecclesion or chapel of the Kariye Camii in Istanbul, from *c.* 1320–1. It shows the Last Judgment. At the top of the scene, an angel holds the heavens, shaped like a swirling white shell; visible in the heavens are a gold moon, gold sun, and gold stars.

Astounded, the elephant looks at the reflection of the moon in the water; Piroz tells the elephant to take some water with his trunk: 'When the elephant's trunk touched the water it rippled, and the elephant thought the moon was moving.'[27] Terrified, the elephants never return. Through the rabbit Piroz's cunning, the moon becomes the source of a great illusion, deceiving the elephant into thinking that the moon is all-powerful and capable of great harm – and all through a reflection. Audiences are invited to imagine the moon as an illusory force, capable of being manipulated and in turn manipulating others.

Tricking the Wolf

The moon as a source of illusion is also central to another animal fable, this one by Scottish poet Robert Henryson (c. 1430–1506). Henryson was an author and schoolmaster.[28] He wrote a large body of work, including a collection of fables in the tradition of Aesop.[29] In fact, Henryson speaks of the 'maister Esope, poet lawriate' ('master Aesop, poet laureate', line 1377).[30] The fable in which the moon makes an important appearance is known as 'The Fox, the Wolf, and the Husbandman', which has been interpreted in various ways; Craig McDonald, for example, argues that the fable itself has a legal under-current.[31] Here we will be concerned with how the moon contributes to the concept of illusion in the tale.

In the tale 'The Fox, the Wolf, and the Husbandman', a fox tricks a wolf by using the reflection of the moon. The wolf had been promised some cheese. Looking into a well, the wolf sees a reflection of the moon: 'The schadow off the mone schone in the well' ('The shadow of the moon shone in the well', line 2392): 'shadow' here means reflection rather than 'shadow' in the way we understand it in modern English.[32] The fox, called Lawrence, then declares:

'Sir,' said Lawrence, 'for once you shall find me trustworthy.
Now do you see not the cheese well yourself,
White as any turnip and round as any seal?
He hung it there so that no man should steal it.
Sir, trust you well, that cheese you see hanging
Might be a present to any lord or king.'

(lines 2392–8)

The wolf is convinced that this reflection of the moon is a block of cheese. There are two buckets attached to the well: the fox leaps into one, pretending to get the cheese, but says it is too big for him to carry on his own. So the wolf gets into the other bucket, which pulls up the one in which the fox is placed. When the wolf asks for help, the fox remarks wryly, 'Thus it fares according to fortune: / As one comes up, so wheels another down' (lines 2418–19). The fox here connects the moving of the buckets to that perennial symbol of shifting fates of people – the Wheel of Fortune. The fable-speaker tells us he does not know who freed the wolf from the bottom of the well, and there ends the tale. A moral explains the meanings of the fable: the wolf is a wicked man; the fox is a fiend; and the cheese is covetousness; the well or 'source' of this vice is all 'fraud and delusion' (line 2451).

Like all Henryson's *Fables*, this text plays with ideas of meaning, truth, and illusion. The moon becomes part of the illusory work of the devil – and perhaps of the fable-writer. As Dorothy Yamomoto remarks, 'Solidity and vacancy, substance and illusion – these are the themes that run through the tale.'[33] This is also applicable to the process of reading: it is full of moments that have solidity and substance, set against moments of vacancy and illusion. At times understanding is solid and substantive, at others vacant and illusory.

Readers of Henryson's *Fables* engaged not only with the stories and their direct morals (at least, the morals as suggested by the author). In fact, in reading the *Fables*, people also engaged with the very idea of what a story is and how someone can find or make meaning from a given story. This whole process itself might sometimes be an illusion, as we try to clutch at a meaning that flits from our grasps. Perhaps we as readers, like the wolf, are forever mistaking the moon for cheese.

The Case of the Disappearing Cliffs

The moon also plays a significant illusory role for Chaucer, as seen in *The Franklin's Tale*. A franklin in medieval English society was someone who owned land: they were not slaves, but nor were they of noble birth. The story told by Chaucer's franklin is, like *Troilus and Criseyde*, based on a tale by Chaucer's Italian contemporary, the poet Giovanni Boccaccio. But Boccaccio is not mentioned, and instead Chaucer's franklin claims that his story is a 'Breton lay': a short story associated with the lands of Brittany, often involving magic and the supernatural. Marie-Françoise Alamichel sees the cycles and movements of the moon in this story as being part of the emphasis throughout the poem of cyclicality and circularity.[34] Throughout, the moon, with all its cyclical movements, is repeatedly associated with change and illusion.[35]

In *The Franklin's Tale*, a young man named Aurelius is desperate to win the affections of a married woman, Dorigen, whose husband is away at sea. In her sorrow at her husband's absence, Dorigen tells Aurelius that she would only be with him if the cliffs disappear from the coast of Brittany. Her meaning is that she would never be with him, since it is presumably impossible for cliffs to just disappear. But Aurelius sees a potential loophole. In a lovelorn speech, Aurelius prays to Phoebus Apollo (the god of the sun) to appeal to his sister, 'Lucina the sheene' ('Lucina the bright' [the moon], line 1045).[36] Specifically, Aurelius asks that in the next 'opposition' of the sun and moon in the zodiacal sign Leo, the moon causes an extremely high tide in order to cover the cliffs (lines 1056–64). Alternatively, he prays for the moon to cause the rocks to sink (line 1073). Aurelius' brother has observed his sadness, and wanting to help, remembers a scholar at Orleans who is learned in the 'operaciouns / Touchynge the eighte and twenty mansiouns / That longen to the moone' ('operations / relating to the twenty-eight mansions [stations] / that belong to the moon', lines 1129–32). The narrator, the franklin himself, dismisses all such things as 'folye' (folly).

But nonetheless, in the world of the tale, the two brothers go to Orleans and enlist the help of this magician-scholar, who engages in complex astrological calculations, all expressed in opaque terminology, with the franklin declaring he does not understand the 'termes of astrologye'. Indeed there follows a thicket of specialist words used almost incomprehensibly:

His tables Tolletanes[37] forth he broght,
Ful wel corrected, ne ther lakked noght,
Neither his collect ne his expans yeris,[38]
Ne hise rootes,[39] ne hise othere geris,
As been his centris[40] and hise argumentz,[41]
And hise proporcionels convenientz[42]
For hise equacions[43] in everything.
And by his eighte speere[44] in his wirking
He knew ful wel how fer Alnath[45] was shove
Fro the heed of thilke fixe Aries[46] above,
That in the ninthe speere considered is;
Ful subtilly he kalkuled al this.[47]
(His Toldean tables he brought forth,
Full well corrected, there lacked nothing,
Neither his collect nor his single-year periods
Nor his tables nor his other equipment,
As be his centres and his arguments,

And his proportions convenient,
For his equation in everything
And by his eight sphere in his calculation
He knew full well how far Alnath was above
From the head of the same fixed Aries above,
That in the ninth sphere is considered to be,
Full subtly he calculated all this.)

All the calculations lead to the scholar being able to calculate the positions of the moon (lines 1285–90), and through this craft, it appears that the cliffs have disappeared. Because of Dorigen's promise, she and her husband agree to Aurelius' demands, albeit with much grief. But seeing the true love between them, Aurelius decides he cannot ruin such a marriage bond, and withdraws his earlier request. Here in Chaucer's *Franklin's Tale*, the moon is unequivocally associated with illusion, and the creation of false sights. The cliffs do not really disappear; it is only that the magician's 'heathen' craft creates the false appearance that they are no longer there. In any case, nothing comes of the illusion. Aurelius decides not to charge ahead with his desire, so in the end, the moon-craft had little efficacy.

The operations of astrology also come under repeated attack by the very teller of this tale. Again and again, the franklin sneers at astrological words and workings, directly announcing his disapproval of the illusory tricks of an astrology not informed by faith in the Christian God. As mentioned above, when Aurelius' brother remembers the scholar of Orleans, the narrator interjects to say that such learning is a mere 'folly' in our (Chaucer's) time, and Holy Church does not allow belief in such an 'illusion' (lines 1131–4). Then, when the scholar completes his calculations, the franklin condemns 'swiche illusiouns and swiche meschaunces / As hethen folk useden in thilke dayes' ('such illusions and such evil doings / As heathen folk used in those days', lines 1292–3). Not only is the moon itself relegated to the realm of illusion; anyone who engages in such moon-craft is also said to belong to a benighted, ignorant time, mired in falsity. The moon's capacity for illusion and falsity is part of the broader concerns of this tale with illusion, including the illusory quality of words themselves – the poet's capacity to delude others.

Abandoned Women

One of Chaucer's lesser-known texts is *The Legend of Good Women*. But it is not isolated from the rest of the poet's work. Carolyn P. Collette sees it as fundamentally linked to Chaucer's corpus: it is 'a story of women's vulnerability in love, grounded in the tragic story of Troilus [in *Troilus and Criseyde*] and looking toward the comedic narratives of the [*Canterbury*] *Tales*'.[48] Before the 1980s, the *Legend of Women* was neglected by scholars, dismissed as poor poetry. This is still often the case today, and it 'remains the ugly duckling of the Chaucer canon'.[49] But there is much value in the *Legend of Good Women*. Chaucer drew on a wealth of sources for his *Legend of Good Women*, including the work of Roman poet Ovid (43 BCE–17/18 CE). Janet Cowen also draws attention to similarities and differences between *The Legend of Good Women* and hagiography (the writing on the lives of saints).[50]

The prologue to this text is framed as a dream vision. This was a very popular kind of writing in the Middle Ages – Chaucer himself wrote four visions (the prologue to *The Legend of Good Women*, *The Book of the Duchess*, *The House of Fame*, and *The Parliament of Fowls*). In this prologue, Chaucer appears as the dreamer. He is visited by the god of love accompanied by Alceste, a loyal princess in Greek mythology who went to the underworld in the place of her husband. Chaucer is reprimanded by the god of love for writing poems that suggest women are faithless and that devalue love:

Thou hast translated the Romaunce of the Rose,
That is an heresye ageyns my lawe,
And makest wyse folk fro me withdrawe.
And of Criseyde thou hast seyd as thee liste,
That maketh men to wommen lasse triste,
That ben as trewe as ever was any steel.

(lines 329–34)

(You have translated the Romance of the Rose
That is a heresy against my law
And make wise folk from me withdraw
And of Criseyde you have said as you want
That makes men to women less trusting,
[women] who be as true as ever was any steel.)

Alceste lessens the god of love's wrath. To make amends, Chaucer must write about 'good' women. After this dream vision there is a series of tales drawn from classical myth about women who are constant and true but suffered because of their constancy. The stories are those of Cleopatra, Thisbe, Dido, Hypsipyle and Medea, Lucrece, Ariadne, Philomela, Phyllis, and Hypermnestra. The poem appears to be unfinished.

The moon emerges repeatedly in *The Legend of Good Women*, as might be expected in a poem so concerned with inconstancy. It appears in the legends of Thisbe, Dido, Ariadne, Phyllis, and Hypermnestra. In all cases, the moon appears to intensify the sense of mutability burdening these women and hints at the capriciousness of men. Fourteenth-century readers saw a moon whose associations of insta-bility and fickleness are sharp; the moon serves to sting readers further in all these painful stories of loss and betrayal – in all cases but Thisbe's, the women suffering at the hands of disloyal and cruel men.

Thisbe

Thisbe and Pyramus are separated lovers who converse through a crack in a wall. They decide to meet one evening. A lion emerges, and Thisbe flees, but not before she drops her veil. The veil becomes bloodied, and Pyramus sees it. Believing Thisbe has died, he takes his life with his sword. Thisbe finds Pyramus dead and takes her life with the same sword. Thisbe is one of the rare cases in *The Legend of Good Women* when the woman is not abandoned by an inconstant husband. Instead, the constancy of love between Thisbe and Pyramus, and the tragic misunderstanding, is what leads to the demise of them both. In a sign of the oncoming tragedy, Thisbe sees by the light of the moon: 'For by the mone she seigh hit wel with-alle' ('For by the moon she saw it well withal', line 812). And the moon shimmers as a clear symbol: 'The mone shoon, men mighte wel y-see' ('The moon shone, people might well see it', line 825). This clear moon stands as a sign for what is to come. Soon Thisbe will lose her beloved Pyramus and lose her life. Reading or hearing this text, medieval audiences engaged with a moon that was a sad sign, one showing the coming of tragedy, not unlike the moon we witnessed in *Troilus and Criseyde* in Chapter 3.

Dido

The hero Aeneas is told by Venus he must woo Dido. The two of them go hunting and find shelter in a cave when it is raining. Aeneas declares his love for Dido and Dido eventually declares her love in return. But subsequently Aeneas falls out of love and decides to leave. Once Dido is abandoned, she takes her own life by a sword after asking her sister to make funeral arrangements. The moon's presence haunts the legend of Dido, as in this description of the moon's illumination: 'When that the mone up-reysed had her light' ('When the moon had raised up her light', line 1163). Dido suffers from Aeneas' inconstancy, and so the moon's light is particularly apt. Just as Dido will be abandoned by Aeneas, so the moon seems to shine almost mockingly – it will abandon her as she will be abandoned by the man she loves. The moon remains a cold and unhelpful witness, not unlike the moon goddess Diana's refusal to help Emily in Chaucer's *Knight's Tale*.

Ariadne

The moon is a bright, searing symbol in the legend of Ariadne. Theseus must face King Minos' 'wicked beast', the Minotaur. The daughters of King Minos, Ariadne and her sister Phaedra, decide to help Theseus; they will guide him out of the maze using thread. Theseus and Ariadne become husband and wife, but in the end, Theseus abandons Ariadne for her sister, because Phaedra is more beautiful. Ariadne is left heartbroken. She and Phaedra, along with Theseus, 'lokeden upon the brighte mone' ('looked upon the bright moon', line 1972). This is the moment at which the sisters hear Theseus' complaint of his predicament. The moon is an unsettling presence in this instance, foreshadowing the abandonment and sorrow that are to come. After her abandonment, Ariadne looks outwards: 'No man she saw, and yit shyned the mone' ('No man she saw, and yet shined the moon', line 2194). The moon glimmers as a sign of Theseus' inconstancy, and amplifies Ariadne's utter dejection and loneliness in this moment as she looks out and finds nobody there.

Phyllis

Phyllis suffers a sad fate. Demophon professes his love and vows to wed her. He takes his leave, promising to come back in one month. But he does not. In a letter she writes as she waits for Demophon, Phyllis wonders why he has not returned. Demophon had claimed he would come back after one moon's circuit – but instead the moon has gone through its circuit four times:

that the mone ones wente aboute.
But tymes foure the mone hath hid her face
Sin thilke day ye wente fro this place,
And foure tymes light the world again.

(lines 2503–6)

(... that the moon once went about,
But four times the moon has hidden her face
Since the day you went from this place
And four times illuminates the world again.)

This image of the moon 'hiding her face', referring of course to the moon's phases and the new moon's covering in complete darkness, is an arresting one. The image metamorphoses the moon: the moon becomes a mourner hiding her face; it is one of those who grieve – like the reader – for Phyllis's tragedy. In this case, the moon is not a static sign of inconstancy and loss; it becomes emotionally implicated in the inconstancy and loss, mourning with human beings for the shifting patterns of the sublunary world.

Hypermnestra

Hypermnestra suffers at the hand of her father. Refusing to follow his orders to kill her husband, she must endure the consequences of his wrath. Her father is abusive and manipulates her. When he is professing his love for her, while manipulating her into killing her husband, he says he would not hurt her 'For al the gode under the colde mone' ('For all the good under the cold moon', line 2638). It is fitting that her abusive father would refer to the 'cold moon' – in the moon's associa-tion with changeability, her father shows how unstable Hypermnestra's life is at his cruel hands. The moon here is also 'cold', referring not only to its perceived qualities of moistness or coldness, but perhaps also to its distance. At last, the moon becomes a cold, objective observer of Hypermnestra's suffering. And as a symbol of inconstancy, it becomes a difficult symbol overseeing the horrors of the world below.

In all these legends of good women, the moon signals and participates in the painful variability of the world and human beings. The moon shines to put a spotlight on the fickleness of the sublunary realm. In these tales, the moon also heightens and complicates the audience's engagement with the women of the stories. Anne Schuurman shows the centrality of pity to *The Legend of Good Women*, and how pity and poetics come hand in hand – in particular, the poem shows how emotion, like poetics, is not entirely our own. Rather, pity is found at the 'interface of self and other'.[51] The moon is also at such an interface, and perhaps becomes the interface itself: the moon is a potent symbol that draws us in and nurtures our concurrent identification and distance from the suffering women. We must navigate whose pain is whose – when we feel compassion, do we mingle self and other, or do the two remain distinct? When we see the moon and all the baggage it carries of inconstancy and pain, do we mourn for Thisbe, Dido, Ariadne, Phyllis, and Hypermnestra – or do we mourn for ourselves, caught as we are with them in this sublunary world?

The Mystery of the Missing Feast

We now leave the world of classical myth to focus on Christian traditions. As seen in Chapter 3, in the medieval Christian imagination, the moon could represent the Church. As the monk Bernard of Clairvaux (d. 1153) put it, God is the true source of light, while the Church is a mere reflection of this light, as the moon merely reflects the sun.[52] And as again witnessed in Chapter 3, this analogy of the moon as Church is a very popular one in the Middle Ages. The symbol of the Church-moon becomes particularly important when we look at a biography in Latin about a holy woman who lived in the region of Liège: the beguine Juliana of Cornillon (c. 1192/3–1258). Beguines were groups of women in the Low Countries who led a devout life but did not take formal vows. Juliana is associated above all with one particular endeavour: fostering devotion to the feast of Corpus Christi, which celebrates the flesh and blood of Jesus Christ. Juliana was a very strong and determined person, and she dedicated most of her life to seeing this feast put in place, despite enduring a great deal of hostility and resistance from others. Her efforts took a toll on her health and wellbeing, but she never gave up. Juliana would not see the feast instituted; this happened after her death, particularly through the efforts of Juliana's friend Eve de St Martin (1190–1265).

Juliana was inspired on her quest by seeing a moon – or rather, a vision of the moon. Her biography records a vision she had around the years 1210–15, in which she repeatedly saw a full moon with a small breakage or missing piece. As is said in her biography:

There appeared to her a full moon in its splendour, yet with a little fracture in its spherical body. When she had seen this sign for a long time, she was amazed, ignorant as to what it might portend. But she could not marvel enough from the fact that, whenever she persisted in prayer, this sign incessantly forced itself upon her vision.[53]

Juliana is baffled and cannot interpret what she sees. So Christ himself appears to her to explain that the moon represents the Church, while the fracture in the moon represents the lack of that one crucial feast, the celebration of his flesh and blood.[54] This may have been inspired by Juliana seeing the wafer of the Christian sacrament of the Eucharist – she would repeatedly see it with part blocked out by the priest's finger.[55] Here the moon is in fragmented form, and it has come to Juliana to present a lack – a missing feast in the calendar of the Church's year.

A Shaming Moon

There were many kinds of religious vocation in the Middle Ages: the beguines, like Juliana of Cornillon, were only one group. One other vocation was that of anchoritism. Anchorites were religious recluses and could be of any gender, although from the thirteenth century onwards there was a growth of women anchorites in particular (sometimes referred to as 'anchoresses', although this term is not a medieval one).[56] Anchorites lived in a cell attached to a church, known as an 'anchorhold', and were expected to live there in solitude until they died. Their existence was defined by suffering, of both a physical and an emotional nature, and they could only look and speak through windows. On entering the anchorhold, the anchorites became dead to the world. They even had the rites of the dead said for them during their enclosure.[57] Being 'dead to the world' meant detaching themselves from all worldly pleasures and attachments. They were meant to sever all ties with their family and friends. Three of these women in England in the early thirteenth century asked for a guidebook to help them in this challenging life, and thus *Ancrene Wisse* (*Guide for Anchoresses*) was born. This is an important text in the history of English literature, and it was also translated from English into Latin and French – a surprising direction for translation to take, given that Latin and French were languages of higher status in this period.[58]

Readers of this text would have encountered a moon with very negative valences. In an adaptation of a verse from the Bible (Ecclesiasticus 22:3),[59] the author explains that a foolish individual, and one who is not devout, is like a 'waning moon':

Filia fatua in deminoratione erit. Þis is Salomones sahe; þet hit limpe to ei of ow, Godd ne leue neauer. 'Cang dohter iwurð as mone i wonunge'; þriueð as þe cangun, se lengre se wurse.[60]

(*A foolish daughter will be made smaller.* This is Solomon's saying. God grant that it never relate to any of you. 'A foolish [worthless] daughter is as the waning moon' – she thrives as the foolish one, the longer the worse.) (43:902–5)

Here those who go backwards in their devotional life, who do not progress forwards, are likened to a moon. The woman as waning moon is also a typical misogynistic image.[61]

And then we have further moon-negativity. Later in the text, the author refers to a verse from the book of Revelation in the Bible:

Apocalypsis: Vidi mulierem amictam sole, et luna sub pedibus ejus. Þis is Sein Juhanes word, Ewangeliste, i þe Apocalipse: 'Ich iseh a wummon ischrud mid te sunne ant under hire uet te mone.' Þe mone woneð ant waxeð ne nis neauer studeuest, ant bitacneð for-þi worltliche þinges, þe beoð as þe mone eauer i change. Þes mone mot te wummon halden under hire uet—þet is, worldliche þinges totreoden ant forhohien—þe wule heouene areachen ant beo þer ischrud mi[d] te soðe Sunne.

(*Apocalypse: I saw a woman clothed in the sun and the moon under her feet.* This is St John's word, the Evangelist, in the Apocalypse: 'I saw a woman covered with the sun and the moon was under her feet.' The moon wanes and waxes, it is never steadfast, and signifies therefore worldly things that are as the moon ever changing. This moon must the woman hold under her feet – that is, worldly things trodden upon and rejected – who will reach heaven and be there clothed with the true sun.) (64:654–61)

The English author is inspired by Gregory the Great (540–604), one of the most famous and fundamental patristic authors. Gregory also interprets Revelation 12:1 and finds that the moon signifies all temporal, worldly things that must be trampled.[62] The moon is just a generic woman, rather than the Virgin Mary (as she is for other interpreters of this verse, as we will see). This moon is explained as embodying everything that is rejected – all the worldly joys and relationships and pleasures that the anchorite must cast away when entering the anchorhold and becoming 'dead to the world'. Not only does the anchorite cast all these earthly things away, but she specifically casts them below her feet. The moon becomes a wasteland, a body of rejection and discard, reminding us perhaps of the moon Astolfo sees in the *Orlando furioso*. Here in *Ancrene Wisse*, the moon is symbolically degraded, not only carrying what has been lost or rejected from the world, but also itself crushed beneath the devotee's powerful feet.

The Moon Beneath One's Feet

The author of *Ancrene Wisse* understands the moon in Revelation to be an unspecified woman. But in many other sources, the woman is the Virgin Mary. One such case is Bernard of Clairvaux:

> Yet the moon usually signifies not only corruption because of its waning, but also a foolish mind, and sometimes truly the church of this time, the former because of its mutability, and the latter because it receives its splendour from elsewhere. Indeed in both, so to speak, the moon may be aptly enough understood to be under Mary's feet, but each in a different way: for *the foolish person changes like the moon, but the wise one remains [unchanging] like the sun.* In the sun indeed is heat and unchanging splendour; in the moon, only a splendour that is altogether changeable and uncertain, and which never remains in one position.[63]

Bernard identifies the woman as the Virgin Mary, and the moon as the Church. Artists were very inspired by this idea of Mary standing on the crescent moon, as seen in a fifteenth-century wall painting in St James the Great in South Leigh, Oxfordshire. Her garment flows softly around the edge of the crescent moon, obscuring it. An early sixteenth-century stained-glass window in the Lady Chapel of the Church of St Mary in Fairford, Gloucestershire, shows an angel holding up the crescent moon as the Virgin Mary stands upon it. A deluge of other images of this subject survives from around Europe. One is a coloured carving from Nuremberg (*c.* 1480) showing the Virgin and Child on the crescent moon. There is also a sculpture from Austria on this theme, from 1450–60,[64] and a woodcut on paper by Albrecht Dürer, from *c.* 1511.[65] There are many fifteenth-century Books of Hours that show this image.[66] A Spanish painting from 1594 in a monastery rule-book shows the same.[67] And finally, there is a German limewood sculpture also showing the Virgin and Child on the crescent moon.[68]

The image of the Virgin Mary standing on a crescent moon finds a powerful but very distinct parallel in another abiding image, showing Mary standing on a full moon. An example of this type, slightly outside of the period of this book, is housed in the National Gallery of Ireland in Dublin; the painting is by Francisco de Zurbarán (1598–1664) and dates to the early 1660s (Plate 11). Zurbarán's painting shows Mary standing on the moon in a soft blue-pink sky filled with angels, and beneath her are the allegories of Hope and Faith. This type of image, the Virgin on a full moon, or in some cases half-moon, represents the Immaculate Conception – the belief that Mary was free from original sin from her conception. Zurbarán produced a number of paintings on this theme. Another example made in 1632, now housed at the National Art Museum of Catalonia, shows the Virgin standing on a half-moon.[69] The different phases of the moon in these contrasting images are important: the full moon and half-moon, on the one hand, are associated with purity and perfection; the crescent moon, on the other, is associated with a broken and soiled world.

It should be noted that not all images of the Virgin and Christ Child with the crescent moon were necessarily negative, however. The Ashmolean Museum in Oxford hosts images showing the Virgin and Child enclosed in crescent moons. This evokes the Revelation verse, which, as seen, could signify a moon that is degraded. But in two images in particular, the crescent moon seems to gently embrace and tenderly hold the Virgin and Child. One sculpture was made in Tuscany in the mid-fifteenth century and is a polychromed cartapesta (Plate 12). It shows the Virgin Mary clasping the infant Christ, who hugs her, and both are held and supported by a crescent moon.

Another example is a metalcut laid on paper, made in Europe between 1460 and 1480, by the printmaker Master of the Clubs,[70] which shows a standing Virgin holding the infant Christ in her arms. They are surrounded by flowers, and the Virgin is wearing a voluminous cloak. Emerging from under it is a large crescent moon; it is revealed that she is standing on this moon as she holds her child. Although this image more closely recalls the Revelation verse, with the moon appearing far below and almost debased when compared to the standing figure with her infant bundle, it still seems to act as a support, as a frame holding this mother and child.

Pearl: A Father's Grief

This mother and child, enclosed in the moon, will suffer a terrible parting when it comes to the Crucifixion. The moon as a companion to grief is also poignantly felt in a poem written by an anonymous contemporary of Chaucer's. The poem is known as *Pearl*, and it is a dream vision, like the prologue to *The Legend of Good Women*, in which a dreamer encounters many wondrous things and is transformed by the vision. *Pearl* is found in a famous manuscript (London, British Library, Cotton Nero A. X/2) that also contains *Sir Gawain and the*

Green Knight. It is generally believed that the speaker of the poem is a father who is grieving the loss of his child.[71] When he encounters his daughter in a dream, she is a bride of heaven, one of the spouses of Christ, and thus she no longer belongs to him. This father's young daughter seems to have grown immeasurably in wisdom but she is also very distant from him. In a move that is painful for father and perhaps audience alike, she chastises him for his possessiveness and his lack of understanding of God's grace.

This whole poem is dominated by the moon. In it, there is an emphasis on how this world of sorrow – and the Dreamer's own limited perception – form a 'sublunary' region of grief and anguish. The Dreamer again and again draws attention to being 'under the moon': he is in the under-the-moon realm, one subject to inconstancy and loss (line 923).[72] In this way, the sublunary world is distinctly unlike the fixed heavens beyond. The moon is actively degraded in this poem:

The mone may thereof acroche no myghte;
To spotty ho is, of body to grym,
And also there ne is never nyght.
What schulde the mone ther compass clym
And to even with that worthly light
That schynes upon the brokes brym?
The planets arn in to pouer a plight
And the selfe sunne ful fer to dym.

(lines 1069–76)

(The moon may therefore acquire no power
Too spotty she is, of body too grim,
And also, [here] there is never night.
Why should the moon its compass/circuit climb,
And to compete with that honourable light,

134

Which shines upon the brook's surface?
The planets are in too poor a state
And the sun itself far too dim.)

The moon is powerless in the hereafter ('The mone may thereof acroche no myghte'), and there is even no night in which the moon might glow. Compared to the light found in the afterlife, the moon is spotted and bleak, severely lacking in beauty. None of the planets can compete with the supremacy of divine light. The father is ultimately ejected from this dream-world in which he encounters the hereafter. For the time being, he remains imprisoned in the sublunary world, far from his daughter and far from understanding her new position in death.[73]

• • •

In *Kalīla and Dimna*, in a story on owls and crows, a crow utters the following words of wisdom: 'The fortune of one who is enlightened by native intelligence and heeds advice is always full, like shadow in a well and not like the light of the moon, which wanes and can be eclipsed.'[74] The crow here highlights what many saw as weaknesses of the moon – its light dims and it can suffer an eclipse, and thus cannot be used as a representation of enlightenment. This chapter has dealt with these sadder and more sinister sides of the moon: how for medieval people, the moon could signal or be associated with failure, emptiness, vice, and grief. We looked at the concept of eclipses and the consumption of the moon during Ragnarok. We considered Juliana of Cornillon's vision, anchoritic women's trampling of the moon – as reflected in the Virgin Mary's own standing on moons – the *Pearl*-Dreamer's sublunary entrapments, and the moon as complicit in illusion, as in *Kalīla and Dimna* and tales by Chaucer and Henryson. The moon can be involved in hurting and tricking human beings, yet also in announcing what may be lacking, what may need to be fixed. With all its sense of inconstancy and brokenness, the moon may thus also be a sign that is gently helpful, gently healing.

6
• • •
THE MOON OF LOVES AND EMBRACES

As fractured as it could be, as fraught with anguish and deficiency, the medieval moon remained beautiful. When medieval people gazed on or thought about the moon, it is clear that they were struck by its shimmering lights, its glow of ivory and silver-white, the dappled shadows like caresses on its surface. In all its splendour, the moon could be used to prophesise and signify weighty theological and philosophical ideas. But it could also be associated with warmer, more intimate states; the moon was linked to that emotion so familiar in this world: love. In this chapter, we will embrace the multi-glance to consider how many medieval readers, listeners, and viewers in Wales, Spain, Arabia, Persia, and India associated the moon with love. The one who is beloved is likened to or even represented by a moon – whether an earthly lover in epic love poetry, or a divine beloved for religious mystics. The moon could also intervene in love trysts, flooding a secret rendezvous with unwelcome light, or casting a gentle, affirming glow upon every loving encounter.

A Welsh Poet

Dafydd ap Gwilym (*c.* 1320–1370) was an important Welsh poet. He was born in Brogynin in Llanbadarn Fawr, Cardiganshire; his parents were Gwilym Gam and Ardudfyl.[1] He is associated with a particular poetic metre, the *cywydd*. The moon appears in a wealth of his poems. 'Cyrchu Lleian' ('Wooing a Nun') refers to the summer moon, for example, whereas 'Yr Adarwr' ('The Fowler') refers to a winter moon. In 'Y Sêr' ('The Stars'), Dafydd ap Gwilym details the stars' relationship with the moon in a series of startling images:

> Flaming plums of the cold harsh moon,
> sparkling berries of the icy moon;
> swollen glands of the hidden moon,
> they are the seeds of fair weather;
> radiance of the moon's large nuts.[2]

These are deeply embodied images of the stars, even being the moon's 'swollen glands'. The images evoke fruitfulness: the plums, the berries, the seeds, the nuts. This casts both moon and stars in a light of abundant fertility. Such an approach also forms a connection between the celestial and earthly realms – the sky becomes fertile land, cultivated and delivering choicest fruits.

In Dafydd ap Gwilym's poetry, the beloved is often personified as the moon. These include his poems 'The Skylark', 'Stealing a Girl', and 'The Heart'. In 'Yr Ehedydd' ('The Skylark'), for example, he refers to the beloved as 'moon of Gwynedd'.[3] Yet the moon could also be a bane for lovers because of its bright, revealing light, as witnessed in Chapter 3 with the moon's revelatory power in a poem by Chrétien de Troyes. In Dafydd ap Gwilym's poem 'Y Lleuad' ('The Moon'), the lover is thwarted by the light of the moon. He intends to meet his married lover in the cover of night, but the moon's brightness prevents secrecy: the speaker of the poem declares with frustration that the moon is worse than the sun in its unwelcome brightness. The speaker curses the moon through various imaginative descriptions of the moon's effects and movements:

> A parish of a saint's construction,
> water planet of all new growth.
> Every fortnight her routine –
> her home beneath heaven is night –
> is to take her course from there
> (I'm deep in thought), growing ever larger
> until she becomes two halves,
> the stars' sun on a bright night.
> She hurls the tide, fair radiance,
> she is the phantoms' sun.[4]

As much as the speaker curses the moon, this shows a deep connection as well – it is as if he is engaged in a lover's quarrel with the moon, even as it is an obstacle to his earthly lover. The speaker continues in this vein, paying close attention to the moon's movements and colours. It is a 'florin', a worthless coin, and a moving flower-shaped tool or spur-rowel. The 'nape of a loaf of frosts' is another of Dafydd ap Gwilym's evocative images. The moon's 'bed' is said to be in a high-up circuit, as wide as the earth. The speaker again looks closely at the moon as it moves through this circuit:

> Her form is that of a finely meshed sieve,
> her rim is familiar with lightning.
> She's a path-walker in heaven's sky,
> the shape of a lace, brass cauldron's brim.

Power of a measuring-lamp of a star-bright field,
a sphere from the bright blue sky.[5]

The 'finely meshed sieve' is such a close-up description, as is 'brass cauldron's brim'. It is an image that brings us near to the very shades and contours of the moon, that moon whose light impeded an encounter between lovers. A parallel can be drawn here with a poem by a contemporary of Dafydd ap Gwilym, Gruffudd Gryg (flourished *c*. 1340–1380), where the April moon impedes his pilgrimage to Santiago di Compostela in Spain.[6] Whereas Gruffudd Gryg's speaker is hindered in a religious journey, Dafydd ap Gwilym's speaker must struggle with the moon's light when meeting a human lover. In both loving journeys, the moon becomes an unbidden but inescapable interlocutor.

Hispano-Arabic Love Poetry

The moon may have been an obstacle to Dafydd ap Gwilym in his romantic endeavours, but elsewhere, the moon is much more of a friend to love. Plate 13 shows a thirteenth-century Syrian *tazza* (footed bowl) inscribed with *naskh* script (one kind of Islamic calligraphy). The words in the *naskh* script compare the beauty of the beloved to the moon.[7] Those who experienced medieval Arabic and Persian poetry would be very familiar with the image of someone's beloved being 'as beautiful as the moon'. This image permeates pre-Islamic and Islamic love poetry. Omid Safi has even suggested the term 'moon beauties' to describe the phenomenon.[8] The image was such a common one that philosopher and physician Avicenna (980–1037) gives the phrase 'as beautiful as the moon' as a basic example in his model of the 'imaginative syllogism', a kind of logical premise in the realm of poetry and poetics.[9]

We also come across this image in the wealth of Hispano-Arabic poetry surviving from Al-Andalus, the Arabic name for the parts of the Iberian Peninsula ruled by Islamic forces from around the year 720. Arab and Berber forces occupied regions of what we now call Spain and Portugal from the eighth century until the fall of Granada to Christian forces in 1492. In fact, by 720 these forces controlled nearly the entirety of the Iberian Peninsula, with the exception of the north-west corner of Spain known as Galicia. Al-Andalus was thus a melting pot of cultures and languages, and its flourishing artforms were nourished by fruitful exchanges between its Jewish, Muslim, and Christian populations.[10]

In Andalusian poetry, we find an array of images related to the beloved being like a moon. The moon is said to rise from the beloved's face, and the beloved one is often said to be a full moon (*badr*). The beloved can be a moon that never wanes – but there are also beloveds likened to crescent moons of striking beauty. Some of the poets who wrote this moon-filled verse include ash-Sharīf at-Talīq (d. 1009):

A branch which sways on a rounded sand dune, and from which my
   heart gathers [a harvest of] fire,
[Is such that] beauty causes a never-waning moon to arise from his
   face.[11]

Ibn Zaidun (1003–1071) talks about the real moon being lesser than his beloved:

Even if the moon [that lights up] the darkness inclined toward us
from the high point of its rising, it would not excite us, I beg your
pardon for mentioning it.[12]

Ibn ʿUbāda al-Qazzāz (eleventh century) creates a flood of images to capture the beloved, above all a crescent moon beyond description:

[He is] like a crescent moon such that when it is observed, it is
beyond description, as well as pure water such that if it were
generously given away, it would overcome the piety of the devout.
A full moon, a midday sun, a stem on a sand dune, fragrant musk;
None more full, none brighter, none more leafy, none more
fragrant.[13]

Ibn ʿUbāda al-Qazzāz also talks about his beloved as a myriad of
moons; the beloved is both a 'new moon' and a 'full moon' in their
beauty:

I loved a new moon unique in its beauty borrowing from the gazelle
its glances and [slender] neck.
A full moon that shone in shapely proportion was proud of its
beauty, desiring no increase.
Grace had adorned him; his figure was graceful!
A full moon that conquered with evident charm, cheek down curling
over a jasmine [complexion].[14]

In describing the joys of romantic and communal drinking, poet
Ḥātim ibn Saʿīd (twelfth century) says: 'A sun drew near to a full
moon: wine and a drinking companion!'[15] And Ibn Sahl of Seville
(1212–1251) portrays the departing beloveds as full moons rising:

O full moons which arose on the day of departure, bright
countenanced, going forth on the path of peril:
My heart bears no sin in loving; instead it is from you that beauty
comes, while from my eye comes the glance.[16]

The moon-beloved is one among a rich reservoir of images in
Arabic Andalusian poetry – along with the flourishing garden, the

intoxicating wine – but still retains its uniqueness. Those who heard or read this poetry would come to associate love and the beloved with the moon. Every time someone looked on a loved one's face, they may have seen the moon. And every time someone looked to the moon above, they may have found inscribed there every beautiful inch of their beloved.

Layla and Majnun

We move now from Arabic to Persian. Nezāmi Ganjavi (1141–1209) was a very famous poet born as Ilyan Ebn Yusuf in Ganjeh, in modern-day Azerbaijan, where he remained for most of his life.[17] He is especially well known for his epic poem *Layla and Majnun* or *Layli and Majnun*, which is replete with the image of the beloved being as beautiful as the moon. The poem tells the story of the doomed love between Layla and Qays, who belong to different tribes. Qays is nick-named Majnun; Majnun is so named because he is driven 'mad' by his love – literally 'possessed with the jinn'; he even flees into the wilderness to dwell among wild animals. In pre-Islamic and Islamic traditions, the 'jinn' are invisible spirits.[18] Layla is forced to marry another man, and both lovers die heartbroken from their separation. The story has its origins in an Arab tale of two lovers who may have actually existed, in the seventh century. There are many versions of the story across languages and periods. As Ferial J. Ghazoul relays the complexities of the narrative:

> Widespread as the story is, to the point of being considered a work of world literature, it has no original text or authentic source. It lies on the borderline between orature and literature. In terms of genre, it is also a hybrid case: both a narrative and a collection of love poems, it offers an account of something that happened as well as

an imaginative construction. The figures in the story, Qays ibn al-Mulawwah (occasionally given other names), known as Majnun (Madman), and his beloved Layla, are (probably) historical figures wrapped in legendary lore.[19]

The specific version of the *Layla and Majnun* story used here is that by Nezāmi. Nezāmi's *Layla and Majnun* survives in a wealth of manuscripts, and the illustrations portray a multitude of scenes, including Layla and Majnun falling in love in school (Plate 14) and Majnun in the wilderness.[20] The lovers, especially Layla, are frequently likened to or personified as moons in their beauty. Describing Qays/Majnun as an infant, the poet says:

> You'd say his milk was mixed with honeycomb
> Or that his cradle was the full moon's home –
> That moon in two weeks was as beautiful
> As is the heavens' moon when she is full. (p. 3)[21]

Even in his infant form, Majnun is as majestically beautiful as the full moon. The adult Majnun is also described at one point as being 'like a slender crescent moon' (p. 192). Layla's/Layli's status as 'moon' is found everywhere in the text. She is as 'splendid as the moon' (p. 4), an 'Arab moon' (p. 5), a 'bright New moon' (p. 9), 'his adored full moon' (p. 17), 'that lovely moon' (p. 60), and 'moon-like Layli' (p. 25). And her power over Majnun is like the moon's power over the sky: 'Just as the skies are governed by the moon / So love for moon-like Layli ruled Majnun' (p. 25). The physical moon cannot compare to her: 'The moon in heaven was envious of her face' (p. 42). As is spoken to Layli directly: 'You are the moon if moons are sweetest things' (p. 110). Majnun is said to be in extreme distress because of 'the moon he couldn't view' (p. 103), in reference of course to Layla. Layla is especially that 'full moon', complete and perfect in her beauty (pp. 15, 53, 65). As Layla grows thin in her grief at being separated from Majnun, she metamorphoses from a full moon to a new moon (p. 234). And in death, her moon-status continues: 'The brightest moon has fallen from the sky' (p. 240).

As in Chaucer's *Troilus and Criseyde*, the moon also plays a vital role in marking the changes of time in the story and signalling shifts in the narrative of these two lovers. For example:

> One evening – when the twilight air was soft
> As silken clothes, the haloed moon aloft
> Was like a shining earring. (p. 13; see also p. 87)

The moon here is a temporal marker, though the audience is specifically invited to look upon the moon as though it is part of a face, adorned with earrings. The moon is almost anthropomorphised. The audience is invited to imagine the moon in human form, linking of course to the 'moon beauties' Layla and Majnun.

Continual references to the moon punctuate the narrative to show the wider, cosmic significance of this love story: 'The moon does not decide when it must rise' (p. 39) – the moon, like all, is subject to the laws of the universe, just as the lovers must be parted. Just as in *Troilus and Criseyde*, the moon's movement through the zodiac is traced: 'The moon moved into Pisces and the night / Was like a black shell brimming with its light, / Its radiance flooded from the shell, a flow / Of bright pearls scattered on the world below' (p. 129). We are treated to views of the moon with its silky texture: 'Like silk the full moon shone with golden light / Its halo was spun linen, pure and white' (p. 139). Or Nezāmi describes the way the moon illuminates the darkness: 'The moon's jewel made earth glimmer in the dusk' (p. 138). The moon permeates the world of this epic love poem; it is woven into the very fabric of the love story.

It has been long acknowledged that Nezāmi is a meta-poetic poet; that is, he draws attention to the nature of the poem he is writing.[22] Nezāmi refers repeatedly to the act of poetic creation, the shape of letters, the sound of poetic metre. This is also important in terms of moon imagery, for his patron, Shirvanshah Akhsetan I (r. 1160–1197), is celebrated as superior to the moon: 'You'd say the shadows on the moon were like / Marks where our glorious monarch's missiles strike' (p. 140). And more directly: 'O Nezāmi, what could be greater than / To serve as we do such a glorious man! / The zodiac itself, the bright moon's phases, / Shake in amazement and proclaim his praises' (p. 140). In these lines, the great love poet draws attention directly to the service he is providing as a poet, flattering his patron – and he turns to the moon to engage in such flattery.

Sufis

We have seen how those who experienced medieval Persian and Arabic poetry were encouraged to think of the beauty of the beloved as the moon through simile – or through the full metaphor (the beloved *is* the moon). Such an image is also translated from the secular to the religious realm. Medieval Sufis, Islamic mystics or contemplatives, use this image of 'moon beauties' in a fundamentally different and radical way. For these poets, the moon becomes representative of Allah, the divine beloved, rather than an earthly lover. This may be shown through two Andalusian poets in particular, writing in Arabic: Muhyddin ibn ʿArabī (1165–1240) and Abu al-Ḥasan al-Shushtarī (1212–1269). We will also compare these to Sufi poets writing in Persian, ʿAṭṭār of Nishapur (1145–1221) and Jalāl al-Dīn Muḥammad Rūmī (1207–1273).

But first it will be useful to give some introductory information about Sufism, and medieval Sufism in particular. Sufism is often understood as a form of Islamic 'mysticism', although there are diffi-culties with such a labelling: 'mysticism' is a term steeped in a Western world, and there are in any case many aspects of Sufism beyond and in dialogue with the 'mystical'.[23] At the heart of a Sufi's quest is the need to overcome the lower self or ego (the *nafs*) to attain union with the divine. There is a fundamental Sufi idea, known as the 'Oneness of Being' (*waḥdat al-wujūd*), that Creation and Creator all form one essence.[24] The Divine Creator is the One True Reality, with Creation a reflection or shadow of this Reality. Medieval Egyptian Sufi poet 'Umar ibn al-Fāriḍ (1181–1235) imagines all of Creation as a shadow-puppet play: there are many shapes and movements, but once the screen is removed, there is only one mover behind it all.[25] A sixteenth-century diagram attributed to Ibn 'Arabī shows how 'many' emanate from one centre. There is a circle in the middle, surrounded by lines and curves to show the emanation of many from one core.[26] The ultimate goal of the Sufi is to dissolve into the oneness of God. Throughout Creation are markers or indications of divine self-manifestation or self-disclosure, labelled with the Qur'anic term *tajalli* (Qur'an 7:143).[27]

Al-Shushtarī was born and raised in Guadix, in what is now Spain; but he also travelled widely, including in regions of today's Middle East.[28] Al-Shushtarī is especially known for using poetic forms invented in this region: the *muwashshaḥ* and the *zajal*. The *muwashshaḥ* may have acquired its name from a coloured belt or girdle, echoing the ways in which the poetic form itself is made up of a myriad languages and a multilayered, interlocking rhyme scheme.[29] The main part of the *muwashshaḥ* poem is in classical Arabic or Hebrew; the closing lines, known as the *kharja* (the exit), are in colloquial Arabic or in a Romance language. The *zajal* is in colloquial Arabic in its entirety.[30] One influ-ential definition of the *muwashshaḥ* was put forward by fourteenth-century writer Ibn Khaldun:

The *muwashshaḥ* consists of branches and strings in great number and different metres. A certain number [of branches and strings] is called a single verse [stanza]. There must be the same number of rhymes in the branches [of each stanza] and the same metre [for the branches of the whole poem] throughout the whole poem. The largest number of stanzas employed is seven. Each stanza contains as many branches as is consistent with purpose and method. Like the *qaṣīda* [classical Arabic ode], the *muwashshaḥ* is used for erotic and laudatory poetry.[31]

In two of Al-Shushtarī's *muwashshaḥah*, both translated in full in the appendix to this book, the closing of the poems refers to the moon of the night when compared to the lover's own moon:

Oh night, long or not long, I must watch you;
But if my Moon [*qamr*] were with me, I would not remain to watch yours.[32]

Al-Shushtarī has borrowed this *kharja* from a poem by Ibn Zaidun: it is not uncommon practice for Andalusian poets to borrow the *kharja* from another poet to make a new poem. In Ibn Zaidun's hands, the *kharja* is used in a secular context. But in Al-Shushtarī's hands, the *kharja* takes on a devotional meaning. Were his beloved to be present he would not watch the night's moon: the Sufi means here that his own moon is infinitely superior to the moon of the night – the divine lover surpasses any moon of the sky. Here Al-Shushtarī plays with the common image of the beloved being like the moon in beauty, capitalizing on this pervasive image in exploring his love for the divine.

This association between moon and divine beloved is all the more pronounced in the work of Ibn ʿArabī, a giant of medieval Sufism. Ibn

'Arabī was a prolific writer, and he is perhaps the most famous medieval Sufi. He was born and raised in Murcia, though like al-Shushtarī he travelled widely in the Middle East, at last dying in Syria.[33] For Ibn 'Arabī, the moon might be read as a sign for or embodiment of humanity: as the moon reflects the sun, so does the perfect human being reflect the divine.[34] As observed above, medieval Sufis understood the human soul as ultimately a reflection or shadow of the one true reality, which is God. And so the moon also captures the divine's beauty in mirror-image form: the moon is like a human being reflecting the beauty of the one true sun.

We will focus here on one collection of Ibn 'Arabī's poems: his *Tarjuman al-Ashwaq* (*The Interpreter of Desires* or *The Translator of Desires*), in which a lover searches for their beloved through the desert. This collection draws on early Islamic and pre-Islamic traditions of the *nasīb* (prelude to a poetic ode). The lover hunts through the desert, often accompanied by the jinn, those invisible spirits in pre-Islamic and Islamic traditions. The *nasīb* form is often associated with the 'Udhra tribe.[35] The moon in *The Interpreter of Desires* acts as a sign of the beloved; there are so many 'moon beauties' populating Ibn 'Arabī's poetry, especially in this collection. These evoke a sensual beloved – one as beautiful as the moon, shimmering with its pulchritudinous light. But in using this well-worn image, Ibn 'Arabī is also expressing the limits of language to express what needs to be said – in particular, the tremendous limitation of language when it comes to encountering the divine.

In *The Interpreter of Desires*, the beloved is likened to a luscious growth like a moon on flourishing trees (p. 208).[36] The moon is a luminescence guiding the lover (p. 132). The full moon is found within the lover's longing soul, but it is also inscribed on the beloved, marking their cheek, for example (p. 108). The 'moonless night' is a source of distress (p. 170), but the beloveds here can replace the missing moon – moon and beloved become interchangeable:

> No moonless night darkened upon me, but I remembered them
>   and walked in moonlight.
> When I ride with them the night becomes like the morning
>   sun. (p. 170)

The lover can cause the moon to rise (p. 236). Elsewhere, the full moon (*badr*) emerges in the lover's soul – the lover is the location of the full moon (p. 136). It is both the beloved and desire itself – for the two are one and the same: 'My love for you is whole; you are the goal of my desire, and from this I am sick. / You are majestic, a full moon risen within me, a moon that never sets' (p. 232). Throughout these poems, Ibn 'Arabī is invoking the common image of the 'moon beauties', using it in a variety of contexts. But in all cases, the beloved is not another human being – the moon-beloved is the divine.

Ibn 'Arabī's engagement with the moon-beloved reaches its apex in the fortieth poem of *The Interpreter of Desires*.[37] In this poem, Ibn 'Arabī refers to a 'moon-girl' who does not move through constellations or time. The poem declares:

> Between Adhri'āt and Buṣrā a fourteen-year-old girl rose to me,
>   a full moon.
> [. . .]
> Each full moon, when it reaches completion must wane again that it
>   may complete a month.
> But this moon does not move through the signs of the zodiac, nor
>   double from odd to even. (p. 174)

The reference to a fourteen-year-old girl is disturbing, and it reminds us that children could be treated as objects of desire in this period. There is, though, another reason for the number fourteen: according to the Islamic calendar, the full moon appears on the fourteenth day of the month. This moon-girl represents the divine, and the girl shows how the divine cannot be encountered through typical human frameworks of thinking and speaking. The usual circuit and phases of the moon do not apply to this moon-girl, for the divine surpasses all time and movement and change. The divine is omnipresent and omnitemporal, and in attempting to encounter the divine we have to try to move beyond – or at the very least acknowledge – the modes of thought and language in which we as humans are trapped. As Sells explains:

> By stating that the moon-girl in question neither moves through constellations nor goes through phases, the poet places her beyond the natural cycles of time and place. The girl-moon thereby transcends the polarities and patterns within the created world and within the act of creation.[38]

These medieval Sufis conjure a moon-beloved who forces us to reflect on the limits of our understanding and our ability to conceive of the universe. The moon-beloved of these medieval thinkers reminds us that we may each be looking at the cosmos through our own veils, our own distortions, our own flickering light. But still, the moon-beloved is there for us to attempt to grasp. She is there for us to behold, and she is there to heal us.

The famous Persian poet Jalāl al-Dīn Muḥammad Rūmī (1207–1273) lived close in time to the Andalusian poets we have discussed, and he also employs the moon to convey the divine beloved. The analogy is that the moon is the generator of light, just as the divine is the one true source of light. When admiring moonlight on a wall, the viewer must remember that its true source is the moon itself – and not become distracted by worshipping the wall; and when there is a reflection of the moon in a well, we should not become fixated on that image, that reflection. We need to turn away, look towards the source – the moon is the goal of the desire, but we become entrenched in focusing only on the reflection. Only when we look to the true source, the moon, will we be freed from unhappy fixation on mere reflections.[39]

ʿAṭṭār of Nishapur is less famous than Rūmī, but he was another brilliant poet in Persian; as his name suggests ("ʿAṭṭār'), he possibly worked as a perfumier or pharmacist. He is best known for his masterpiece *Manṭiq-ut-ṭair* (*The Conference of the Birds* or *The Speech of the Birds*), dating to the 1170s. The poem is in couplets, in the *masnavi* form; in addition to an overarching frame narrative, the poem is filled with miniature stories within a story. The frame narrative tells the story of the birds of the world seeking their leader. The hoopoe comes to guide them, teaching them of their worthy leader the Simorgh, a legendary bird in Persian mythology associated with but distinct from the phoenix. The birds undertake an excruciating and devastating journey to the Simorgh. When at last they find him, they in fact see a reflection of themselves. This poem works as an allegory for the quest of the Sufi as they seek to be annihilated and 'oned' with the divine through *fanā* (annihilation) and *baqā* (remaining, endurance in God).[40] In many ways, it is a poem about love – about suppressing and destroying the lower self or ego (*nafs*) to realise the true, divine love and be at one with the divine beloved.

The Andalusian Sufis invoked the common image of 'moon beauties' to try to approach the divine beloved, and this is partly the case for ʿAṭṭār too. His allegorical poem is filled with beloveds compared in their beauty to the moon. In one of the stories within story, a king's daughter is described as having a face 'like the full moon in its radiant grace' (p. 212).[41] But the moon also plays another role. For ʿAṭṭār, in his *The Conference of the Birds*, the moon is part of a cosmos that is all in longing for the divine. This resonates with a Sufi idea that Creator and Creation both long for each other. Early on in the poem, ʿAṭṭār says: 'From fish to moon, all particles attest / To Him, and make His essence manifest' (p. 5). This image captures the Sufi doctrine that God is present in everything, that all of Creation is a mirror image or shadow of the True Reality that is God. Every atom, every creature, every possible thing is suffused with the essence of God, just as soaked wool is full of water (an image of Ibn ʿArabī's).[42] The phrase 'from fish to moon' is common in Persian poetry; it conveys the sense of 'from the depth to the heights'.[43]

In describing the intense, overarching love of the cosmos for the divine, both sun and moon are implicated in the intensity of ardour:

For love of You the sun goes mad, each night
It smears its face with mud, and hides its light;
The moon too melts for You – we see it yield
To You in awe, and throw away its shield. (p. 8)

The sense here is that the moon's shifting shape reflects its love for the divine. As it moves from full to gibbous and crescent forms, it is as though the moon 'melts'. As it shifts away from being a full moon, it is as though it casts away its 'shield' in absolute love of the divine. Furthermore, the moon is also used to convey the destruction of the self in the search for the divine – the 'head' of the self should be severed, and instead: 'seek out the moon and fly / Beyond the utmost limits of the sky' (p. 41). Here the moon represents the seeking of a love beyond the earthly realm. Seeking the moon is to cast off the stifling layers of the self and find the true, pure love of the divine.

The culminating story in *The Conference of the Birds* is of the love shared between a king and a young man. The king rashly orders the young man's death, soon regrets his action, and wastes away in grief, becoming like a crescent moon in his consumptive despair. But thankfully, the young man had not in fact been killed. The once-absent lover in ʿAṭṭār's *The Conference of the Birds* is likened to a moon emerging from the clouds:

> The youth appeared
> Like moonlight when the heaven's clouds have cleared.
> Dressed all in white he knelt before the king,
> And wept as clouds weep raindrops in the spring.
> Then, when the wakened monarch saw the boy,
> There were no words that could express his joy.
> They knew that state of which no man can speak;
> This pearl cannot be pierced, We are too weak.
> The absence that the king endured was gone
> And they withdrew, united now as one. (p. 244)

In this climax of *The Conference of the Birds*, the moon captures the many shifts of love and longing of the Sufis in their quest to be united with the Divine. Tormented by the beloved's absence, we have a crescent moon – recalling the crescent moons of sorrows we encountered in Chapter 5. But in the healing of the love bond and the fulfilment of the lover's ardent desire for the beloved, the emergence of the beloved is like the flooding of moonlight. We have now seen how medieval Sufis such as ʿAṭṭār, Rūmī, Ibn ʿArabī, and al-Shushtarī read the moon. Reclaiming the image of 'moon beauties', Sufis imagined the divine beloved as the ultimate moon. And the moon itself is also part of a cosmos that is all absorbed in intense, overwhelming love for the divine. But these Sufis are not alone in using the moon in their devotional encounters. They are joined by a Hindu lover of Krishna.

Mīrābāī

Mīrābāī was an Indian woman who lived in the sixteenth century (*c.* 1500–1546), and is still revered today. Twentieth-century images of her show a beautiful person singing and dancing joyfully as Krishna looks on and participates with her; or the posters depict her sitting peacefully, surrounded by avatars of the god.[44] There are many versions of her life story, but we can deduce that she was a member of the royalty who gave up her status and devoted herself to her beloved Krishna rather than the husband with whom she had an arranged marriage.[45] She suffered years of persecution because of her calling.[46] Although she was not one of them, she aligns herself with the *gopis* (women from Vrindavan who left their husbands to dedicate themselves to their devotion to Krishna).[47] Many songs in the Rajasthani language are attributed to Mīrābāī; these are outpourings of love and longing for Krishna. It remains difficult, however, to know which songs are authentically hers, as there is no early manuscript version.[48] Given her life and her devotional songs, Mīrābāī has been understood in the West as a Hindu 'mystic', though as Nancy M. Martin observes, 'to label her as either a "saint" or a "mystic" is to impose categories that belong to Christian Europe rather than to *bhakti*'.[49]

If we take the bare standard definition in English, *bhakti* is simply 'religious devotion, piety, or devoted faith, as a means of salvation'.[50] But as we dig deeper, *bhakti* is much more than this. As the translator A.J. Alston observes, the word *bhakti* comes from the root *bhaj*, meaning 'to share': 'The basic idea is that God (termed "Bhagavan, also from the root "bhaj") allows His devotees (His "Bhaktas") to share in His own nature and His own Consciousness, if they offer themselves to Him in sincere love.'[51] Martin has noted that Mirabai's songs are all about 'intersubjective meaning creation'.[52] And in John Stratton Hawley's words:

'Bhakti', as usually translated, is devotion, but if that word connotes something entirely private and quiet, we are in need of other words. Bhakti is heart religion, sometimes cool and quiescent but sometimes hot – the religion of participation, community, enthusiasm, song, and often of personal challenge.[53]

Mīrābāī has invited comparative reading with European writers. Holly Hillgardner finds a shared, shifting dynamic of 'longing and letting go' in the work of Mīrābāī and the Flemish mystic Hadewijch (thirteenth century).[54] Alexandra Verini has written about models of female friendship in the writings attributed to Mīrābāī and *The Book of Margery Kempe* from the fifteenth century.[55]

We have many songs in which Mīrābāī expresses her love for her beloved Krishna. And these are filled with references to the beloved as the moon. In one poem, she imagines her existence without Krishna as a terrible thing, like a night without a moon:

My darling, grant me Your sight,
I cannot exist without You.
Life without You
Is like a pond without a lotus,
Or a night without the moon. (p. 75)[56]

Just as a night sky would be barren without a moon, just as a lotus would become desiccated without a pond, so is the lover without the divine beloved. Here, if we delve deeper into how the image works, Mīrābāī is imagining Krishna himself as a moon. The night sky is her life, only truly vivified when graced by and illuminated with her beloved moon.

In another song, she likens herself to a lotus or moon-flower that opens joyfully on seeing the moon. As the flower opens in pleasure on encountering the moon, so is she when she can see her beloved:

The lotus expands
When it beholds the moon,
And great will be my joy, too,
When I can see Thee. (pp. 83–4)[57]

In this song, the touch of the moon causes an 'opening' of the self. The spreading petals of the lotus are akin to the human self – the longing soul – expanding outwards and receiving the healing touch of the beloved. We can see here how the moon is associated with nourishment, the luminescence of the moon-beloved a nurturing caress on the human soul.

In another song, Mīrābāī imagines herself to be like a 'moonbird' gazing enraptured at the moon: 'As the moonbird looks, absorbed, at the moon, / So have I lost my heart to you, O Lord' (p. 93). The moonbird refers to the *chakor* who is desperately in love with the moon.[58] Mīrābāī, and more generally any devoted human soul, becomes like the *chakor*, this bird afflicted with such intense longing for the moon. Krishna is very clearly likened to the moon in these lines.

In the tradition of sharing and of the communal creation of meaning nurtured by *bhakti*, we can see how these songs of a moon-beloved encourage a range of individuals to utter their love-longing for the beloved Krishna. The songs tap into a reservoir of shared images of the moon – a moonless night, a moon-flower, a moon-bird – to imagine and find ways to express devotion to Krishna. It is a communal well of devotion, many people dipping in to speak of a night, a flower, a bird, all in agonising longing for a moon-beloved.

• • •

In this chapter, we have looked at traditions where the moon has a beautiful reach – it is a moon of loves and embraces. From such a viewpoint, the moon is both gentle and powerful. Not only does it reach into the soft, soothing parts of love, but it also embodies the pain of love, the absences and pangs of love-longing. We began with the Welsh poet Dafydd ap Gwilym, for whom the moon is a strong, at times even frustrating, presence in love. Dafydd relays the moon's beauty in startling detail, and it shimmers as a witness in all love relationships on earth. We then turned to the notion of 'moon beauties' in Arabic and Persian traditions. The image of the loved one being as beautiful as the moon pervades Persian and Arabic poetry, as seen in a wide range of Andalusian poets, for example. In the Persian love epic *Layla and Majnun*, the moon is an abiding force in the lovers' relationship, as we saw it was for Troilus and Criseyde. The moon particularly draws attention to the intimate dance between earthly and cosmic events.

Sufi and Hindu poets reclaimed the image of 'moon beauties'. For poets like al-Shushtarī, Ibn 'Arabī, Rūmī and 'Aṭṭār, the moon beauty is the divine beloved, beyond all cosmic measurements and cycles – and the moon itself wastes away in longing for the divine beloved. The Hindu poet Mīrābāī might be treated alongside the Sufi poets, because she too speaks of a divine moon-beloved. For Mīrābāī, Krishna is her moon: without him, she is like a moonless night; and in longing for him, she is like a moon-flower or moon-bird, caught in perpetual longing and need for the moon. For medieval audiences of writing and images, the moon is a witness and even at times a participant in the languages of human love. When speaking the language of love, many medieval people spoke the language of the moon.

7

...

THE MOON OF WORLDS AND TALES: AN EPILOGUE

In this journey through medieval moons, using a multi-glance, we have seen the earth's moon from many aspects. It is riddling, planetary, influential, powerful, adventurous, signifying, healing, loving – and much more. Medieval people's reading, hearing, and viewing of the moon nurtured their bond with the earth itself, and the moon had an enduring link with the human imagination. The abundant reservoir of written and visual sources available from the years 700–1600, from around the world, reveals a spectrum of medieval moons. This book has told lunar stories pulsing with endeavour and emotion, excitement and fear, power and vulnerability, anguish and love. In telling these stories as though through 'alchemical' moonlight, I have sought to give a much-needed focus on the medieval centuries, even as 'medieval' is, as seen in the Introduction, a fraught term. This book of medieval moons has hoped to exhibit a medieval world that is not purely Western, embracing instead a richly global Middle Ages.

THE MEDIEVAL MOON

In the Introduction, we imagined viewing the medieval world through imperfect but transformative moonlight, each encounter with the past an alchemical reaction that shifted depending on its participants. In doing so, we confronted the terminological and methodological challenges in a book of this nature. Both the avian and multi-glance methodologies are useful in attempting comparative work: comparative study can be imagined as a bird's flight or as a multifaceted 'glance' across cultures. This book has in particular harnessed the methodology of the multi-glance to traverse many moons across a range of cultures, seeking to give distinct traditions an equal footing. The multi-glance allows a look across a spectrum of 'moons' from around the medieval world. The methodology does not work immaculately, and the coverage – like the moonlight through which we view the past – has at times been imperfect.

In Chapter 1, we considered medieval definitions of the moon; this chapter posited that the moon itself forms a kind of riddle in the medieval world with its baffling array of qualities and meanings, and it is indeed found at the centre of riddling traditions in Old English and Old Norse. Through alchemical encounters with the past, it becomes clear that the moon-planet – moist, cold, and phlegmatic – was understood throughout the world to have immense influence on earth. The moon was believed to impact trees, tides, people's movement, and much more. And in its complexity, the moon was embodied in the form of powerful goddesses and gods, differing from tradition to tradition, though our spotlight particularly fell on the Greco-Roman Artemis/Diana and the Chinese Chang'e. Both are goddesses of immense power and splendour.

In Chapter 2, we studied stories related to travel to and from the moon; this chapter suggested that the moon invited medieval audiences and viewers to navigate the similarities and the differences between 'self' and 'other'. We journeyed through moonlight with a Japanese nun, we called out to the moon with a concerned medieval citizen of England, and we witnessed the spectacular voyages to and from the moon by Astolfo and Kaguya-hime in *The Frenzy of Orlando* and *The Tale of the Bamboo Cutter*. All these expeditions raise central questions about how to define home and the 'foreign', and what exile truly means. The moon is intimately tied with earth in these stories, becoming at times a many-hued mirror reflection of earth, or coming close to earth to reveal its flaws. Through all these stories of travel and adventure, the moon shifts between being an otherworld and being an extension of our earthly homeland.

In Chapter 3, we examined the moon's potent symbolic or 'semiological' role, fundamental to acts of prophecy, as a sign of future events, or as a symbol in religious contexts. This chapter contended that the moon was central to how medieval people understood and navigated their present and future lives. The moon was crucial in people finding hidden meanings around them, and in shaping people's conceptions of their futures. This chapter covered a wealth of materials and subjects. The first half focused on the moon as foreteller of the future – from the moon as portent in a tragic-epic poem of Chaucer's, to moon prognostication practices in England and Polynesia, to the moon's centrality in prophetic activity in European literature. The second half dwelt on religious symbolism, including interpretations of an Islamic moon miracle, the moon as a sign in Christian history or as a symbol in Christian doctrine, and the moon's pervasiveness in Christian iconography.

In Chapter 4, we pondered the moon's central role in medieval diagnosis and treatment of ill-health of both a physical and mental nature; this chapter underscored that for medieval people, the moon had a deep and visceral connection with human bodies and minds. The chapter highlighted the concept of melothesia – the idea that particular signs of the zodiac corresponded to particular parts of the body – visualised in images of the 'zodiac man'. We spent time with Islamic medicine and English 'moonbooks' that focused on illness and treatment, and we traced the strong connections between the moon and mental ill-health and epilepsy. We also revealed the story of a lunar king's wasting disease in South Asian traditions, and the invocation of the moon for healing feuds in Old Norse. Through all these examples, it became clear that the moon, linked as it was to illness and treatment regimens, had an inescapable part to play in healing practices.

In Chapter 5, we reflected on more painful readings of the moon, with its links to states of suffering and to falsity; this chapter demonstrated that the moon could signify sadness and illusion for medieval people. It first focused on medieval understandings of eclipses, bound as these are with the concurrent strength and vulnerability of the moon. It then moved through various traditions which reveal the more fraught and sinister aspects of the moon: the chasing wolf of Old Norse; the deceived elephant of *Kalīla and Dimna* and the equally deceived wolf of Henryson's *Fables*; the moon illusion in Chaucer's *Franklin's Tale* and the mournful moon of his *Legend of Good Women*. All these examples were bolstered by the moon of Juliana of Cornillon emerging to show an absence she saw in her world; the shaming moon of an English anchoritic text, echoed in the Virgin Mary standing on the moon; and the moon that torments the grieving father of *Pearl*.

In Chapter 6, we contemplated the moon's abiding associations with love in a range of secular and religious contexts. This chapter showed that the moon was fundamental to how medieval people experienced and talked about love in its myriad forms. Dafydd ap Gwilym is fixated on the moon in much of his love poetry, where the beloved may be as beautiful as the moon but the moon itself may thwart a romantic rendezvous. Hispano-Arabic poetry is replete with 'moon beauties' (Omid Safi), and we witnessed how this image is reclaimed for devotional purposes by a range of Andalusian and Persian Sufis, as well as by the Hindu Mīrābāī, who speaks of her love for Krishna as a love-longing for the moon, like a flower or bird starved of lunar nourishment. So although the previous chapter revealed a harsher, less compassionate moon, Chapter 6 discovered a moon that emanates love.

In this final and brief chapter, which acts as an epilogue to the book, we will dwell with the moon in its role in telling stories and in forming worlds. For this, we will pause on three varied sources, each speaking of the moon's intimacy with earth and of its immense creative power: a twelfth-century illustration of the 'land of the moon'; medieval Korean poems; and a fourteenth-century fresco from a church-mosque in Istanbul.

The Land of the Moon

A story in the Latin *Marvels of the East* tells of a 'land of the moon' and a 'land of the sun'. This text survives in both Latin and English and is a collection of accounts of wondrous places or beings in an imagined 'East'. In the English version, there is a moon-lake rather than a moon-land. But in this Latin version's land of the moon, it is cold by day and hot by night; in the land of the sun, it is hot by day and cold by night. In the manuscript with which we opened this book, we see a soft blue illustration of the land of the moon (Plate 15).[1] Like Princess Kaguya's tale in *The Tale of the Bamboo Cutter*, this story and illustration of *The Marvels of the East* help audiences to imagine a distinctive moon-land, far from earth, yet still with a powerful and unbreakable connection with the earth in which they dwell.

The Rhythms of the Moon

A deep connection with the moon is also found among medieval Korean poets. Korean *sijo* poetry is a kind of verse form related to *haiku* with very old roots; it is three-line verse composed in the vernacular.[2]

The moon appears repeatedly in medieval *sijo* poetry as a fundamental part of poets' encounters with the world. The poet Lee Hyun-bo (1467–1555) thinks of his relationship with the outside world by imagining the moon: 'As the white moon reflects upon the surface, / I grow indifferent to that world' (p. 47).[3] The poet Lee Hwang (1501–1570) says that the moon and the winds are his 'only companions' (p. 61). In 'Songs of a fisherman's four seasons', poet Yun Seon-do (1587–1671) describes the glittering beauty of the moon's role in nature: 'White dew glistens as it trickles down the grassy bank. / The bright moon rises above' (p. 91). And then the poet describes a particular sight on the moon: 'A jade hare on the moon pounds out the medicine' (p. 91). This has been identified as an image that many people thought they saw on the moon when looking at its shadows.[4] Just as European viewers thought they saw a man on the moon, as seen in Chapter 2, people in Asia saw a jade hare. Yun Seon-do also expresses various yearning encounters with the moon: 'I intended to ascend to the pines-embraced hermitage / To watch the dawn moon' (p. 93), and 'I will lean against the pine tree window / Until the winter moon passes over the western peak' (p. 101). For these poets, the moon is an indispensable part of the rhythms of their lives, as it was for so many in the medieval world. And for Yun Seon-do, the moon itself forms an object of desire, as the poet actively seeks out a meeting with the dawn and winter moons. Another *sijo* poet, Jeong Cheol (1536–1593), adopts a woman's voice to appeal to a beloved one:

If only I were able to cut out my heart
To make that moon
Immeasurably high in the sky,
Hanging proudly,
I could follow its beam
To find my precious love there. (p. 63)

Here the poet imagines (through a woman's voice) forming one's heart into a moon in order to find and reach the one who is beloved.[5] As witnessed in Chapter 6, the moon is frequently invoked in love relationships, at times to describe the beloved – or at times, as here, to describe that bewildering path to the beloved.

A Church-Mosque

Let us now end with one final medieval image which encapsulates the profundity of the moon's relationship with earth and all that is in it (Plate 16). This image also demonstrates how the moon continuously forms a borderland between the earth and the cosmos beyond. It is found in the Kariye Camii, a Greek Orthodox church building in Istanbul now used as a mosque. The building is replete with mosaics and frescoes from the Byzantine period. Its layered history – as both church and mosque – also speaks to the mosaic of cultures this book has sought to attend to. A fresco in this church-mosque dating to *c.* 1320–1 shows the Last Judgment. In this scene is a detail of an angel rolling up the scroll of heaven. The image is found in the domed vault of a parecclesion (a side chapel).

The western half of the image shows the moon, the sun, and the stars swirling in a large white shell-like shape. This is the cosmos embodied, and the moon is a fundamental part of it: the moon circles with the sun and stars in an angel's grasp. As we look upon it, spiralling in an angelic dance, we might imagine all that the moon meant for medieval people: it was an endlessly powerful planet, a deep and inescapable part of how medieval readers, authors, listeners, and viewers made sense of their world. It gave up a wealth of meanings, stories, imaginings. As it is held by an angel, we might imagine the moon too as a rich frontier, signalling for medieval people that border between earth and the wider cosmos, between this life and the life beyond. In its silver-gold swirl, the Kariye Camii moon reminds us of how it has spoken to the human imagination across centuries. Even as we may look back to the 'Middle Ages' through imperfect moonlight, the moon's powerful presence for medieval people continues to be felt. We look at the moon that medieval people looked upon, in all its myriad colours and forms, its hauntings and its blessings; we gaze with them; and, I hope, we feel our imaginations ignite.

Appendix

• • •

TRANSLATIONS FROM MIDDLE ENGLISH MOONBOOKS AND ARABIC SUFI POETRY

This appendix provides texts to accompany the discussions in this book, particularly those in Chapters 3, 4, and 6. The Middle English moonbooks have been chosen for their centrality to wisdom regarding the moon, wisdom disseminated in a major vernacular of Europe. The texts selected (all dating to the fifteenth century) give a representative sample of the different approaches and concerns of Middle English moonbooks. These excerpts are complemented by Arabic Sufi poetry that focuses intimately on the moon and forms a focal point of discussion in Chapter 6. These Sufi poems have been translated elsewhere, as indicated in the notes placed next to the titles, but those translations are not widely available.

Excerpts from *The Book of Hippocrates*[1]

This is the Book of Hippocrates. In this book, he teaches how to know by planets sickness, life, and death, and the times thereof.

Hippocrates first says that a physician should take heed of the moon when it is full. Then waxes blood and marrow and brain and other humours which are moist and cold or moist and hot. The same sickness that is cold and dry or hot and dry shows also the course of the moon. Wherefore, when you take a cure, be it of physic or else of surgery, take heed of the moon and of the time when the sickness took and in which sign it began. [. . .]

When a moon is in a sign that is called Aries, in English a ram, this sign connects to the head and the chin of the human being. This sign is of the type of fire, hot and dry, choleric. Wherefore, when [there is] a planet that is called Mars or else the sun, which is also hot and dry, the sickness must needs be in the head, of heat and of fires, and he may not well speak and the lungs and the breast burn from heat. [. . .]

When the moon is in a sign that is called Taurus, that sign is of the type of the earth, cold and dry. And if a planet that is called Saturn is with the moon in this sign and Mars, that is a planet that is contrary to the moon, this sickness shall be of coldness and dryness. This sign connects to the human throat. The sickness shall be of fiery intermittent fever, cold gout, cold dropsy, and others that are passions of the spleen. Wherefore, if the moon is in this sign and the planet with him [the moon] is cold, that sickness may not be healed. [. . .]

When a man has this sickness and the moon is in this sign [Gemini] and other planets are contrary, then it is good to give medicine. But if Saturn and Mars are together when this sickness takes him, within twenty-five days he shall die. This sign connects to a human's arms and shoulders and all that sickness that belongs to them. [. . .]

Cancer is a sign that is cold and moist of the type of phlegm. When the moon is in this sign, he [the moon] is in his own house. If a man falls sick at that time and the sickness be of phlegm that is cold and moist as is dropsy, daily fever and morbid swelling that be in colour white and in feeling soft, they may not be cured until the moon comes into a sign that is called Leo. [. . .] And winds that come out of the north are contrary and cause increase of the sickness. Cancer connects to the breast, and sickness of the breast are in this time most grievous. [. . .]

Leo is a sign that is hot and dry, of the type of fire. [. . .] If a man falls sick while the moon is in this sign and Mars and the Sun are with the moon, he shall die in the hot summer within two years by day when the sun is hottest, that is, about noon. This sign connects to a man's stomach and liver and gall. Therefore, all sickness and pains that are of the gall and of the liver are most troublesome when the moon is in this sign. [. . .]

Virgo is a sign that is cold and dry of the type of the earth [. . .]. If the moon has with him Saturn, he shall die soon after harvest September. All manner of sickness that is from the navel to the stomach trouble more when the moon is in this sign. [. . .]

Libra is a sign that is hot and moist. [. . .] If the moon has with him the sun or Mars, the sickness shall never leave him in his life. This sign connects to a human's body the kidneys and the loins and the bladder. Therefore, all sickness that is in these members trouble most while the moon is in this sign. [. . .]

Scorpio is a sign cold and moist, of the kind of water. [. . .] If Venus and Mercury are with the moon in this sign, in certain times they shall bleed, that is when the moon meets with Mercury and Venus. [. . .]

Sagittarius is a sign hot and dry, of the kind of fire. When the moon is in this sign, if a man falls into any sickness in the haunch or in the thigh from the knee to the hip bone, as in the passion sciatica, shall no medicine be given thereto for him before the moon comes into a sign that is called Capricorn or Virgo. If the moon has with him a planet that is called Venus, this sickness is incurable, for it shall turn into a palsy within two years, the which shall take him his limbs from the waist downward. All manner of passions that are from the hip-bone to the knee grieve most while the moon is in that sign, for this sign belongs to this part of a man. [. . .]

Capricorn is a sign that is cold and dry, of the kind of earth. When the moon is in this sign, all manner of sickness in the knee of coldness and dryness shall no medicine receive until the moon is in a sign that is called Aquarius or Libra or Gemini. If the moon has with him Saturn or Venus, or if the sign is contrary and the knee has no swelling, that passion is incurable. This sign connects to a human's knee and the part of the leg behind the knee, and therefore all grievances that fall thereto when the moon is in this sign are incurable. [. . .]

Aquarius is a sign that is hot and moist. When the moon is in that sign, all manner of sickness that are from the knee to the ankle shall take no medicine, as in cramp in the calf of the legs and ulcers and the dropsy. If the moon has with him Jupiter and Saturn, that sickness that he takes in the limb shall last him till the moon has gone three times about, that is, a quarter of a year. But do your medicine whatever time you will, save when the moon is in this sign. [. . .]

Pisces is a sign that is cold and moist. When the moon is in this sign, all manner of sickness that is in the foot [. . .] shall no medicine take while the moon is in this sign. And if the sun or Mars or Saturn is with the moon in this sign, it is incurable, but if it so be that the medicine be given thereto anon after the moon and Saturn depart, and so of the sun and Mars afterwards, a man may ease him and with medicine cure him. [. . .]

Excerpts from *The True Knowledge of Astrology*[2]

Here begins the marvellous and true knowledge of astrology founded and proved true [. . .]. It is honourable and profitable to know every day throughout the year in which sign the moon is, for as the philosopher [Ptolemy] says, the moon is the next planet to the earth and therefore it has the most strength and effect than any other planet with regard to earthly things and more relevance to the human creature. So that by the moon and by the complexion of the sign that the moon is in, you may know what is good to do or not, leave or take, begin or rest [...].

March/Aries

Know you well without doubt that when the moon is in the Sheep [...], in that day it is good to let blood. For if a man takes sickness in that time, fear it not for he will soon be whole. It is good to go with merchandise, to buy in to the east. It is good to be bathed. It is good to melt metal and to make bells and guns and to work all that belongs to metal and to fire. [...] The thief that steals will be found, and he who breaks out of prison and flees will be found again. [...] For know you well if there is thunder in that time, the moon shall become all dark. And great pestilence in the region will be, and herbs will want strength. And many folk will be sick, and worms will multiply. And that betokens great famine in the east country and great disease in many cities and towns that year. [...]

April/Taurus

And when the moon is in the sign that is called Taurus, which is in English a bull, it is good to begin all things that belong to stability and long it will endure. [...] It is good to wed a woman [...] or to buy lands or tenements, or corn or beasts, or a good horse. [...] It is not good to begin a long journey as to Rome or to Saint Katherine's mount. It is not good to begin with great wrath or anger towards any man [...]. The male child that is born in that [time] will have his mark in his front or in his arm, for he shall be amiable and a good body and fair and proud of himself. [...] The maiden child will have her mark in the left arm, for she will be much loved and made of with many men for her beauty and she may live as long as the male. [...]

May/Gemini

And when the moon is in the sign that is called Gemini, do not let blood on your arm [. . .]. It is not good to be stewed, nor to cut your nails of your fingers, nor of your toes. [. . .] It is good to speak of peace, or of accord, or of matrimony, or contract of wedding. It is good to set children to school or to learn subtle crafts and minstrelsy. It is good to plead before judges and advocates and to ask steady judgement in governments of tenements. It is good to take laxative medicine for man's health. [. . .] If it thunders in that sign, great rain will be, and great plenty of corn and namely of wheat. The winter will be grievous, and great infirmity will there be in many countries and many great marvels and wonders will fall. [. . .]

June/Cancer

And when the moon is in the sign that is called Cancer, in English tongue a crab, it is evil to wed a wife, for often times they will be at debate and strife. It is not good to begin anything that should be stable, as castles or towers or formal agreements that should last long. [. . .] Evil it is to heal the breast, for whomsoever falls to be burned or hurt there, it is peril of death. Good it is to go on a journey where you will soon come back again. Good it is to begin all things that you desire soon to have an end of. It is a good time to take medicine, for the moon is then in its own house and is full of moistness. Good it is to bathe or to stew or to do all manner of thing that belongs to water. [. . .]

July/Leo

And when the moon is in the sign that is called Leo, in English tongue a lion, that sign is firm and stable. And beware of taking any medicines within the body, for if you do you must cast it out or be in peril of death. [...] It is not good to begin no cause against your adversary nor begin anything that you desire soon to have end of. [...] Good time it is to buy clothes of green colour. This sign betokens all this, and it is hot and dry, burning of nature, like fire or to the parts of the Orient, which is eastward. [...] And if it thunders in that sign, the moon being in that sign, great contention and strife will there be that year between the king and the commons. Fruit will be good but they will be dear, but at the year's end there shall be much and namely of wheat. [...]

August/Virgo

When the moon is in the sign that is called Virgo, and it is called in English tongue a Maiden, good it is to set and sow and to do all things that belong to the earth. It is good to travel through the country and to send letters and to do other things that you desire soon to be ended to the good, to buy clothes of green colour [...]. The child who is born in this sign has his mark in his right hand or in his knees. He shall be good of body and fair and simple of understanding. [...] The maiden has her sign in the cheek, and she will be hard-working and pleasant in all manner of working, and she is good to wed for man's profit. And she may live as the man does, but I advise to keep them both from falling in water for dread of death that may befall from that. [...]

September/Libra

When the moon is in the sign that is called Libra, and in English tongue called the Scales, then it is good to go southward in to places of merchandise. And it is good to buy furs and all white clothing and all white money and stones of that colour and all white doves and swans and all birds of this colour. [. . .] And evil it is to begin anything that needs to be stable, like building or establishing towers or castles [. . .]. And things stolen will be returned. And the man or woman who takes sickness in that time will be in peril of death. And a man who breaks out of prison or flees away will return or soon be found. [. . .]

October/Scorpio

When the moon is in the sign that is called Scorpio, in English tongue a scorpion, it is evil to be clothed in new clothing or to make them. And it is evil to make fellowship, or to speak to a king or great lords for any profitable purpose. It is evil to write letters or to hear tidings. It is not a good time to begin a journey on the sea nor land nor to do anything that you would soon have success in, nor is it good to let blood but for great need, nor to take medicine in your body but for great need. [. . .] The male child that is born in that sign has his mark in the left foot or beside the nose. He will be full of vices and evil of conditions, and a liar and a thief, and a man-slayer. [. . .] The woman will be pleasant to her husband. [. . .]

November/Sagittarius

When the moon is in the sign that is called Sagittarius, and in English tongue called an archer, good it is to buy gold or silver, to win in merchandise and clothes of green colour or blood-red colour. It is good to speak to princes or to great lords, and new clothes to wear [. . .]. Good it is to be a man of religion, to be advanced in the holy church, and good to go with merchandise into the north country. [. . .] And if it thunders in that time, much fruit will fall through great frosts. And the Greeks say it betokens great tribulation against merchants who work in strong countries. [. . .]

December/Capricorn

When the moon is in the sign that is called Capricorn, in English tongue a goat, it is good to go northward by the sea in the water for merchandise and for other needs also. And it is good to set and to sow, to till and to cut trees, and to do all things that belong to the earth, and it is a good time to buy lead or iron, and to do all things that you would soon have end of, and it is evil to go southward, or to take any medicines or to let blood. [...] And things stolen will never be found. And whoever flees will turn again to his home. And whoever falls sick will soon die by nature. [...]

January/Aquarius

When the moon is in the sign that is called Aquarius, and it is called in English tongue the sign of a man, it is good to buy all things that will be stable, as to take foundations for castles or towers, or to enter into a great dignity or office, or of marriage, or to move to a new house to dwell in, or to move from one house to another to dwell in, and good to speak with kings or great lords, or to great scholars or advocates, to bring legal action before them or before judges. [...] And it is good to buy things that are of black colour, as furs, or black horses, or black beasts, and a good time to take wild fowl, and to wed a woman, and good to bleed on the arm. [...]

February/Pisces

When the moon is in the sign that is called Pisces, in English tongue called a fish, it is good to work in things belonging to the water, for fishing, or for water mills, or to go to the sea, or to other waters, and good to take medicines, and good to speak to a woman to have her as a paramour. [...] And it is good to set children to school to learn subtle crafts as playing the organ or stringed musical instrument or any subtle minstrelsy, or to be subtle in argument or of letters [. . .].

Excerpts from *The Moon of Ptolemy*[3]

Here begins *The Moon of Ptolemy*, founded by old doctrine of astrology [. . .]. If the moon is in the sign that is called Aries, in English tongue a sheep, go not for peril of death. And if the moon is in the sign that is called Taurus, in English tongue a bull, it is great peril. And if the moon is in the sign that is called Gemini, go securely, for you will have your purpose and your winnings and welfare. And if it is in the sign that is called Cancer, in English tongue a crab, go without peril. And if it is in the sign that is called Leo, in English tongue a lion, it is good to go against lords or princes [. . .]. And in the sign that is called Virgo, in English tongue a maiden, it is not good to go north [. . .]. And if it is in the sign that is called Libra, in English tongue the scales, go not, for you shall find enemies in your way to deter you, or to do harm to you. And if the moon is in the sign that is called Scorpio, in English tongue a scorpion, go not then for it is the most perilous of death. If it is in the sign that is called Sagittarius, in English tongue an archer, go boldly, for you will win thereof and find some great profit. And if it is in the sign that is called Capricorn, in English tongue a goat, it is not good to go. And if it is in the sign that is called Aquarius, in English tongue the sign of a man, go then, for you will gain much of your desire. And if the moon is in the sign that is called Pisces, in English tongue a fish, that is the last sign of the year, go not for peril of death, for it is unfortunate.

And all these have been proven for the most part. It fails men never, so that a man knows well the sign of the month that he is in, and the moon and the change and the prime of the day, and the hour and the eclipses that here are called dismal days. No unlearned man can learn to use the astrolabe or quadrant, unless a scholar through his own knowledge teaches him in the English tongue. For if an ordinary man were to do the teaching, scholars would be as though unlearned and the world would be undone, and it were against all reason.

Excerpts from 'He Who Will Harken of Wit'[4]

He who will harken of wit
Which is witnessed in holy scripture,
Listen to me a moment.
A story I will you tell,
What time is good to buy and to sell,
As it is found in books.
[...]

Day I

The first day of the moon
God knew well what was to do,
That day he made Adam.
[...]
That day is good, in truth to tell,
For to buy and to sell,
And to pass the sea.
All that is done that same day,
It will have good speed in faith,
Good luck and also fair grace.
[...]

Day II

On the second day of the moon,
All good things are good to do.
That day God made Eve.
[...]

Day III

The third day of the moon was Cain born,
Who in Hell is forlorn,
For he his brother killed.
[...]
He who flees that day, certainly,
He will be found soon again
Without any fail
And whomsoever does in sickness fall,
It will destroy all his strengths.
No doctor may avail him.
[...]

Day IV

The fourth day was born Abel.
That day is good, I tell you well,
Works to begin.
The child in truth who is born then
He will be a full good man,
And long live and prosper.
[...]

Day V

The fifth day is evil and bitter.
He who falls sick or gets pain
He will die from it.
That day it is a great folly
House or land to buy
In field or in bower.
[...]

Day VI

The sixth day Daniel was born,
Who helped Susanne, through God's grace,
Out of worldly shame.
He who is born that day, truly,
He will be noble and hardy,
And a man of very good fame.
[...]

Day VII

The seventh day of the moon
Abel fled away soon
From his brother Cain,
But that day Abel was slain.
[...]
He who so takes sickness or pain,
He might be saved through medicine,
His pains to abate.
[...]

Day VIII

The eighth day of the moon,
All things are good to do,
I warn you before.
For that day, I tell you,
That the rich king Methuselah
Of his mother was born.
[...]

Day IX

The ninth day of the moon,
You will have your dream soon
Within the fourth day.
But he who falls sick that day
It will hold him long, I guess,
I there well the truth say.
[…]

Day X

The tenth day of the moon
I will tell you what is to do.
That day was Lameth [son of Methuselah and father of Noah] was born.
That day is neither good nor ill.
[…]

Day XI

The eleventh day of the moon
All things are good to do,
Which do not belong to sin.
If you that day buy or sell,
Or take wife, truly to tell,
In it you will prosper.
[…]

Day XII

The twelfth day of the moon
All things are good to do,
And profitable enough.

That day Ham, Noah's son
Was ordained in to this world to dwell
And born without woe.
[...]

Day XIII

The thirteenth day of the moon,
If you have anything to do,
Then begin no thing.
[...]

Day XIV

The fourteenth day of the moon
All things are good to do,
As long as no sin be wrought.
For that day God's priest Aaron
Blessed old Simeon.
But take care that you do not flee.
If you that day, without lie,
Fall in any malady,
Soon it will go from you.
And if a child is born that day,
He will be a shrew in faith,
Wicked and false also.
[...]

Day XV

The fifteenth day of the moon,
No matter how much you have to do,

Take care not to begin.
[…]
The Tower of Babylon that day
Begun was, truth to say,
A giant let it set.
Dismal day it is.
Whoever begins anything, indeed,
That day were better left.
[…]

Day XVI

The sixteenth day of the moon,
All things are good to do,
House to set and sea to pass,
Both to buy and sell.
[…]
That same day was Nahor [brother of Abraham] born.
[…]

Day XVII

The seventeenth day of the moon
The earth opened very suddenly,
Then sank five cities,
Sodom, Adman, and Gomorrah,
Also Zeboiim and Zoar
[…]
Whomsoever that day begins to sell,
Through luck he may speed well,
And in good stead stand.
[…]

Day XVIII

The eighteenth day of the moon,
Buy and do what is to do,
[…]
For Isaac that day was born,
And he overcame all the sorrows that chafe,
Through the might of God's grace.
[…]

Day XIX

The nineteenth day of the moon
Abide, if you have anything to do,
Until a better time comes.
[…]
But if a child that day is born,
Great joy is laid before him.
Most holy he will be,
For Elizabeth was born that day,
Who bore John the Baptist, indeed,
That holy man so noble.
[…]

Day XX

The twentieth day of the moon,
Securely do what is to be done,
For good speed it will have.
[…]
For Isaac, truth to say,
Blessed Jacob his son that day.

Through God's holy virtue.
[…]

Day XXI

The twenty-first day of the moon
Begin and do what is to be done,
For it is a very good time
To buy and to sell in every place,
House to set or sea to pass,
Also the letting of blood.
He who is born that day, truly,
He will be noble and hardy,
I tell you before.
For that day was Esau [son of Isaac],
Who God gave so great virtue,
Of his mother born.
[…]

Day XXII

The twenty-second day of the moon,
Begin whatever you have to do,
Without any dread.
[…]

Day XXIII

The twenty-third day of the moon
Do whatever you have to do,
That day is good and able.
That day was Moses born

To keep the law, God chose him,
He was so true and stable.
[...]

Day XXIV

The twenty-fourth day of the moon,
I will you say what is to do.
That day was Aaron born.
He who grows sick that day,
I say to you truly, without denial,
His life will soon be forlorn.
[...]

Day XXV

The twenty-fifth day of the moon,
Jesus Christ from pains soon,
Into Egypt went.
[...]
The child, indeed, who is born then,
He will be a sinful man.
[...]

Day XXVI

The twenty-sixth day of the moon,
All things are good to do,
I tell you most well.
That day led Moses
God his people, without lie,
Throughout Israel.
[...]

Day XXVII

The twenty-seventh day of the moon,
No matter how much you have to do,
Wait for the second day,
For whatever thing you do,
It will not turn out well for you.
Your dreams betoken sorrow.
[...]

Day XVIII

The twenty-eighth day of the moon,
Begin no thing to do,
Abide a better time.
But your dreams that same night
Will turn to joy, I believe,
Within the tenth day.
[...]
But that child who is born then,
He will be a reckless man,
And full wicked of mind.
[...]

Day XXIX

The twenty-ninth day of the moon,
All thing is good to do,
And dreams are very good
which will turn to joy and bless,
For Christ that day blessed, indeed,
who for us died on the Cross.
[...]

Day XXX

The thirtieth day of the moon,
Abide if you have anything to do.
[...]
But what you dream that night
Within nine days, I believe,
You will find it true.
[...]

Epilogue

Now have you heard a fair story
Every man to rule him by,
How it is best to do.
[...]
When you see clearly
What time of the moon it is
Whether the moon is old or new
Go to this story again
And do right as it will say to you
Or else you will rue it.

Excerpts from John Metham's *Book of Destiny*[5]

As Albohazen witnesses, [...] the moon should, because of her propinquity, have many influences on nature's workings. [...] This treatise is compiled to give knowledge to the listeners which day is the most expedient to begin any work upon, to take voyage over the sea, to bleed for any sickness, to know what should befall him who falls sick in any day of the moon, and of other things it deals with, as the readers will find. [...]

The first day of the moon is fortunate to begin every good work. [...] The person who is born the first day of the moon should be disposed to be wise and discreet and to live long, disposed to have great vexation and great labour, but he should by great labour overcome it at last. [...]

The second day of the moon is prosperous to begin all works. He who weds a wife that day should live long with his wife in prosperity for the most part. This day is good for diviners, if it be that the sun is in the house of Saturn. [...]

The third day of the moon is not fortunate to begin any work. [...] A man should no journey take upon this day. [...] He who is born that day should be disposed to theft and covetousness, and die mischievously. [...]

The fourth day is good to begin every worldly occupation, and principally to seek springs for wells of water, to seek also veins of metal and mines of sand, gravel, and clay. He who is born that day should be greatly disposed to lechery, and he should have great vexation, but he should well overcome it. [...]

The fifth day is not successful to begin any work. He who is born that day should be a lunatic or else foolish. He who falls sick that day, unless he begins to improve within twenty-four hours, he should soon die. It is perilous to pass the sea that day. Whatever a man dreams that night after midnight should befall the next day by some similitude. [...]

The sixth day of the moon is lucky for those who will go hunting and hawking, if the weather is temperate. He who is born that day should be happy, be good, bold, hardy, and wise. If a woman is born that day, she should be fortunate to have a good husband. [...] That day is good to begin building places, and to begin all other works, and also to bleed. [...]

The seventh day is fortunate to begin all works. The person born that day should be disposed to be subtle of wit and diverse of conditions, and changeable, and disposed to live long. And if a body falls in sickness that day, he should soon recover. [...]

The eighth day is fortunate for all works. He who is born that day should be greatly disposed to lechery. [...] If a man falls in sickness that day, he should within four days recover and heal, or else die. That day is fortunate to pass the sea with merchandise, if the wind serves. [...]

The ninth day of the moon is lucky to begin all works. He who is born that day should be gracious and come to worship, and be disposed to have great wit. [...]

The tenth day is good to begin all works, to make agreements, to pass the sea with merchandise, and to wed a wife. He who is born that day should never be steadfast, but always wandering from one country to another. [...]

The eleventh day is good to begin all works. He who is born that day should be fortunate to good and a great purchaser, kind of heart, serious, and stable. He who falls sick upon that day should soon recover. This day is happy to buy and to sell, and it is fortunate to set children to school, and to wed a wife. [...]

The twelfth day is fortunate to begin all works, but most especially those who will divine and prognosticate and win a singular battle, to take a voyage over the sea, to buy and to sell. [...]

The thirteenth day is fortunate to begin all works, especially for astronomers to calculate. A man child that is born that day should be disposed to be evil taught, and to be angry and full of vice, but he should live only a short time. A woman that is born that day should be greatly disposed to lechery, or else she should die soon after her birth. [...]

The fourteenth day is fortunate to begin all works. He who is born that day should be disposed to be wise and rich and strong and short of life. If a man falls into sickness that day, he should never recover. A man may for need bleed for all sicknesses on this day. [...]

The fifteenth day is not successful to begin any work, for it is ungracious. And my author says that a man should not send his servant any message to speed well upon this day. [...] What a man dreams should turn only to fantasy. [...]

The sixteenth day is fortunate to begin all works, to buy and to sell and to wed a wife. He who is born that day should be disposed to be gracious and true, and of long life, but he should not be rich. He who falls sick that day should be long sick, but at the last he should recover. [...]

The seventeenth day is fortunate to begin all works. [...] He who falls sick that day should long continue in his sickness, but at the last with good governance he should escape it. Whatever a man dreams that night should turn to truth. [...]

The eighteenth day is fortunate to begin all works. He who is born that day should be malicious, disposed to malice, and backward of conscience and disposed to pride, but he should live but a short time. He who falls sick should be long sick and struggle to recover. What a man dreams that night should turn to truth by some similitude. [...]

The nineteenth day is good and lucky to begin all works, especially to buy and to sell and to pass the sea. [...] It is perilous to bleed that day. [...]

The twentieth day is fortunate to begin all works. He who is born that day should greatly increase in worldly goods, and be disposed to be subtle of wit and fortunate. [...]

The twenty-first day is fortunate. He who is born that day should be strong of complexion and of great wit, disposed to lechery and to many other vices. He who falls sick that day should die of that sickness. [...]

The twenty-second day is ungracious to begin any work, save only to buy and to sell. It is peril to pass the sea on that day. [...]

The twenty-third day is fortunate to begin all works. He who is born that day should be greatly disposed to vices, and most especially to lechery, and he should die mischievously. [...]

The twenty-fourth day is good to begin every work. He who is born that day should be wise and come to worship and be disposed to be a man of war. And if it be a woman that is born on that day, she should have many husbands and be rich and come to great worship. This day is profitable to buy and to sell, to pass the sea with merchandise, and to go on pilgrimage. [...]

The twenty-fifth day is fortunate to go hunting, and to sell. [...] It is peril to pass the sea. [...] If a man or woman falls sick on this day, they should never be clean of it. [...]

The twenty-sixth day is fortunate to hunt deer in the forest, but it is not fortunate to wed a wife, nor to pass the sea, nor fortunate to begin any work. [...]

The twenty-seventh day is fortunate to begin all works. He who is born that day should be disposed to be wise and true, and he should have many friends and be gracious and good of governance. [...]

The twenty-eighth day is fortunate to begin all works. What child is born that day should live with great travail, ever busy and ever in tribulation, but he should be right true of condition. He who falls into sickness should long be vexed with it, but at the last he should escape it. [...]

The twenty-ninth day is neither good nor fortunate to begin any works. A man child that is born that day should be fortunate to great worship, but he should be disposed to lechery, and should be made through marriage. If a woman be born that day, she should be demure and beauteous and modest, and she should come to great worship in marriage. [...]

The thirtieth day is fortunate to set children to school [...] and to begin all worldly occupations and to pass the sea with merchandise. He who is born that day should be disposed to be wise and greatly loved of women for seemliness of person and beauty of face. And if it is a maid that is born that day, she should be amiable and seemly and come to great worship. [...]

In this *Book of Destiny* you shall conceive, notwithstanding, that here is written how a man or woman should be disposed who is born on various days of the moon, whether to worship or to misfortune. You should not singularly for truth take it that it should be so, for bad raising may cause that a man shall never come to worship, though he be born to come to worship. [. . .] And of other things, you must look that the time is reasonable, for men should not begin nor do any worldly occupations on holy days, nor should men bleed in winter, nor pass the sea in tempests. Wherefore a consideration in all things must be had by discretion and reason.

Excerpts from 'Aries, prima mansio'[6]

Aries, prima mansion [first mansion]. The first mansion of the moon is temperate [. . .]. When the moon is in this mansion it is good to receive medicines, to put beasts to their pasture, to begin a journey, except in the second hour of the day. But wed not while the moon is in this mansion nor in the sign of the Ram. Buy no servant, for he will be a shrew, disobedient or fugitive. Buy tame beasts. Ride and make your journey by water if you will, for you shall have good passage. Take no acquaintance of new fellowship, for it shall not last. He that is taken shall be sore imprisoned. Make your armour, plant your trees. Cut your hair and your nails. Make your clothes and wear them. But see in all these things that the moon is free from unfortunate aspects of the wicked planets. [. . .]

The second mansion of the moon is dry [. . .]. When the moon is in this mansion, sow your seeds, begin your journey, but it is perilous to pass by water. Be not wedded. Buy tame beasts. Take no new fellowship, especially of those that are mightier than you. If you be taken prisoner, you are likely by cause of your good to be long imprisoned. This mansion is good for all things that are made with fire and for hunting. Buy no cows nor sheep. Plant no trees. Wear no new clothes. [...]

The third mansion of the moon is temperate [...]. When the moon is in this mansion, attend to your merchandise. [...] Make no marriage. Buy tame beasts. If you go by water, you shall have dread and peril. Take no fellowship, especially of your better. If you be taken, you shall long abide in prison and lose your good. Work with fire. Hunt; buy no cows nor sheep, plant no trees, sow no seeds. Wear no new clothes. [...]

The fourth mansion of the moon is moist [...]. When the moon is in this mansion, sow your seeds, wear new clothes. Wed not. Buy prisoners. Begin to build, for it will be durable. Buy tame beasts. Enter into no ship for passing the sea, for you will have a tempest of waves. Take no new fellowship. If you are taken, you shall have a long captivity. Build, dig for conduits [for water]. [...]

The fifth mansion of the moon is dry [...]. When the moon is in this mansion, make matrimony, put children to learn law or scripture, or write or make medicines, or take a journey. Buy servants. Build; go by water. Take no evil fellowship. If you are taken prisoner, you will pay and well escape. Wash your head; shear your hair. [...]

The sixth mansion of the moon is temperate [...]. When the moon is in this mansion, kings may begin to war and to lay sieges and pursue enemies and malefactors. Sow no seeds. Send no messenger. Borrow not. Take your journey by water, for though you tarry, you shall well come to your way's end. Take fellowship boldly, for they shall be faithful to you. [...] Take no medicines nor spices, nor cure any wounds [...].

The seventh mansion of the moon is moist [...]. When the moon is in this mansion, sow all manner of seeds [...]. Ride such beasts as you will. Take no journey except at the very end of the night. If you go by water, you shall speed well, though you will be delayed in the journey. Take fellowship, for they shall be true. [...] Buy no lands; deal with no physicians. [...]

The eighth mansion of the moon is temperate [...]. When the moon is in this mansion, receive medicine. [...] If it rains while the moon is in this mansion, it shall do good. Begin no journey. Weddings that are made will last in one accord only a little while. The servant who is bought shall accuse his lord. Enter into a ship, for you shall safely pass and quickly come again. [...]

The ninth mansion of the moon is dry [...]. When the moon is in this mansion, sow no seeds. Take no journey. [...] Wear no new clothes lest you be drowned in them. Make strong your gates and locks. Move your corn from place to another. Organise your beds and also your curtains. [...]

The tenth mansion of the moon is moist [...]. When the moon is in this mansion, make weddings. Take no journey. Borrow not. Wear no new clothes; do not provide clothes for your wife. Build, for it shall be durable. Take fellowship, for it is good. Beware of being taken for long imprisonment. [...]

The eleventh mansion of the moon is temperate [...]. When the moon is in this mansion, let out no prisoner. Besiege cities. Sow and plant what you will. [...] Lay foundations and build. Take fellowship and you shall win. Wear no new clothes. Shear your hair if you will. [...]

The twelfth mansion of the moon is moist [...]. When the moon is in this mansion, begin to build, give a lease, sow and plant. Wed and wear new clothes and provide clothes for your wife. Take your journey in the first or in the third part of the day. And leave nothing for you shall not recover it again except with great hostility and labour. If you enter any ship, you shall have peril and labour to escape. Buy servants and beasts, but buy them after the moon has gone out of the Lion [Leo] and into the Maiden [Virgo]. [...]

The thirteenth mansion of the moon is temperate [...]. When the moon is in this mansion, put grain in your land, sow your seeds. Take your journey. Wed. Deliver prisoners. Good it is to wed a woman who has been corrupted, evil to wed a virgin, for they will last a little while in company. Buy servants and they will be true. If you enter any ship, your coming again will be long delayed. [...] Receive new medicines. Make new clothes. Build, be merry. Go before every lord that you have business with. Wash your head and shear your hair [...].

The fourteenth mansion of the moon is temperate [...]. When the moon is in this mansion, wed women but no virgins. Receive medicines. Sow and plant. Take no journey. [...] Buy servants; they shall be true. Enter ships. Take fellowship boldly. If you are taken, you will soon escape. [...]

The fifteenth mansion of the moon is moist [...]. When the moon is in this mansion, dig pits and conduits [for water]. Take no journey; receive medicines for infirmity of wind and no other. Matrimony made in this mansion shall little while endure in accord. If you lend money, you will not recover it again. Eschew all journeys by water and by land. Take no new fellowship. Change your dwelling. [...] Shear not your hair. Buy servants. [...]

The sixteenth mansion of the moon is moist [...]. When the moon is in this mansion, take no journey. Receive no medicine. Attend to no merchandise. Do not provide clothes for your wife. Do not make or wear new clothes. In matrimony there will be no accord. Buy servants. Take no new fellowship. If you are taken prisoner, you will soon be delivered. [...]

The seventeenth mansion of the moon is moist [...]. When the moon is in this mansion, buy sheep and beasts and put them to pasture. Wear new clothes. Besiege towns. Wed no maiden. Build and it will last well. And if you enter into a ship, you will have anger and sorrow, but you will escape. [...]

The eighteenth mansion of the moon is dry [...]. When the moon is in this mansion, build, buy land, give leases on your land. Receive dignity and worship; if it rains it will do good. Take your journey towards the East. If the moon is with Mars and you wed, you shall find that your wife is not a virgin. Buy no servants. Build, enter into ships. Take no new fellowship. Plant trees and herbs. Wear no new clothes. Shear not your hair. Receive and make medicines. [...]

The nineteenth mansion of the moon is moist [...]. When the moon is in this mansion, lay siege to castles, plead with your adversary. Take your journey. [...] Buy no servants. Enter no ship, for she is likely to be broken. [...]

The twentieth mansion of the moon is moist [...]. When the moon is in this mansion, buy beasts. For a journey it is neutral. Rain that falls will do good and no harm. [...]

The twenty-first mansion of the moon is temperate [...]. When the moon is in this mansion, build, sow, buy sheep, land, beasts, and ornaments for women and clothes. It is neutral for a journey. A woman who is deprived of her husband by death or departing will never be wedded again. If you buy a servant, he shall be disobedient and not subservient to you. [...]

The twenty-second mansion of the moon is moist [...]. When the moon is in this mansion, buy, take your journey in the third part of the day. Wear new clothes. Wed not, for you and your wife will be divided and you will die six months before your wife at least. And your wife will be in discord with you and treat you wrongly. Buy no servants in any way. [...]

The twenty-third mansion of the moon is moist [...]. When the moon is in this mansion, receive medicine. Wear new ornaments and new clothes [...] Wed not. Buy no servants. Enter no ship. Take fellowship. [...]

The twenty-fourth mansion of the moon is temperate [...]. When the moon is in this mansion, attend to no merchandise, buy no ornaments, wear no new clothes. Take no wife. Take medicines. Send your knights and your hosts. Buy servants. Enter no ship. Take no new fellowship. If you are taken, you will soon be delivered. [...]

The twenty-fifth mansion of the moon is temperate [...]. When the moon is in this mansion, besiege towns and castles and pursue your enemies. Send your messengers. Wed not. Sow not. Buy no beasts. Buy no sheep. Take your journey to the South. Buy servants. Enter into ships. Take no new fellowships. [...]

The twenty-sixth mansion of the moon is dry [...]. When the moon is in this mansion, take your journey in the first part of the day [...]. Wed not. Buy servants. Build. Enter into ships. Take no fellowship. Beware that you are not taken. [...]

The twenty-seventh mansion of the moon is moist [...] When the moon is in this mansion, sow your seeds. Do your merchandise. Wed. [...] Take no journey in the third part of the day of the night in no way. Enter into no ship. Buy no servant. Take no fellowship. If you are taken, you will not escape. [...]

The twenty-eighth mansion of the moon is temperate [...]. When the moon is in this mansion, attend to merchandises. Sow. Receive medicine. [...] Wed, if you will. Take no journey in the third part of the night, if you can. Buy no servant. Take no fellowship. If you are taken, you will not escape.

Excerpts from 'For Journeying'[7]

When you would do anything or begin anything, look in what sign the moon makes its course. And if you find it in Aries, soon and well you will fulfil your journey. If she [the moon] is in Taurus, you will suffer harm. If she is in Gemini, you will have profit and men you will find as your friends. If she is in Cancer, dread you not to go if your way is short. If she is in Leo [...] you will be much grieved. If she is in Virgo, go not for you will be constrained with your fortune. If she is in Libra, dread for to go for you will find enemies. If she is in Scorpio, you will be sorry; go not nor begin anything. If she is in Sagittarius, do your journey and what you desire in goodness will come to you. If she is in Capricorn, [. . .] go not. If she is in Aquarius, you should eschew to go, for you will have contrariness. If she is in Pisces, if you go poor you will not come back poor.

Al-Shushtarī's 'Moon Song I'⁸

To me, from me, he is the goal:
hey you, how are you doing?
You will find me running and the path
leads to me, so that I might see you.
I am never absent from my presence.
There is no veil before me.
The peak of presence is my absence
I long that you can see me, and the truth.
All truth is in my disappearance
For if not, I would not be discovered.
For I continue and continue,
Setting up traps for my essence.
I trapped myself and thus I know
I am alone in the traps.
I have no like and no equal
I say to myself in every moment:
I am the signifier and the signified.
In me it is proven for sure.
I am the rich and also the poor,
Garments of clay veil me from myself.
Shadows are the illusions
My garment is my own;
I disrobe, for better is nakedness,
And I will accept the consequences.

I seek myself in myself,
Absent to myself, I ask:
In truth, my beloved:
Do you see me and not a fantasy?
So I said to myself:
Absolutely, absolutely, I have no copy.
I have achieved my deepest self,
I have seen the one who imaged you.
You return and tell me I make things up;
The others have changed you.
My wine is a delicate wine,
It intoxicated me a long while ago.
It is so good I break open the cache,
And its breaking is not in vain.
My story is all wonders:
I am the tablet and the pen.
My essence was so divided:
Me? I do not know you.
When I put aside the mirror
And everything in your image?
I felt in myself and the feelings
Were manifest from me to me:
All the names were for me a peel.
My essence is the heart of the issue.
While hidden from sight,
I sang out to the moon one night:
Oh night, whether long or not long
I must watch you.
But if my moon were with me,
I would not remain to watch yours.

Al-Shushtarī's 'Moon Song II'⁹

O hidden one and eternal
How manifest and clear you are.
You have disappeared from my sight,
But in the eyes of my heart, I see you.
You never disappear from me,
nor does your secret disappear from me
Your command and your judgment and your decree
Affect the living and the dead.
I look at the world and see
Your kindness present in everything.
You are eternal with no end
Your judgement is victorious over humanity.
The guilty and the innocent among us,
how can they break free from your command?
Oh you who wish to see God,
Look at the togetherness of being
Silent, or speaking, or frozen
In animal or plant
In everything you will see God
With no divisions or sides.
With no sides or divisions,
You will see the God who provided for you.
And all of him is dispersed;
He wants to test you.
One; he has no equal, no copy or likeness
By remembering the beautiful one,
I shortened the long night.
Forgive the singer who says,
And the one to whom he says:

Oh night, whether long or not long
I must watch you.
But if my moon were with me,
I would not remain to watch yours.

Ibn ʿArabī's 'Moon Girl'[10]

Between Adhriʿāt and Busra she appeared,
a girl of fourteen, full moon emerging.
In pride and glory, she exceeds
the movements of time itself.
Each full moon, when it reaches completion
must wane again that it may complete a month.
But this moon does not move through the signs of the zodiac,
nor double from odd to even.
You are responsible for each delicious smell,
You are a garden bringing forth flowers and spring.
Beauty has become full in you.
In all that is made there is nothing like you.

•••

NOTES

Introduction

1. Edgar Williams, *Moon: Nature and Culture* (London: Reaktion Books, 2014), p. 107.
2. Carol Ann Duffy, ed., *To the Moon: An Anthology of Lunar Poems* (London: Picador, 2009), p. xvii.
3. I take my inspiration here from the early modern lyric or ballad attributed to Tom O'Bedlam, which refers to a 'Book of Moons'. I am indebted to Professor Peter Davidson for drawing my attention to this text. See Harold Bloom, *How to Read and Why* (London: Fourth Estate, 2000), pp. 104–10.
4. See Scott L. Montgomery, *The Moon and the Western Imagination* (Tucson: University of Arizona Press, 1999); Williams, *Moon: Nature and Culture*; James Attlee, *Nocturne: A Journey in Search of Moonlight* (London: Hamish Hamilton, 2011); and Bernard Brunner, *The Moon: A Brief History* (New Haven, CT: Yale University Press, 2010): Hannah Pang, *The Moon* (London: 360 Degrees, 2018).
5. For one introduction to medieval manuscripts in Old and Middle English, see Elaine Treharne, 'The Context of Medieval Literature', in David Johnson and Elaine Treharne, eds, *Readings in Medieval Texts: Interpreting Old and Middle English Literature* (Oxford: Oxford University Press, 2005), pp. 7–14. For examples of studies on literacy in particular regions, see further: Sarah Rees Jones, ed., *Learning and Literacy in Medieval England and Abroad* (Turnhout: Brepols, 2003); Agnieszka Bartoszewicz, *Urban Literacy in Late Medieval Poland* (Turnhout: Brepols, 2017); Arnved Nedkvitne, *The Social Consequences of Literacy in Medieval Scandinavia* (Turnhout: Brepols, 2004); Kristina Richardson, *Roma in the Medieval Islamic World: Literacy, Culture and Migration* (London: I.B.

Tauris, 2021); Rebecca Shuang Fu, 'Women's Literary Practices in Late Medieval China (600–1000)' (unpublished dissertation, University of Pennsylvania, 2015).

6. Attlee, *Nocturne*, p. 5.

7. For the Russian context, see further Janet Martin, *Medieval Russia, 980–1584* (Cambridge: Cambridge University Press, 2007); and Basil Dmytryshyn, *Medieval Russia: A Source Book, 850–1700* (London: Harcourt Brace Jovanovich, 1991). For the Chinese context, see further Denis C. Twitchett, ed., *The Cambridge History of China*, vol. 3, *Sui and T'ang China, 589–906 AD, Part One* (Cambridge: Cambridge University Press, 1979).

8. See further Jacques Le Goff, who discusses these and other ideas, in *My Quest for the Middle Ages*, in collaboration with Jean-Maurice de Montremy, translated by Richard Veasey (Edinburgh: Edinburgh University Press, 2003), especially pp. 1–44.

9. Jonathan Hsy, *Antiracist Medievalisms: From 'Yellow Peril' to Black Lives Matter* (Leeds: Arc Humanities Press, 2021), p. 19.

10. On Galileo, see further Montgomery, *The Moon and the Western Imagination*, pp. 114–34.

11. See the useful summary by Williams, *Moon: Nature and Culture*, pp. 133–4.

12. See further Geraldine Heng, *The Global Middle Ages: An Introduction* (Cambridge: Cambridge University Press, 2021), p. 4; and Geraldine Heng, 'A Global Middle Ages', in Marion Turner, ed., *A Handbook of Middle English Studies* (Hoboken, NJ: Wiley, 2013), pp. 413–29.

13. A.S. Lazikani, *Emotion in Christian and Islamic Contemplative Texts: Cry of the Turtledove* (New York: Palgrave Macmillan, 2021), p. 9.

14. Hans Belting, *Florence and Baghdad: Renaissance Art and Arab Science*, trans. Deborah Lucas Schneider (Cambridge, MA: Belknap Press, 2011), p. 4.

15. Belting, *Florence and Baghdad*, p. 5.

16. Liz Herbert McAvoy and Sue Niebrzydowski have also written on multi-directional gazing across medieval traditions, but the term 'multi-glance' is my own. See further Liz Herbert McAvoy and Sue Niebrzydowski, 'Introduction: Medieval Women's Literary Cultures and Thinking beyond the Local', in Kathryn Loveridge et al., eds, *Women's Literary Cultures in the Global Middle Ages: Speaking Internationally* (Cambridge: D.S. Brewer, 2023), pp. 1–20 (at p. 7).

17. See Belting, *Florence and Baghdad*, p. 5.

18. María Rosa Menocal, *The Arabic Role in Medieval Literature: A Forgotten Heritage* (Philadelphia: University of Pennsylvania Press, 2004); Karla Mallette, *European Modernity and the Arab Mediterranean: Toward a New Philology and a Counter-Orientalism* (Philadelphia: University of Pennsylvania Press, 2010); Karla Mallette, *Lives of the Great Languages: Arabic and Latin in the Medieval Mediterranean* (Chicago, IL: University of Chicago Press, 2022); Suzanne Conklin Akbari, 'The Persistence of Philology: Language and Connectivity in the Mediterranean', in Suzanne Conklin Akbari and Karla Mallette, eds, *A Sea of Languages: Rethinking the Arabic Role in Medieval Literary History* (Toronto: University of Toronto Press, 2013), pp. 3–22; and Shazia Jagot, 'Averroes, Islam, and Heterodoxy in the Spanish Chapel "Triumph of St Thomas Aquinas"', *Interfaces: A Journal of Medieval European Literature* 6 (2019), 7–32, especially pp. 23 and 28–9.

19. See further Charles Burnett, 'Arabic into Latin', in Peter Adamson and Richard C. Taylor, eds, *The Cambridge Companion to Arabic Philosophy* (Cambridge:

Cambridge University Press, 2004), pp. 370–404; Charles Burnett, 'The Coherence of the Arabic–Latin Translation Program in Toledo in the Twelfth Century', *Science in Context* 14:1–2 (2001), 249–88, especially pp. 257, 260–3; and Peter King, 'Emotions in Medieval Thought', in Peter Goldie, ed., *The Oxford Handbook of Philosophy of Emotion* (Oxford: Oxford University Press, 2010), pp. 167–87.

20. For a summary of sources, see Nicholas Campion, *A History of Western Astrology*, vol. 2, *The Medieval and Modern Worlds* (London: Bloomsbury, 2013), pp. 43–66; and Laurel Means, ed., *Medieval Lunar Astrology: A Collection of Representative Middle English Texts* (Lewiston, NY: E. Mellen, 1993), pp. 50, 60–1. On Ibn al-Haytham, see Shazia Jagot, 'Chaucer and Ibn al-Haytham (Alhacen): *Perspectiva*, Arabic Mathematics, and the Acts of Looking', *Studies in the Age of Chaucer* 44 (2022), 27–61.

Chapter 1: The Moon of Riddles and Mysteries

1. Translation my own. All the riddles with other translations can be found on this website: https://theriddleages.wordpress.com/riddles-by-number. To read more about the Exeter Book riddles, see further Jonathan Wilcox, '"Tell Me What I Am": The Old English Riddles', in David Johnson and Elaine Treharne, eds, *Readings in Medieval Texts: Interpreting Old and Middle English Literature* (Oxford: Oxford University Press, 2005), pp. 46–59; Patrick J. Murphy, *Unriddling the Exeter Riddles* (University Park, PA: Penn State University Press, 2011); Dieter Bitterli, *Say What I Am Called: The Old English Riddles of the Exeter Book and the Anglo-Latin Riddle Tradition* (Toronto: University of Toronto Press, 2009); and Harriet Soper, *The Life Course in Old English Poetry* (Cambridge: Cambridge University Press, 2023), pp. 25–60.

2. See further Murphy, *Unriddling the Exeter Riddles*, p. 128.

3. Patrick Murphy suggests it may, additionally, be describing the Harrowing of Hell, a story widespread in Anglo-Saxon times in which Christ is said to have descended into Hell after his Crucifixion, rescuing all the 'virtuous' souls condemned there: Murphy, *Unriddling the Exeter Riddles*, pp. 123–39.

4. *Bosworth Toller's Anglo-Saxon Dictionary Online*, hrinan (v.), https://bosworth-toller.com/19775 [accessed 21 August 2024].

5. Neville Mogford, 'Moon and Tide: A New Interpretation of Exeter Riddle 22 Based on the Medieval Science of Computus', *Review of English Studies* 73 (2022), 201–18.

6. *The Poetic Edda: A Dual-Language Edition*, ed. and trans. Edward Pettit (Cambridge: Open Book Publishers, 2023), verse 13, p. 372. Translation my own.

7. *The Poetic Edda*, ed. and trans. Pettit, verse 14, p. 372. Translation my own. In addition to Pettit's dual-language edition above, readers can find a full translation of the poem by Carolyne Larrington, *The Poetic Edda* (Oxford: Oxford University Press, 2014). To read more about this text, see Paul Acker, 'Dwarf-Lore in *Alvíssmál*', in Paul Acker and Carolyne Larrington, eds, *The Poetic Edda: Essays on Old Norse Mythology* (New York: Routledge, 2002), pp. 213–27; and John Lindow, 'Poetry, Dwarfs, and Gods: Understanding *Alvíssmál*', in Judy Quinn, Kate Heslop and Tarrin Wills, eds, *Learning and Understanding in the Old Norse World: Essays in Honour of Margaret Clunies Ross* (Turnhout: Brepols, 2007), pp. 285–303.

8. 'The Liflade ant te Passiun of Seinte Margarete', in *The Katherine Group MS Bodley 34*, ed. Emily Rebekah Huber and Elizabeth Robertson (Kalamazoo, MI:

Medieval Institute Publications, 2016), Online, https://d.lib.rochester.edu/teams/text/liflade-ant-passiun-of-seinte-margarete, 32:4 [accessed 24 June 2024].

9. Uranus was not discovered until the eighteenth century; Neptune was not discovered until the nineteenth century. See further William Herschel, 'The Discovery of Uranus', https://www.rmg.co.uk/stories/blog/astronomy/discovery-uranus [accessed 24 June 2024]; and John Uri, '175 Years Ago: Astronomers Discover Neptune, the Eighth Planet', https://www.nasa.gov/history/175-years-ago-astronomers-discover-neptune-the-eighth-planet/#:~:text=On%20the%20night%20of%20Sept,orbit%20of%20the%20planet%20Uranus [accessed 24 June 2024].

10. C.S. Lewis, *The Discarded Image: An Introduction to Medieval and Renaissance Literature* (1964; repr. Cambridge: Cambridge University Press, 2012), p. 96. See also the explanation by Peter Adamson in his work on the Arabic author Al-Kindi, who follows Aristotle: Peter Adamson, *Al Kindi* (Oxford: Oxford University Press, 2007), pp. 181–2.

11. See further Campion, *History of Western Astrology*, vol. 2, *The Medieval and Modern Worlds*, pp. 43–66; and Means, ed., *Medieval Lunar Astrology*, pp. 50, 60–1. See also David Juste et al., eds, *Ptolemy's Science of the Stars in the Middle Ages* (Turnhout: Brepols, 2020).

12. See further Brunner, *The Moon: A Brief History*, p. 2; and Kelli Hansen, 'Johannes de Sacrobosco and the Sphere of the Universe', https://library.missouri.edu/news/special-collections/johannes-de-sacrobosco [accessed 21 August 2024].

13. Guillaume de Lorris and Jean de Meun, *Le Roman de la Rose*, ed. and trans. Armand Strubel (Paris: Livre de Poche, 1992), pp. 880–2, lines 16840–54. Translation from *The Romance of the Rose*, trans. Frances Horgan (Oxford: Oxford University Press, 1994; repr. 2008), p. 260. © Frances Horgan 1994; reproduced with permission of the Licensor through PLSclear.

14. *Le Roman de la Rose*, ed. and trans. Strubel, pp. 882–4, lines 16885–98; *The Romance of the Rose*, trans. Horgan, p. 261. © Frances Horgan 1994; reproduced with permission of the Licensor through PLSclear.

15. *The Romance of the Rose*, trans. Horgan, p. 348. © Frances Horgan 1994; reproduced with permission of the Licensor through PLSclear.

16. Montgomery, *The Moon and the Western Imagination*, p. 70.

17. From *The Divine Comedy* by Dante Alighieri, published by Penguin Classics. Copyright © Robin Kirkpatrick, 2006, 2007, 2012. Reprinted by permission of Penguin Books Limited. The full reference is Dante Alighieri, *The Divine Comedy: Inferno, Purgatorio, Paradiso*, trans. Robin Kirkpatrick (London: Penguin, 2012), p. 326. For the Italian, see 'Digital Dante', Columbia University Libraries (2019), https://digitaldante.columbia.edu/dante/divine-comedy/paradiso/paradiso-2/ [accessed 11 June 2024].

18. See further 'Digital Dante', https://digitaldante.columbia.edu/text/library/the-convivio/book-02/#N_36_ [accessed 10 February 2025].

19. Mark Williams, *Fiery Shapes: Celestial Portents and Astrology in Ireland and Wales, 700–1700* (Oxford: Oxford University Press, 2020), p. 161.

20. Translation of the text from https://library-artstor-org.ezproxy-prd.bodleian.ox.ac.uk/#/asset/BARTSCH_3390042;prevRouteTS=1702487441096 [accessed 13 December 2023].

21. Gervase of Canterbury, *Opera historica*, ed. W. Stubbs (London: Longman & Co., 1879), vol. 1, p. 276. Translation my own.

22. Gervase of Canterbury, *Opera historica*, p. 276. Translation my own.

23. Giles E.M. Gasper and Brian K. Tanner, '"The Moon Quivered like a Snake": A Medieval Chronicler, Lunar Explosions, and a Puzzle for Modern Interpretation', *Endeavour* 44:4 (2020), 1–9 (at p. 6).

24. On moon as shepherd, see Tamara M. Green, *The City of the Moon God: Religious Traditions of Harran* (Leiden: Brill, 1992), p. 25. See also László Sándor Chardonnens, *Anglo-Saxon Prognostics 900–1100: Study and Texts* (Leiden: Brill, 2007), p. 393.

25. *Ælfric's Catholic Homilies: The First Series*, ed. Peter Clemoes (Oxford: Oxford University Press, 1997), p. 230. Translation my own.

26. See further Roy Michael Liuzza, 'Anglo-Saxon Prognostics in Context: A Survey and Handlist of Manuscripts', *Anglo-Saxon England* 30 (2001), 181–230.

27. See further Roy Michael Liuzza, 'Anglo-Saxon Prognostics in Context'.

28. *Bedae Opera de temporibus*, ed. Charles W. Jones (Boston, MA: Medieval Academy of America, 1943), p. 231. Translation from *Bede: The Reckoning of Time*, trans. Faith Wallis (Liverpool: Liverpool University Press, 1999), p. 80.

29. *Bedae Opera de temporibus*, ed. Jones, p. 231; *Bede: The Reckoning of Time*, trans. Wallis, pp. 80–1.

30. *Bedae Opera de temporibus*, ed. Jones, p. 232; *Bede: The Reckoning of Time*, trans. Wallis, p. 82.

31. *Bedae Opera de temporibus*, ed. Jones, p. 234; *Bede: The Reckoning of Time*, trans. Wallis, p. 84.

32. On medieval bestiaries in Europe, see further Elizabeth Morrison and Larisa Grollemond, *Book of Beasts: The Bestiary in the Medieval World* (Los Angeles: J. Paul Getty Museum, 2019); Megan Cavell, ed. and trans., *The Medieval Bestiary in English: Texts and Translations of the Old and Middle English 'Physiologus'* (Peterborough: Broadview Press, 2022); Debra Higgs Strickland, *Medieval Bestiaries: Text, Image, Ideology* (Cambridge: Cambridge University Press, 1995); Debra Higgs Strickland, ed., *The Mark of the Beast: The Medieval Bestiary in Art, Life, and Literature* (New York: Garland, 1999); and Sarah Kay, *Animal Skins and the Reading Self in Medieval Latin and French Bestiaries* (Chicago, IL: University of Chicago Press, 2017).

33. https://www.abdn.ac.uk/bestiary/ms24/f12v [accessed 25 June 2024].

34. https://www.abdn.ac.uk/bestiary/ms24/f76v [accessed 25 June 2024].

35. https://www.abdn.ac.uk/bestiary/ms24/f23v [accessed 25 June 2024].

36. Tamarah Kohanski and C. David Benson, eds, *The Book of John Mandeville* (Kalamazoo, MI: Medieval institute Publications, 2007), https://d.lib.rochester.edu/teams/text/kohanski-and-benson-the-book-of-john-mandeville-introduction [accessed 21 August 2024].

37. *Oxford English Dictionary*, 'astrolabe: noun'.

38. *A Treatise on the Astrolabe*, in *The Riverside Chaucer*, third edition, ed. Larry D. Benson and F.N. Robinson (Oxford: Oxford University Press, 2008), p. 662.

39. Translation my own.

40. *Oxford English Dictionary*, 'volvelle: noun'.

41. https://collections.ashmolean.org/collection/search/per_page/25/offset/0/sort_by/relevance/object/139546 [accessed 21 August 2024].

42. https://digital.bodleian.ox.ac.uk/objects/079272ec-cca8-4742-b626-aed3b0dfd5bf/surfaces/1bd5c214-b5f2-4ceb-86a7-809aeed652ba/ [accessed 10 February 2025].

43. https://viewer.library.wales/4393492#?xywh=495%2C239%2C1636%2C2629&cv=12 [accessed 21 August 2024].

44. Johannes Fabricius, *Alchemy: The Medieval Alchemists and their Royal Art* (Copenhagen: Rosenkilde and Bagger, 1976), p. 25.

45. For further discussion, see Niall McCrae, *The Moon and Madness* (Exeter: Imprint Academic, 2011), p. 39.

46. For a study of *The Canon's Yeoman's Tale*, see Mark Bruhn, 'Art, Anxiety, and Alchemy in the *Canon's Yeoman's Tale*', *Chaucer Review* 33 (1999), 288–315.

47. 'The Martyrdom of Sancte Katerine', https://d.lib.rochester.edu/teams/text/martyrdom-of-sancte-katerine, 6:1 [accessed 21 August 2024].

48. Translation my own.

49. Snorri Sturluson, *The Prose Edda*, trans. Jesse L. Byock (London: Penguin Classics, 2005), p. 53.

50. Snorri Sturluson, *Prose Edda*, trans. Byock, p. 52.

51. Madi Williams, *Polynesia, 900–1600* (Leeds: Arc Humanities Press, 2021), p. 44.

52. https://www.metmuseum.org/art/collection/search/38344 [accessed 6 March 2025].

53. *Popol Vuh: The Definitive Edition of the Mayan Book of the Dawn of Life and the Glories of Gods and Kings*, trans. Dennis Tedlock (New York: Touchstone, 1996), p. 141.

54. Irene Silverblatt, *Moon, Sun, Witches* (Princeton, NJ: Princeton University Press, 1987), p. 47.

55. Blas Valera, quoted in Silverblatt, *Moon, Sun, Witches*, p. 47.

56. Jordan Paper, *Through the Earth Darkly: Female Spirituality in Comparative Perspective* (London: Bloomsbury, 2018), pp. 111–26.

57. Silverblatt, *Moon, Sun, Witches*, p. 50.

58. See further Jacqueline de Weever, 'Chaucer's Moon: Cinthia, Diana, Latona, Lucina, Proserpina', *Names* 34:2 (1986), 154–74.

59. Weever, 'Chaucer's Moon', 166.

60. Geoffrey Chaucer, *Troilus and Criseyde, with Facing-Page Il Filostrato*, ed. and trans. Stephen A. Barney (New York: Norton, 2006), lines 2051–72.

61. *The Riverside Chaucer*, third edition, lines 2075–82. All subsequent references are to this edition.

62. On Selene see further Claire Préaux, *La Lune dans la pensée grecque* (Brussels: Palais des Académies, 1973); Robert Parker, 'Selene', in *Oxford Classical Dictionary*, https://oxfordre.com/classics [accessed 6 March 2025]; and Karen ní Mheallaigh, *The Moon in the Greek and Roman Imagination: Myth, Literature, Science and Philosophy* (Cambridge: Cambridge University Press, 2020), especially pp. 23–4.

63. David Leeming, *A Dictionary of Asian Mythology* (Oxford: Oxford University Press, 2002), https://www.oxfordreference.com/display/10.1093/acref/9780195120523.001.0001/acref-9780195120523 [accessed 6 March 2025]. See also Eugene Y. Wang, 'Mirror, Moon, and Memory in Eighth-Century China: From Dragon Pond to Lunar Palace', *Cleveland Studies in the History of Art* 9 (2005), 42–67 (especially p. 59); and Yanlin Pan, 'Paradigm Shifts, Iconographic Changes: The Moon Goddess Chang'e and Other Beauties in Paintings of the Mid Ming' (unpublished dissertation, University of California Davis, 2013).

64. https://www.metmuseum.org/art/collection/search/45754 [accessed 6 March 2025].

65. Excerpted from Wen C. Fong's translation of Tang Yin's poem from 'The Moon Goddess Chang E' in *The Met Collection* online. Published by The Metropolitan Museum of Art, New York. Copyright © 2002–2024. Available at https://www. metmuseum.org/art/collection/search/45754. Reprinted by permission.

66. See further Yugong Gao, 'Cranes and People in China: Culture, Science, and Conservation' (unpublished dissertation, University of Texas at Austin, 2001); and Shuxian Ye, *A Mythological Approach to Exploring the Origins of Chinese Civilization* (Singapore: Springer, 2002), pp. 437–40.

67. Wang, 'Mirror, Moon, and Memory in Eighth-Century China', p. 59.

68. 'Chang E [*sic*], the Moon Goddess', in 'Art of the Buddhist Relic Online Exhibition', https://exhibitions.library.vanderbilt.edu/hart3164w-art-budhist-relic/chang-e-the-moon-goddess/ [accessed 5 January 2025]. On the significance of the hare, see Wang, 'Mirror, Moon, and Memory in Eighth-Century China'.

69. https://www.artic.edu/artworks/110823/chang-e-the-moon-goddess [accessed 16 September 2024].

Chapter 2: The Moon of Travels and Adventures

1. Stephen Owen, 'The Cultural Tang (650–1020)', in Kang-I Sun Chang and Stephen Owen, eds, *The Cambridge History of Chinese Literature*, vol. 1, to 1375 (Cambridge: Cambridge University Press, 2010), pp. 286–380 (at pp. 310–11).

2. Nathaniel Isaacson, 'Locating *Kexue Xiangsheng* (Science Crosstalk) in Relation to the Selective Tradition of Chinese Science Fiction', *Osiris* 34:1 (2019), 139–57 (at p. 152).

3. Williams, *Moon: Nature and Culture*, p. 107.

4. For a translation of this text, see *True Story; Lucius, or the Ass*, trans. Paul Turner (Richmond: Alma Classics, 2018). For a study, see Karen ní Mheallaigh, *Reading Fiction with Lucian: Fakes, Freaks, and Hyperreality* (Cambridge: Cambridge University Press, 2014), especially pp. 216–27.

5. Edwin O. Reischauer, 'The Izayoi Nikki (1277–1280)', *Harvard Journal of Asiatic Studies* 10:3–4 (1947), 255–387 (at p. 269).

6. Christina Laffin, *Rewriting Medieval Japanese Women: Politics, Personality and Literary Production in the Life of Nun Abutsu* (Honolulu: University of Hawai'i Press, 2013), p. 1.

7. See Reischauer, 'The Izayoi Nikki (1277–1280)', p. 269.

8. See Reischauer, 'The Izayoi Nikki (1277-1280)', p. 269; and Christina Laffin, 'Medieval Women's Diaries', in Haruo Shirane and Tomi Suzuki with David Lurie, eds, *The Cambridge History of Japanese Literature* (Cambridge: Cambridge University Press, 2016), pp. 268–79 (especially pp. 273–5).

9. Laffin, *Rewriting Medieval Japanese Women*, p. 2.

10. See Laffin, *Rewriting Medieval Japanese Women*, pp. 136–72.

11. James A. Wren, 'Salty Seaweed, Absent Women, and Song: Authorizing the Female as Poet in the *Izayoi nikki*', *Criticism* 39:2 (1997), 185–204.

12. All quotations are from Reischauer, 'The Izayoi Nikki (1277–1280)'; page numbers are incorporated in the text. Another translation is: Helen Craig McCullough, trans., 'The Journal of the Sixteenth-Night Moon', in Helen Craig

McCullough, ed., *Classical Japanese Prose: An Anthology* (Stanford, CA: Stanford University Press, 1990), pp. 340–76.

13. Duffy, *To the Moon*, p. 6.
14. Duffy, *To the Moon*, p. 10.
15. Albert of Saxony, *Quæstiones in Aristotelis De cælo*, ed. Benoît Patar (Louvain-la-Neuve: Editions de l'Institut Supérieur de Philosophie, 2008), Book II, Question 7, p. 284. Translation my own. For a discussion, see Claudia Kren, 'The Medieval Man in the Moon', *Mediaevalia* 7 (1981), 221–38.
16. See further Montgomery, *The Moon and the Western Imagination*, p. 67.
17. All quotations from the Bible are from the Douay-Rheims version, www.drbo. org [accessed 24 June 2024].
18. These stories are described in S. Baring-Gould, *Curious Myths of the Middle Ages* (London: Rivingtons, 1873), pp. 190–4. I have not been able to corroborate the sources elsewhere.
19. Dante, *The Divine Comedy*, trans. Kirkpatrick, p. 326.
20. My translation and an accompanying commentary on the poem are also available here: https://www.english.ox.ac.uk/article/the-moon-an-anonymous-medieval-lyric [accessed 11 February 2025].
21. Matti Rissanen, 'Colloquial and Comic Elements in "The Man in the Moon"', *Neuphilologische Mitteilungen* 81:1 (1980), 42–6.
22. All quotations are from '81: Mon in the mone stond ant strit', in *The Complete Harley 2253 Manuscript*, vol. 3, ed. and trans. Susanna Greer Fein, David Raybin, and Jan Ziolkowski (Kalamazoo, MI: Medieval Institute Publications, 2015), https://d.lib.rochester.edu/teams/publication/fein-harley2253-volume-3 [accessed 21 August 2024]. Translations my own.
23. 'Introduction', in *The Complete Harley 2253 Manuscript*, vol. 3, ed. and trans. Fein, Raybin, and Ziolkowski, https://d.lib.rochester.edu/teams/text/fein-harley2253-volume-1-Introduction [accessed 11 August 2021].
24. '80: Talent me prent de rymer e de geste fere', in *The Complete Harley 2253 Manuscript*, vol. 3, ed. and trans. Fein, Raybin, and Ziolkowski, https://d.lib. rochester.edu/teams/text/fein-harley2253-volume-3-article-80 [accessed 11 August 2023]. Translation my own.
25. From *Orlando Furioso* by Ludovico Ariosto, published by Penguin Classics. Copyright © Barbara Reynolds, 1977. Reprinted by permission of Penguin Books Limited. The full reference is: *A Romantic Epic of Ludovico Ariosto: Orlando Furioso (The Frenzy of Orlando), Part Two*, trans. Barbara Reynolds (London: Penguin, 1991); page numbers are incorporated in the text. For another translation, see *Orlando Furioso: A New Verse Translation*, trans. David R. Slavitt (Cambridge, MA: Harvard University Press, 2010). For the Italian, see *Orlando furioso*, commentary by Emilio Bigi, ed. Cristina Zampese (Milan: Rizzoli, 2012).
26. Ita Mac Carthy, 'Ariosto the Lunar Traveller', *Modern Language Review* 104:1 (2009), 71–82 (at p. 74).
27. Jeffrey T. Schnapp, 'The Chatter of People and Things', *Modern Language Quarterly* 72:3 (2011), 319–39 (at p. 330).
28. Daniel Leisawitz, 'Ironic Geography in Ariosto's *Orlando furioso*', *Renaissance Quarterly* 75:2 (2022), 367–402.
29. Ladina Bezzola Lambert, *Imagining the Unimaginable: The Poetics of Early Modern Astronomy* (Brill: Leiden, 2022), p. 13.

30. See Donald Keene, 'The Tale of the Bamboo Cutter', *Monumenta Nipponica* 11:4 (1956), 329–55; and Joshua S. Mostow, 'Early Heian Court Tales', in Shirane and Suzuki with Lurie, eds, *The Cambridge History of Japanese Literature*, pp. 121–8 (at p. 121).

31. H. Richard Okada, *Figures of Resistance: Language, Poetry, and Narrating in the Tale of the Genji and Other Mid-Heian Texts* (Durham, NC: Duke University Press, 1991), p. 54.

32. All quotations of this text are from Keene's translation, 'The Tale of the Bamboo Cutter'. Numbers within brackets refer to pagination. Permission to quote was granted by Seiki Keene, son of the late Donald Keene.

33. See Jonathan Stockdale, *Imagining Exile in Heian Japan: Banishment in Law, Literature, and Cult* (Honolulu: University of Hawai'i Press, 2015), pp. 43–4.

34. Mostow, 'Early Heian Court Tales', p. 121.

35. Stockdale, *Imagining Exile in Heian Japan*, p. 44. See also Michael F. Marra, *The Aesthetics of Discontent: Politics and Reclusion in Medieval Japanese Literature* (Honolulu: University of Hawai'i Press, 1991).

36. Stockdale, *Imagining Exile in Heian Japan*, p. 51.

Chapter 3: The Moon of Prophecies and Signs

1. C.H. Talbot, ed., *The Anglo-Saxon Missionaries in Germany* (London: Sheed and Ward, 1954). See also the discussion in Katherine O'Brien O'Keeffe, *Stealing Obedience: Narratives of Agency and Identity in Later Anglo-Saxon England* (Toronto: University of Toronto Press, 2012), pp. 65, 73.

2. See further Liana Saif, 'Homocentric Science in a Heliocentric Universe', in Nicholas Campion and Dorian Gieseler Greenbaum, eds, *Astrology in Time and Place: Cross-Cultural Questions in the History of Astrology* (Newcastle-upon-Tyne: Cambridge Scholars Publishing, 2015), pp. 159–72 (at p. 166).

3. Campion, *A History of Western Astrology*, vol. 2, p. 82.

4. All references are to *Troilus and Criseyde*, ed. Stephen Barney, with book and line numbers given in the text. Translations are my own. For introductions to the poem, see Jennifer Nuttall, *Troilus and Criseyde: A Reader's Guide* (Cambridge: Cambridge University Press, 2012); and Barry Windeatt, *Oxford Guides to Chaucer: Troilus and Criseyde* (Oxford: Oxford University Press, 2005).

5. See Means, ed., *Medieval Lunar Astrology*, pp. 1, 68.

6. Leona O'Desky, 'Chaucer's *Troilus and Criseyde*: Astrology and the Transference of Power' (unpublished dissertation, Rutgers University, 1974), p. 61.

7. M. Stokes, 'The Moon in Leo in Book V of *Troilus and Criseyde*', *Chaucer Review* 17:2 (1982), 116–29 (at p. 116).

8. *Troilus and Criseyde*, ed. Barney, p. 173, n. 9.

9. R.M. Liuzza, 'Anglo-Saxon Prognostics in Context', pp. 186–7.

10. *Ælfric's Catholic Homilies: The First Series*, ed. Clemoes, p. 229. Translation my own.

11. Quotations are from R.M. Liuzza, ed., *Anglo-Saxon Prognostics: An Edition and Translation of Texts from London, British Library, MS Cotton Tiberius A. iii* (Woodbridge: Boydell & Brewer, 2011); page numbers are incorporated in the text.

12. Chardonnens, *Anglo-Saxon Prognostics*, p. 470.

13. Means, ed., *Medieval Lunar Astrology*, p. 1.

14. Means, ed., *Medieval Lunar Astrology*, p. 1.

15. Quotations are from Means, ed., *Medieval Lunar Astrology*; page numbers are incorporated in the text. Translations are my own.

16. Williams, *Polynesia, 900–1600*, p. 2.

17. Williams, *Polynesia, 900–1600*, p. 46.

18. Williams, *Polynesia, 900–1600*, p. 55.

19. Daniel Hikuroa, 'Mātauranga Māori: The ūkaipō of Knowledge in New Zealand', *Journal of the Royal Society of New Zealand* 47:1 (2017), 5–10 (at p. 7).

20. Hikuroa, 'Mātauranga Māori', p. 7.

21. Isaac Warbrick et al., 'Te Maramataka: An Indigenous System of Attuning with the Environment, and Its Role in Modern Health and Well-Being', *International Journal of Environmental Research and Public Health* 20:3 (2023), 1–12 (at p. 2).

22. Williams, *Polynesia, 900–1600*, p. 56.

23. Mere Roberts, Frank Weko, and Liliana Clarke, 'Maramataka: The Maori Moon Calendar', *AERU*, Research Report no. 238 (Canterbury: Lincoln University, August 2006), p. 15.

24. Roberts, Weko, and Clarke, 'Maramataka: The Maori Moon Calendar', pp. 7-11.

25. Hikuroa, 'Mātauranga Māori', p. 6.

26. Hikuroa, 'Mātauranga Māori', p. 8.

27. Hikuroa, 'Mātauranga Māori', p. 8.

28. Mere Roberts, Frank Weko, and Liliana Clarke, 'Maramataka: The Maori Moon Calendar', Lincoln University. Agribusiness and Economics Research Unit (2006), p. v, https://researcharchive.lincoln.ac.nz/server/api/core/bitstreams/6eb5e823-90ba-4063-b596-100e293fe183/content [accessed 6 March 2025]

29. Geoffrey of Monmouth, *The History of the Kings of Britain*, trans. Lewis Thorpe (Harmondsworth: Penguin, 1966), p. 168.

30. See further Elizabeth J. Bryan, 'Astronomy Translated: *Caput Draconis* and the Pendragon Star in Geoffrey of Monmouth, Wace, and Laȝamon', *Arthuriana* 26:1 (2016), 141–63.

31. Geoffrey, *The History of the Kings of Britain*, trans. Thorpe, p. 202.

32. See further 'NASA Eclipse Web Site', https://eclipse.gsfc.nasa.gov/SEhelp/moonorbit.html#:~:text=The%20node%20where%20the%20Moon%27s,respect%20to%20the%20ascending%20node [accessed 12 August 2024].

33. Bryan, 'Astronomy Translated', p. 142. For a parallel image used differently, see Marilina Cesario, '*Fyrenne Dracan* in the *Anglo-Saxon Chronicle*', in Maren Clegg Hyer, ed., *Textiles, Text, Intertext: Essays in Honour of Gale R. Owen-Crocker* (Woodbridge: Boydell & Brewer, 2016), pp. 153–70.

34. Bryan, 'Astronomy Translated', pp. 154–5. For a definition and consideration of 'Anglo-Norman' (French of England) texts, see Ruth J. Dean with Maureen B.M. Boulton, eds, *Anglo-Norman Literature: A Guide to Texts and Manuscripts* (London: Anglo-Norman Text Society, 1999); and the now classic study by Dominica M. Legge, *Anglo-Norman Literature and Its Background* (Oxford: Clarendon Press, 1963).

35. Geoffrey, *The History of the Kings of Britain*, trans. Thorpe, p. 184.

36. *The Book of John Mandeville*, ed. Kohanski and Benson, lines 2647–9.

37. For scholarship on this text, see for example Mark Bradshaw Busbee, 'A Paradise Full of Monsters: India in the Old English Imagination', *LATCH* 1 (2008),

51–72; Brian McFadden, 'The Social Context of Narrative Disruption in *The Letter of Alexander to Aristotle*', *Anglo-Saxon England* 30 (2001), 91–114; and Susan M. Kim, '"If One Who Is Loved Is Not Present, a Letter May Be Embraced Instead": Death and the *Letter of Alexander to Aristotle*', *Journal of English and Germanic Philology* 109 (2010), 33–51 (at p. 34).

38. Quotations are from *The Beowulf Manuscript: Complete Texts and the Fight at Finnsburg*, ed. and trans. R.D. Fulk (Cambridge, MA: Harvard University Press, 2010); page numbers are incorporated in the text. Translations are my own.

39. McFadden, 'The Social Context of Narrative Disruption', p. 109.

40. Kate Perillo, 'The Limits of *Ongietenisse*: Translating Global Imagination in the Old English *Letter of Alexander to Aristotle*', *Parergon* 35:2 (2018), 67–89 (at p. 81). See also Omar Khalaf, 'The Old English *Alexander's Letter to Aristotle*: Monsters and Hybrids in the Service of Exemplarity', *English Studies* (2013), 659–67.

41. *Christ* in *The Exeter Book*, ed. George Philip Krapp and Elliott Van Kirk Dobbie (New York: Columbia University Press, 1936), lines 1174–6. For a discussion, see Frances McCormack, 'Those Bloody Trees: The Affectivity of *Christ*', in Alice Jorgensen, Frances McCormack, and Jonathan Wilcox, eds, *Anglo-Saxon Emotions: Reading the Heart in Old English Language, Literature, and Culture* (Farnham: Ashgate, 2015), pp. 143–61.

42. Both poems, *Christ in Judgement* and *The Dream of the Rood*, are available with facing-page translations in: *Old English Poems of Christ and His Saints*, ed. and trans. Mary Clayton (Cambridge, MA: Harvard University Press, 2013). *The Dream of the Rood* may also be found in most anthologies of Old English. For example: *A Choice of Anglo-Saxon Verse*, ed. and trans. Richard Hamer (London: Faber & Faber, 2015).

43. *The Conference of the Birds*, trans. Afkham Darbandi and Dick Davis (London: Penguin, 2011), p. 18.

44. See further Bilha Moor, 'The Jew, the Orthodox Christian, and the European in Ottoman Eyes, ca. 1550–1700', in Hakan T. Karateke, H. Erdem Çipa and Helga Anetshofer, eds, *Disliking Others: Loathing, Hostility, and Distrust in Premodern Ottoman Lands* (Boston, MA: Academic Studies Press, 2018), pp. 75–106.

45. References to the Qur'an are from *The Qur'an*, trans. Abdel Haleem (Oxford: Oxford University Press, 2008).

46. For a discussion of the event and its interpretations, see Richard Netton, *Islam, Christianity, and the Realms of the Miraculous* (Edinburgh: Edinburgh University Press, 2018), pp. 171–83.

47. Quoted and translated in Netton, *Islam, Christianity, and the Realms of the Miraculous*, p. 174.

48. Quoted and translated in Netton, *Islam, Christianity, and the Realms of the Miraculous*, p. 175.

49. Annemarie Schimmel, *And Muhammad Is His Messenger: The Veneration of the Prophet in Islamic Piety* (Chapel Hill: University of North Carolina Press, 1985), pp. 69–70.

50. On Chrétien de Troyes, see further Norris J. Lacy and Joan T. Grimbert, eds, *A Companion to Chrétien de Troyes* (Cambridge: D.S. Brewer, 2005).

51. Chrétien de Troyes, *Cligés*, lines 1672–90, in 'Dictionnaire Electronique de Chrétien de Troyes' (University of Ottawa), http://zeus.atilf.fr/dect/ [accessed

2 September 2024]. Translation my own. For a full translation of the text, see Chrétien de Troyes, *Arthurian Romances*, trans. W.W. Kibler and C.W. Carroll (London: Penguin, 1991), p. 143.

52. Quotations are from *The Old English Martyrology: Edition, Translation, and Commentary*, ed. and trans. Christine Rauer (Woodbridge: Boydell & Brewer, 2013); page numbers are incorporated in the text. Translations are my own.

53. 'Medieval Sourcebook: Innocent III (r. 1198–1216): Letters on Papal Policies', https://sourcebooks.fordham.edu/source/inniii-policies.asp [accessed 9 August 2022].

54. On the *glossa ordinaria*, see *Biblia Latina cum Glossa Ordinaria: Facsimile Reprint of the Edito Princeps Adolph Rusch of Strassburg, 1480/1481* (Brepols: Turnhout, 1992), vol. 2, p. 587. See further Miri Rubin, *Corpus Christi: The Eucharist in Late Medieval Culture* (Cambridge: Cambridge University Press, 1991), pp. 169–72. For Ambrose, see *Patrologia Latina* (henceforth *PL*), 14:203–6: *Patrologiae cursus completus: series Latina*, ed. J.P. Migne, 221 vols (Paris: Migne, 1844–55, 1862–5), https://about. proquest.com/en/products-services/patrologia_latina/ [accessed 6 March 2025]. For Isidore: *De natura rerum* XVIII 6, in *Isidore of Seville: Traité de la Nature* (Bordeaux: Féret et Fils, 1960), p. 243. For Bede: *PL* 91, col. 197B; for Rabanus: *PL* 109, col. 172C; for Gerhoh: *PL* 194, col. 846B; for Peter Lombard: *PL* 191, col. 149A. See also Anthony Cassell, '"Luna est Ecclesia: Dante and the "Two Great Lights"', *Dante Society of America* 119 (2001), 1–26 (especially pp. 9–10).

55. *PL* 36, col. 132.

56. *English Wycliffite Sermons*, ed. Anne Hudson (Oxford: Oxford University Press, 2022), pp. 392–3. On Wycliffite sermons, see further Kantik Ghosh, 'After Wyclif: Philosophy, Polemics and Translation in *The English Wycliffite Sermons*', in L. Campi and S. Simonetta, eds, *Before and After Wyclif: Sources and Textual Influence* (Basel: Fédération Internationale des Instituts d'Etudes Médiévales, 2022), pp. 167–86; David Lavinsky, 'Knowynge Cristes Speche: Gender and Interpretive Authority in the Wycliffite Sermon Cycle', *Journal of Medieval Religious Cultures* 38:1 (2012), 60–83; Jennifer Illig, 'Preparing for Easter: Sermons on the Eucharist in English Wycliffite Sermons', in J. Patrick Hornbeck and Michael van Dussen, eds, *Europe after Wyclif* (New York: Fordham University Press, 2016), pp. 247–64.

57. See further Mordecai Schreiber, *The Shengold Jewish Encyclopedia* (Rockville, MD: Schreiber Publishing, 2007), p. 194.

58. On this point on Crucifixion scenes, see further Ellen M. Ross, *The Grief of God: Images of the Suffering Jesus in Late Medieval England* (Oxford: Oxford University Press, 1997), p. 152, n. 107.

59. Moshe Barasch, *Gestures of Despair in Medieval and Early Renaissance Art* (New York: New York University Press, 1976), p. 97.

60. John Beckwith, *Early Medieval Art: Carolingian, Ottonian, Romanesque* (London: Thames & Hudson, 1964), p. 48; and Montgomery, *The Moon and the Western Imagination*, p. 62.

61. For the image, see Beckwith, *Early Medieval Art*, p. 48; see also pp. 109, 111.

62. Beckwith, *Early Medieval Art*, pp. 112, 115.

63. https://www.dorchester-abbey.org.uk/wall-paintings/ [accessed 30 December 2023].

64. Anne Marshall, 'Medieval Wall Painting in the English Parish Church', https://reeddesign.co.uk/paintedchurch/kempley-christ-in-majesty.htm [accessed 21 August 2024].
65. Marshall, 'Medieval Wall Painting in the English Parish Church'.
66. Marshall, 'Medieval Wall Painting in the English Parish Church'.
67. Marshall, 'Medieval Wall Painting in the English Parish Church'.
68. https://www.abdn.ac.uk/bestiary/ms24/f103v [accessed 25 June 2024].

Chapter 4: The Moon of Illnesses and Cures

1. Campion, *A History of Western Astrology, Vol II*, pp. 77–8.
2. Lynn Thorndike, *A History of Magic and Experimental Science* (New York: Columbia University Press, 1923), vol. 3, pp. 281–93.
3. The text: Pseudo-Hippocrates, *Libellus de medicorum astrologia*, trans. Petrus de Abano (Venice: Erhard Ratdolt, 1447–1527), p. 46. See also Laurel Braswell, 'The Moon and Medicine in Chaucer's Time', *Studies in the Age of Chaucer* 8 (1986), 145–56 (at p. 147). On Peter of Abano, see further Enrico Berti, 'La classificazione aristotelica delle scienze in Pietro d'Abano', *Trans/Form/Ação* 37:3 (2014), 17–32.
4. Cornelius O'Boyle, 'Astrology and Medicine in Later Medieval England: The Calendars of John Somer and Nicholas of Lynn', *Sudhoffs Archiv* 89:1 (2005), 1–22 (at p. 5).
5. See further McCrae, *The Moon and Madness*, p. 35. For an introduction to medieval medicine, see Faith Wallis, *Medieval Medicine: A Reader* (Toronto: University of Toronto Press, 2010).
6. McCrae, *The Moon and Madness*, p. 35.
7. O'Boyle, 'Astrology and Medicine in Later Medieval England', p. 5.
8. For a brief biography of Nicholas of Lynn, see Douglas Gray, 'Lenne, Frer N.', in Douglas Gray, ed., *The Oxford Companion to Chaucer* (Oxford: Oxford University Press, 2003), https://www.oxfordreference.com/display/10.1093/acref/9780198117650.001.0001/acref-9780198117650 [accessed 6 March 2025]. See also Nicholas of Lynn, *The Kalendarium of Nicholas of Lynn*, ed. Sigmund Eisner, trans. Gary Mac Eoin and Sigmund Eisner (Athens: University of Georgia Press, 1980), p. 2; 'Somer J., John Somer' in Gray, ed., *The Oxford Companion to Chaucer*; and John Somer, ed., *The Kalendarium of John Somer*, ed. Linne R. Mooney (Athens: University of Georgia Press, 1998), p. 3.
9. https://digital.bodleian.ox.ac.uk/objects/82a37a79-d751-41bb-b080-538e7039f048/ [accessed 12 May 2025].
10. https://digital.bodleian.ox.ac.uk/objects/63d46734-a46b-4251-a6c6-9c83387ac83b/ [accessed 17 September 2024].
11. https://digital.bodleian.ox.ac.uk/objects/2f0a34b9-9168-4ebd-b19f-da1252084abc/surfaces/7d3e48c9-71a0-4c60-b78a-a0622839ca98/ [accessed 17 September 2024].
12. https://www.jstor.org/stable/community.12395057 [accessed 9 March 2025].
13. https://digital.bodleian.ox.ac.uk/objects/5d71a452-789d-4a7f-bfd5-8460607599d3/surfaces/eb61004a-fbb7-4eef-acf6-49cc2d3bb5d2/ [accessed 17 September 2024].
14. https://digital.bodleian.ox.ac.uk/objects/989ccf57-3ae3-4d6c-9d26-30c936a4c940/surfaces/ab10ac94-bc6a-4927-be4e-cfdd67a555d9/ [accessed 17 September 2024].

15. https://digital.bodleian.ox.ac.uk/objects/0031fe59-7408-4012-9662-c793bbdaebc1/surfaces/ddf3d11c-3d4f-4b85-8b52-dbf93696f7d2/ [accessed 17 September 2024].

16. https://digital.bodleian.ox.ac.uk/objects/eca53671-3a29-46ef-acae-3aa2b3b48195/surfaces/b77a89c3-970d-4591-b87e-2563469a9c05/ [accessed 17 September 2024].

17. https://www.jstor.org/stable/community.11663914 [accessed 9 March 2025].

18. See further Manfred Ullmann, *Islamic Medicine* (Edinburgh: Edinburgh University Press, 2008), p. 114.

19. Cyril Elgood, *A Medical History of Persia and the Eastern Caliphate: From the Earliest Times until the Year AD 1932* (Cambridge: Cambridge University Press, 1951), p. 362.

20. See further Norzakiah binti Saparmin, 'History of Astrology and Astronomy in Islamic Medicine', *International Journal of Academic Research in Business and Social Sciences* 9:9 (2019), 282–96.

21. Ullmann, *Islamic Medicine*, p. 112.

22. Felix Klein-Franke, *Iatromathematics in Islam: A Study on Yuḥanna Ibn aṣ-Ṣalt's Book on Astrological Medicine: Edited for the First Time* (Hildesheim: Georg Olms Verlag, 1984), p. 107.

23. See further Peter Pormann and Emilie Savage-Smith, *Medieval Islamic Medicine* (Edinburgh: Edinburgh University Press, 2022), p. 155.

24. Elgood, *A Medical History of Persia and the Eastern Caliphate*, p. 362.

25. Ullmann, *Islamic Medicine*, p. 113.

26. Ullmann, *Islamic Medicine*, p. 113.

27. Elgood, *A Medical History of Persia and the Eastern Caliphate*, p. 360.

28. See also Chardonnens, *Anglo-Saxon Prognostics, 900–1100*, pp. 394–5. For a detailed study of Middle English moonbooks, see Irma Taavitsainen, *Middle English Lunaries: A Study of the Genre* (Helsinki: Société Néophilologique, 1988). Excerpts from various moonbooks are available in the appendix to the present book.

29. The text is available in *Medieval Lunar Astrology*, ed. Means, pp. 210–22.

30. Braswell, 'The Moon and Medicine in Chaucer's Time', p. 152.

31. Quotations are from *Anglo-Saxon Prognostics*, ed. Liuzza, with page numbers incorporated in the text; translations are my own.

32. The term 'catalyst' is from Means, *Medieval Lunar Astrology*, p. 306.

33. All quotations are from *Medical Writings from Early Medieval England*, ed. M.A. D'Aronco and John D. Niles (Cambridge, MA: Harvard University Press, 2023), with page numbers incorporated in the text. Translations are my own.

34. *Lanfranc's 'Science of Cirurgie'*, ed. Robert V. Fleischhacker (London: Kegan Paul, 1894), pp. 9–10.

35. John Pearn, 'Master John of Arderne (1307–1380): A Founder of Modern Surgery', *ANZ Journal of Surgery* 82:1–2 (2012), 46–51. See also Marion Turner, 'Illness Narratives in the Later Middle Ages: Arderne, Chaucer, and Hoccleve', *Journal of Medieval and Early Modern Studies* 46 (2016), 61–87.

36. See further Braswell, 'The Moon and Medicine in Chaucer's Time', p. 154.

37. John Arderne, *Treatises of Fistula in Ano*, ed. D'Arcy Power (Oxford: Oxford University Press, 1910), p. 16. Translation my own.

38. Arderne, *Treatises of Fistula in Ano*, p. 16.

39. Arderne, *Treatises of Fistula in Ano*, p. 16.
40. Arderne, *Treatises of Fistula in Ano*, p. 16
41. Arderne, *Treatises of Fistula in Ano*, pp. 18–19.
42. Joseph S. Alter, 'Heaps of Health, Metaphysical Fitness: Ayurveda and the Ontology of Good Health in Medical Anthropology', *Current Anthropology* 40:1 (1999), 43–66.
43. Alter, 'Heaps of Health', p. 55.
44. On this, see Anthony Michael Cerulli, *Somatic Lessons: Narrating Patienthood and Illness in Indian Medical Literature* (Albany: State University of New York Press, 2012), p. 112. My thanks are due to Dr William McGrath for pointing me to this resource.
45. See David Gordon White, *The Alchemical Body: Siddha Traditions in Medieval India* (Chicago, IL: University of Chicago Press, 2012), p. 24.
46. For further discussion see Cerulli, *Somatic Lessons*, pp. 108, 117.
47. Alter, 'Heaps of Health', p. 56.
48. White, *The Alchemical Body*, p. 24.
49. William A. McGrath, 'Vessel Examination in the Medicine of the Moon King', in C. Pierce Salguero, ed., *Buddhism and Medicine: An Anthology of Premodern Sources* (New York: Columbia University Press, 2017), pp. 501–13; and Ronit Yoeli-Tlalim, 'Re-Visiting "Galen in Tibet"', *Medical History* 56:3 (2012), 355–65.
50. See further M.A. Riva et al., 'The Disease of the Moon: The Linguistic and Pathological Evolution of the English Term "Lunatic"', *Journal of the History of the Neurosciences* 20:1 (2011), 65–73.
51. See 'Paracelsus', in Andrew Louth, ed., *The Oxford Dictionary of the Christian Church* (Oxford: Oxford University Press, 2022), https://www.oxfordreference.com/display/10.1093/acref/9780199642465.001.0001/acref-9780199642465 [accessed 6 March 2025].
52. See 'Paracelsus', in Miquel Porta and John M. Last, eds, *A Dictionary of Public Health* (Oxford: Oxford University Press, 2018), https://www.oxfordreference.com/display/10.1093/acref/9780191844386.001.0001/acref-9780191844386 [accessed 6 March 2025].
53. See further McCrae, *The Moon and Madness*, p. 40.
54. Riva et al., 'The Disease of the Moon'.
55. As a starting point, see https://medievaldisabilityglossary.hcommons.org/lunacy/ [accessed 14 December 2023].
56. *The Early South English Legendary, or, Lives of Saints*, ed. Carl Horstmann (London: N. Trübner & Co., 1887), p. 369. See also the *Oxford English Dictionary* entry for 'lunatic'.
57. *The Early South English Legendary*, p. 369.
58. *Middle English Dictionary*, definition 1a of 'lunatik', adjective: https://quod.lib.umich.edu/m/middle-english-dictionary/dictionary/MED26340/track?counter=2&search_id=68638174 [accessed 21 May 2024].
59. See further Riva et al., 'The Disease of the Moon'.
60. *Middle English Dictionary*, definition 1a of 'lunatik', adjective.
61. *English Wycliffite Sermons*, ed. A. Hudson and P. Gradon, 5 vols (Oxford: Clarendon Press, 1983–96), 2.23.
62. *Middle English Dictionary*, definition 1b of 'lunatik', adjective.

63. *Lydgate's Reson and Sensuallytee*, ed. Ernst Sieper (London: Kegan Paul, Trench, Trübner & Co., 1901), p. 162.
64. *Bosworth Toller's Anglo-Saxon Dictionary Online*, https://bosworthtoller. com/23122 [accessed 14 December 2023].
65. *Bosworth Toller's Anglo-Saxon Dictionary Online*, https://bosworthtoller. com/23116 [accessed 14 December 2023].
66. 'Dictionary of Old English Corpus', https://doe.artsci.utoronto.ca [accessed 6 March 2025].
67. See also discussion in Emily Kesling, *Medical Texts in Anglo-Saxon Literary Culture* (Cambridge: D.S. Brewer, 2020), pp. 130–52.
68. Quoted from the *Middle English Dictionary* (Online), definition 1b of 'lunatik', adjective: https://quod.lib.umich.edu/m/middle-english-dictionary/dictionary/ MED26340/track?counter=2&search_id=68638174 [accessed 21 May 2024].
69. *The Book of John Mandeville*, ed. Kohanski and Benson, chapter 13, line 1532.
70. *English Mediaeval Lapidaries*, ed. Joan Evans and Mary S. Serjeantson (London: Oxford University Press, 1933; repr. 1990), p. 77.
71. Cited from Williams, *Moon: Nature and Culture*, p. 95.
72. Larrington, *The Poetic Edda*, p. 13.
73. *The Poetic Edda: A Dual-Language Edition*, ed. Pettit, verse 137, p. 110. Translation my own.
74. On the name Loddfafnir, see Larrington, *The Poetic Edda*, p. 287, n. 112.
75. Larrington, *The Poetic Edda*, p. 287, n. 137.

Chapter 5: The Moon of Sorrows and Illusions

1. Sarah Harlan-Haughey, 'The Circle, The Maze, and the Echo: Sublunary Recurrence and Performance in Chaucer's *Legend of Ariadne*', *Chaucer Review* 52:3 (2017), 341–60.
2. On eclipses' links to storms and wars, see Roberto de Andrade Martins, 'André do Avelar and the Teaching of Sacrobosco's Sphaera at the University of Coimbra', in Matteo Valleriani, ed., *De sphaera of Johannes de Sacrobosco in the Early Modern Period: The Authors of the Commentaries* (Cham: Springer Nature, 2020), pp. 313–58 (at p. 321).
3. William H. Smith, 'John of Sacrobosco', in Robert E. Bjork, ed., *The Oxford Dictionary of the Middle Ages* (Oxford: Oxford University Press, 2010), https:// www.oxfordreference.com/display/10.1093/acref/9780198662624.001.0001/ acref-9780198662624 [accessed 6 March 2025].
4. Lynn Thorndike, ed. and trans., *The Sphere of Sacrobosco and Its Commentators* (Chicago, IL: University of Chicago Press, 1949), pp. 141–2.
5. Thorndike, *The Sphere of Sacrobosco and Its Commentators*, p. 142.
6. *Layli and Majnun*, trans. Dick Davis (London: Penguin, 2021); page numbers are given in the text.
7. Thorndike, *The Sphere of Sacrobosco and Its Commentators*, p. 142.
8. María José Martínez Usó and Francisco J. Marco Castillo, 'Occultation of Planets by the Moon in European Narrative Medieval Sources', *Journal for the History of Astronomy* 50:2 (2019), 192–220.
9. For one useful source, see F.R. Stephenson, L.V. Morrison, and C.Y. Hohenkerk, 'Measurement of the Earth's Rotation: 720 BC to AD 2015', *Proceedings:*

Mathematical, Physical and Engineering Sciences 472:2196 (2016), 1–26. See also Justin D. Schove, *Chronology of Eclipses and Comets, AD 1–1000* (Woodbridge: Boydell Press, 1984).

10. See further Tayra M.C. Lanunza Navarro, 'Pedro Sánchez Ciruelo: A Commentary on Sacrobosco's *Tractatus de sphaera* with a *Defense of Astrology*', in Valleriani, ed., *De sphaera of Johannes de Sacrobosco*, pp. 53–89.

11. E. Nenci, 'Francesco Capuano di Manfredonia', in Valleriani, ed., *De sphaera of Johannes de Sacrobosco*, pp. 91–100 (at p. 95).

12. Peter Barker, 'John of Glogów', in Valleriani, ed., *De sphaera of Johannes de Sacrobosco*, pp. 137–60 (at p. 143).

13. F. Richard Stephenson and Said S. Said, 'Records of Lunar Eclipses in Medieval Arabic Chronicles', *Bulletin of the School of Oriental and African Studies* 60:1 (1997), 1–34.

14. Stephenson and Said, 'Records of Lunar Eclipses in Medieval Arabic Chronicles', p. 4.

15. Stephenson and Said, 'Records of Lunar Eclipses in Medieval Arabic Chronicles', p. 14.

16. Stephenson and Said, 'Records of Lunar Eclipses in Medieval Arabic Chronicles', p. 20.

17. Stephenson and Said, 'Records of Lunar Eclipses in Medieval Arabic Chronicles', p. 20.

18. Bernard R. Goldstein, 'Colors of Eclipses in Medieval Hebrew Astronomical Tables', *Aelph* 5 (2005), 11–34.

19. Snorri Sturluson, *The Prose Edda*, trans. Jesse L. Byock (London: Penguin, 2005), p. 14.

20. See further Anders Andrén, 'Sun and Moon', in Jens Peter Schjødt, John Lindow, and Anders Andrén, eds, *The Pre-Christian Religions of the North: History and Structures* (Turnhout: Brepols, 2020), pp. 1465–80.

21. *The Prose Edda*, trans. Byock, p. 53.

22. *The Prose Edda*, trans. Byock, p. 54.

23. *The Prose Edda*, trans. Byock, p. 108.

24. A helpful summary of the text and its history can be found in Lourdes Maria Alvarez, '*Calila e Dimna*', in Bjork, ed., *The Oxford Dictionary of the Middle Ages*. See also '*Kalīla wa-Dimna*', in Marlé Hammond, *A Dictionary of Arabic Literary Terms and Devices* (Oxford: Oxford University Press, 2018). See further *Calila e Dimna*, ed. Juan Manuel Cacho Blecua and María Jesús Lacarra (Madrid: Clásicos Castalia, 1984); and *Kalīla and Dimna*, trans. Wheeler Thackston (Indianapolis, IN: Hackett Publishing, 2019), pp. ix–x. For a discussion of the text, see Marianne Marroun, '*Kalila wa Dimna*: Inception, Appropriation, and Transmimesis', *Comparative Literature Studies* 48:4 (2011), 512–40.

25. Bettina Krönung, trans. Angela Kinney, 'The Wisdom of the Beasts: The Arabic Book of Kalila and Dimna and the Byzantine Book of Stephanites and Ichnelates', in Carolina Cupane and Bettina Krönung, eds, *Fictional Storytelling in the Medieval Eastern Mediterranean and Beyond* (Leiden: Brill, 2016), pp. 427–60.

26. *Kalīla and Dimna*, trans. Thackston, p. 79.

27. *Kalīla and Dimna*, trans. Thackston, p. 80.

28. For a biography, see Robert Henryson, *The Complete Works*, ed. David J. Parkinson (Kalamazoo, MI: Medieval Institute Publications, 2010), https://d.lib.rochester.

edu/teams/text/parkinson-henryson-complete-works-introduction [accessed 11 December 2023].

29. On the *Fables*, see Gillian Rudd, 'Lions, Mice, and Learning from Animals in Henryson's *Fables*', in Bruce Boehrer, Molly Hand, and Brian Massumi, eds, *Animals, Animality, and Literature* (Cambridge: Cambridge University Press, 2018), pp. 88–102.
30. All quotations are from *The Complete Works*, ed. Parkinson; line numbers are incorporated in the text. Translations are my own.
31. Craig McDonald, 'The Perversion of Law in Robert Henryson's Fable of the *Fox, the Wolf, and the Husbandman*', *Medium Ævum* 49:2 (1980), 244–53.
32. On this use of 'shadow' for reflection, see further Henryson, *The Complete Works*, ed. Parkinson, n. 2392.
33. Dorothy Yamomoto, *The Boundaries of the Human in Medieval English Literature* (Oxford: Oxford University Press, 2000), p. 70.
34. Marie-Françoise Alamichel, '"This Wyde World, Which That Men Seye Is Round": Movement and Meaning in *The Franklin's Tale*', *Etudes anglaises* 67:3 (2014), 259–73 (see especially pp. 267–9).
35. Chauncy Wood, *Chaucer and the Country of the Stars: Poetic Uses of Astrological Imagery* (Princeton, NJ: Princeton University Press, 1970; repr. 2015), p. 271.
36. See further Angela Lucas, 'Astronomy, Astrology and Magic in Chaucer's *Franklin's Tale*', *Maynooth Review* 8 (1983), 5–16 (at p. 6). All quotations are from *The Riverside Chaucer*, ed. Benson and Robinson, third edition; line numbers are incorporated in the text and translations are my own.
37. Astronomical tables made in Toledo.
38. The 'tables Tolletanes' provides planetary positions in single-year periods ('expans yeeris') and in twenty-year periods ('collect').
39. Dates as bases from which astronomical calculations are made.
40. Table of distances between parts of the equator.
41. Angles in calculating astronomical positions/motions.
42. Tables for calculating planetary positions/motions.
43. Divisions of the sphere into astronomical houses.
44. Eighth sphere, i.e. sphere of the fixed stars.
45. Medieval astronomers defined 'Alnath' as being a star in the constellation of Aries. The name also referred to the first mansion of the moon. See further *Riverside Chaucer*, p. 899.
46. The first point of Aries.
47. *The Franklin's Tale*, lines 1266–84, in *The Canterbury Tales*, ed. Jill Mann (London: Penguin, 2005), pp. 426–7. For an explanation of these lines, see further pp. 956–8 in Mann's edition and the *Riverside Chaucer*, p. 899. See further Lucas, 'Astronomy, Astrology and Magic'.
48. Carolyn P. Collette, *Rethinking Chaucer's Legend of Good Women* (Woodbridge: Boydell & Brewer, 2014), p. 117.
49. Betsy McCormick, Leah Schwebel, and Lynn Shutters, 'Introduction: Looking Forward, Looking Back on the *Legend of Good Women*', *Chaucer Review* 52:1 (2017), 3–11 (at p. 3).
50. Janet M. Cowen, 'Chaucer's *Legend of Good Women*: Structure and Tone', *Studies in Philology* 82:4 (1985), 416–36.

51. Anne Schuurman, 'Pity and Poetics in Chaucer's *Legend of Good Women*', *PMLA* 130:5 (2015), 1302–17 (at p. 1313).

52. *Sancti Bernardi Opera*, ed. J. Leclercq, C.H. Talbot and H.M. Rochais (Rome: Editiones Cistercienses, 1957–77), vol. 5, p. 264.

53. *Fête-Dieu (1246–1996)*, vol. 2, *Vie de Sainte Julienne de Cornillon*, ed. Jean-Pierre Delville (Louvain-la-Neuve: Institut d'Etudes Médiévales, 1999), p. 120. Translation my own. Readers can find a full translation of this text here: 'The Life of Juliana of Cornillon', trans. Barbara Newman, in Anneke B. Mulder-Bakker, ed., *Living Saints of the Thirteenth Century: The Lives of Yvette, Anchoress of Huy; Juliana of Cornillon, Author of the Corpus Christi Feast; and Margaret the Lame, Anchoress of Magdeburg* (Turnhout: Brepols, 2011), pp. 143–302.

54. *Fête-Dieu (1246–1996)*, vol. 2, ed. Delville, p. 122.

55. See Anneke B. Mulder-Bakker, *Lives of the Anchoresses: The Rise of the Urban Recluse in Medieval Europe*, trans. Myra Heerspink Scholz (Philadelphia: University of Pennsylvania Press, 2005), p. 86; and 'The Life of Juliana of Cornillon', trans. Newman, p. 162.

56. On anchoritism, see especially Ann. K. Warren, *Anchorites and Their Patrons in Medieval England* (Berkeley: University of California Press, 1985). On the difficulties of the term 'anchoress', see Liz Herbert McAvoy, 'Introduction', in Liz Herbert McAvoy, ed., *Anchoritic Traditions of Medieval Europe* (Woodbridge: Boydell, 2010), pp. 1–21 (at pp. 11–12).

57. See further E.A. Jones, 'Ceremonies of Enclosure: Rite, Rhetoric and Reality', in Liz Herbert McAvoy, ed., *Rhetoric of the Anchorhold: Space, Place and Body within the Discourses of Enclosure* (Cardiff: University of Wales Press, 2008), pp. 34–49. See also E.A. Jones, ed., *Hermits and Anchorites in England, 1200–1550* (Manchester: Manchester University Press, 2019), p. 17.

58. For an introduction to the text, see the essays in Yoko Wada, ed., *A Companion to Ancrene Wisse* (Cambridge: D.S. Brewer, 2003). For a full translation of this text, see *Ancrene Wisse: Guide for Anchoresses: A Translation Based on Cambridge, Corpus Christi College, MS 402*, trans. Bella Millett (Exeter: University of Exeter Press, 2009).

59. 'A son ill taught is the confusion of the father: and a foolish daughter shall be to his loss.'

60. Quotations are from: *Ancrene Wisse: A Corrected Edition of the Text in Cambridge, Corpus Christi College, MS 402 with Variants from other Manuscripts*, ed. Bella Millett, 2 Vols, EETS O.S. 325 and 326 (London: Oxford University Press, 2005–2006); references, to page and line number respectively, are in the text. Translations are my own.

61. Nicholas Watson, '"With the Heat of the Hungry Heart": Empowerment and *Ancrene Wisse*', in Mary C. Erler and Maryanne Kowaleski, eds, *Gendering the Master Narrative: Women and Power in the Middle Ages* (Ithaca, NY: Cornell University Press, 2003), pp. 52–70 (at p. 60).

62. Gregory the Great, *Moralia in Iob* (Turnhout: Brepols, 1953), p. 1750.

63. *Sancti Bernardi Opera*, vol. 5, p. 264; emphasis in the original.

64. https://www.jstor.org/stable/community.15631257 [accessed 9 March 2025].

65. https://www.jstor.org/stable/community.15645437 [accessed 7 March 2025].

66. https://www.jstor.org/stable/community.14640246 [accessed 7 March 2025]; https://www.jstor.org/stable/community.14638864 [accessed 7 March 2025].

67. https://www.jstor.org/stable/community.15040603 [accessed 7 March 2025].

68. https://www.jstor.org/stable/community.18801978 [accessed 7 March 2025].

69. https://www.museunacional.cat/en/colleccio/immaculate-conception/francisco-de-zurbaran/065578-000#:~:text=Description%3A,cherubim%20occupying%20a%20half%20moon. [accessed 17 September 2024].

70. https://collections.ashmolean.org/collection/search/per_page/25/offset/0/sort_by/date/object/81075 [accessed 21 August 2024].

71. For a full translation of the poem, see *The Poems of the Pearl Manuscript in Modern English Translation: Pearl, Cleanness, Patience, Sir Gawain and the Green Knight* (Exeter: Exeter University Press, 2008). For an introduction to this poem, see John M. Bowers, *An Introduction to the Gawain-Poet* (Gainesville: University Press of Florida, 2013); and Ad Putter, *An Introduction to the Gawain-Poet* (London: Longman, 1996). For further scholarship on the poem, see Cecilia A. Hatt, *God and the Gawain-Poet: Theology and Genre in Pearl, Cleanness, Patience, and Sir Gawain and the Green Knight* (Cambridge: D.S. Brewer, 2015); and David Coley, *Death and the Pearl-Maiden: Plague, Poetry England* (Columbus: Ohio State University Press, 2019).

72. All quotations to *Pearl* (with line numbers incorporated in the text) are from *Pearl*, ed. Sarah Stanbury (Kalamazoo, MI: Medieval Institute Publications, 2001), https://d.lib.rochester.edu/teams/text/stanbury-pearl [accessed 21 January 2024].

73. Further discussion of *Pearl*, *Ancrene Wisse*, Juliana of Cornillon, Bernard of Clairvaux, and images of the Virgin Mary on the crescent moon can be found in A.S. Lazikani, 'The Broken Moon: Lunar Semiotics in *Ancrene Wisse* and *Pearl*', *Chaucer Review* (forthcoming).

74. *Kalīla and Dimna*, trans. Thackston, p. 76.

Chapter 6: The Moon of Loves and Embraces

1. Maria Teresa Agozzino, 'Dafydd ap Gwilym', in Bjork, ed., *The Oxford Dictionary of the Middle Ages*, https://www.oxfordreference.com/display/10.1093/acref/9780198662624.001.0001/acref-9780198662624 [accessed 6 March 2025]. For a discussion, see also Helen Fulton, *Dafydd ap Gwilym and the European Context* (Cardiff: University of Wales Press, 1989); the outline of Fulton's study is available on pp. ix–xiii.

2. The translation is from Swansea University's Dafydd ap Gwilym page: A. Cynfael Lake, https://dafyddapgwilym.net/eng/3win.php [accessed 18 March 2024].

3. Dafydd Johnston, https://dafyddapgwilym.net/eng/3win.php [accessed 14 December 2023].

4. Huw Meirion Edwards, https://dafyddapgwilym.net/eng/3win.php [accessed 18 March 2024].

5. Huw Meirion Edwards https://dafyddapgwilym.net/eng/3win.php [accessed 18 March 2024].

6. For this poem, 'The April Moon', see Joseph P. Clancy, ed., *Medieval Welsh Poems* (Dublin: Four Courts Press, 2003), pp. 210–12. See also R. Geraint Gruffydd, 'Gruffudd Gryg', in the *Oxford Dictionary of National Biography*, https://www.oxforddnb.com [accessed 6 March 2025].

7. https://www.metmuseum.org/art/collection/search/444717 [accessed 9 March 2025].

8. Omid Safi, '"The Real Intention Was My Beloved": The Moon in Persian Sufi Poetry', in Christiane Gruber, ed., *The Moon: A Voyage through Time* (Toronto: Aga Khan Museum, 2019), pp. 35–44.

9. Deborah L. Black, 'The "Imaginative Syllogism" in Arabic Philosophy: A Medieval Contribution to the Philosophical Study of Metaphor', *Mediaeval Studies* 51 (1989), 242–67; Vincent Gillespie, '*Ethice Subponitur?* The Imaginative Syllogism and the Idea of the Poetic', in Philip Knox, Jonathan Morton, and Daniel Reeve, eds, *Medieval Thought Experiments: Poetry, Hypothesis, and Experience in the European Middle Ages* (Turnhout: Brepols, 2018), pp. 297–327. See also L.E. Goodman, *Avicenna* (London: Routledge, 1992), p. 222; and Balqis al-Karaki, 'Dissimilar Premises, Similar Conclusions: On the Partial Rationality of Metaphor – A Comparative Study', *Journal of Near Eastern Studies* 70:1 (2011), 81–100 (especially pp. 95–7).

10. See further María Rosa Menocal, Raymond P. Scheindlin, and Michael Anthony Sells, eds, *The Literature of Al-Andalus* (Cambridge: Cambridge University Press, 2000).

11. See further James T. Monroe, ed. and trans., *Hispano-Arabic Poetry: A Student Anthology* (Piscataway, NJ: Gorgias Press, 2004), p. 154, lines 1–2.

12. Monroe, ed., *Hispano-Arabic Poetry*, p. 184, line 47.

13. Monroe, ed., *Hispano-Arabic Poetry*, p. 222, lines 12–14.

14. Monroe, ed., *Hispano-Arabic Poetry*, p. 218, lines 2–5.

15. Monroe, ed., *Hispano-Arabic Poetry*, p. 302, line 1.

16. See further Monroe, ed., *Hispano-Arabic Poetry*, p. 304, line 3.

17. *Layli and Majnun*, trans. Davis, p. xii.

18. On jinn, see Amira El-Zein, *Islam, Arabs, and the Intelligent World of the Jinn* (Syracuse, NY: Syracuse University Press, 2009); on Majnun in particular, see pp. 118–20.

19. Feria J. Ghazoul, '*Majnun Layla:* Translation as Transposition', in Sandra Bermann and Catherine Porter, eds, *A Companion to Translation Studies* (Malden, MA: John Wiley & Sons, 2014), pp. 375–87.

20. Other relevant images include: Walters manuscript W.605, folio 83b (Iran, 1486–95): Majnun among wild animals; Walters manuscript W.624, folio 115a (Lahore, 1597–8): the lovers meet in the wilderness; Walters manuscript W.624, folio 98a (Lahore, 1597–8): Layla and Majnun fall in love at school.

21. Translations are from *Layli and Majnun*, trans. Davis; page numbers are given in the text.

22. See further Kamran Talattof and Jerome W. Clinton, eds, *The Poetry of Nizami Ganjavi: Knowledge, Love, and Rhetoric* (New York: Palgrave, 2000); and Kamran Talattof, *Nezami Ganjavi and Classical Persian Literature: Demystifying the Mystic* (Cham: Palgrave Macmillan, 2022).

23. See further Lloyd Ridgeon, 'Mysticism in Medieval Sufism', in Lloyd Ridgeon, ed., *The Cambridge Companion to Sufism* (Cambridge: Cambridge University Press, 2014), pp. 125–49.

24. See further Alexander Knysh, 'Waḥdat al-Wujūd', in Ibrahim Kalin, ed., *The Oxford Encyclopedia of Philosophy, Science, and Technology in Islam* (Oxford: Oxford University Press, 2014), https://www.oxfordreference.com/display/10.1093/acref:oiso/9780199812578.001.0001/acref-9780199812578 [accessed 6 March 2025].

25. This is in his poem *Naẓm al-sulūk* (*Poem of the Sufi Way*), lines 679–706. A translation of the poem is available in *'Umar Ibn al-Fāriḍ: Sufi Verse, Saintly Life*, trans. Th. Emil Homerin (Mahwah, NJ: Paulist Press, 2001). An edition of the Arabic is: Abd al-Khāliq Mahmūd, ed., *Dīwān Ibn al-Fāriḍ: tahqīq wa-dirāsah naqdīyah* (al-Haram [Jīzah]: 'Ayn lil-Dirāsāt wa-al-Buḥūth al-Insānīyah wa-al-Ijtimā'īyah, 1995); and for a transliteration: A.J. Arberry, *The Mystical Poems of Ibn al-Fāriḍ: Edited in Transcription from the Oldest Extant Manuscript in the Chester Beatty Collection* (London: Emery Walker, 1952).

26. The diagram is in the keeping of the University of California, San Diego: https://www.jstor.org/stable/community.13885468 [accessed 7 March 2025].

27. For introductions to Sufism, see Alexander D. Knysh, *Islamic Mysticism: A Short History* (Leiden: Brill, 2000); and Alexander Knysh, 'Sufism', in Robert Irwin, ed., *The New Cambridge History of Islam*, vol. 4, *Islamic Cultures and Societies to the Eighteenth Century* (Cambridge: Cambridge University Press, 2010), pp. 60–104.

28. See further Lourdes María Alvarez, trans., *Abū al-Ḥasan al-Shushtarī: Songs of Love and Devotion* (Mahwah, NJ: Paulist Press, 2009), p. 17.

29. *The Penguin Anthology of Classical Arab Literature*, ed. and trans. Robert Irwin (London: Penguin, 1999), p. 276.

30. See further Hammond, *Dictionary of Arabic Literary Terms and Devices*.

31. Quoted in *The Penguin Anthology of Classical Arab Literature*, ed. and trans. Irwin, p. 276.

32. Translation my own; based on the transliterated edition of the Arabic provided here: *Poesía Estrófica (Cejeles Y/O Muwassaḥāt) Atribuida al Místico Granadino As-Sustarī Siglo XIII. d.C.*, ed. F. Corriente (Madrid: Consejo Superior de Investigaciones Científicas, Instituto de Filologia, Departamento de Estudios Arabes, 1988), p. 68. For another translation of the full poem, along with others by al-Shushtarī, see Alvarez, trans., *Abū al-Ḥasan al-Shushtarī: Songs of Love and Devotion*.

33. For an account of Ibn 'Arabī's life, see Claude Addas, *Quest for the Red Sulphur: The Life of Ibn 'Arabī*, trans. Peter Kingsley (Cambridge: Islamic Texts Society, 1993).

34. See further Esmé L.K. Partridge, 'The Celestial "Polished Mirror": The Mystical Dimension of the Moon according to Muḥyddin Ibn 'Arabī', *Journal of the Muḥyddin Ibn 'Arabī Society* 68 (2020), 103–16 (at p. 104).

35. See further Michael Sells, 'Bewildered Tongue: The Semantics of Mystical Union in Islam', in Moshe Idel and Bernard McGinn, eds, *Mystical Union in Judaism, Christianity, and Islam: An Ecumenical Dialogue* (1996; repr. London: Bloomsbury, 2016), pp. 87–124 (at p. 91).

36. Translations are my own, based on the edition in Michael Sells, ed. and trans., *The Translator of Desires* (Princeton, NJ: Princeton University Press, 2021); page numbers for the Arabic poems are incorporated in the text.

37. A translation of this poem is available in the appendix to this book.

38. Sells, trans., *The Translator of Desires*, p. 268.

39. *Islamic Mystical Poetry: Sufi Verse from the Early Mystics to Rumi*, ed. and trans. Mahmood Jamal (London: Penguin, 2009), p. 154.

40. See further Andrew Wilcox, 'The Dual Mystical Concepts of Fana' and Baqa' in Early Sufism', *British Journal of Middle Eastern Studies* 38:1 (2011), 95–118.

41. From *The Conference of the Birds* by Farid 'Aṭṭār published by Penguin Classics. Copyright © Afkham Darbandi and Dick Davis, 1984. Reprinted by permission of Penguin Books Limited. The full reference is: *The Conference of the Birds*, trans.

Afkham Darbandi and Dick Davis (London: Penguin, 2011); page numbers are incorporated in the text.

42. For this image, see R.W.J. Austin, trans., *The Bezels of Wisdom* (Mahwah, NJ: Paulist Press, 1980), p. 92.

43. See *The Conference of the Birds*, trans. Darbandi and Davis, p. 264, n. 14.

44. A range of such images is available through a keyword search on Google images, including the terms 'Mīrābāī' and 'Krishna'.

45. For an account of the various legends of her life, see Nancy M. Martin, 'Rajasthan: Mirabai and Her Poetry', in Edwin F. Bryant, ed., *Krishna: A Sourcebook* (New York: Oxford University Press, 2007), pp. 241–54 (at pp. 242–3). See further Nancy M. Martin, 'Invoking Mirabai: Elision and Illumination in the Global Study of Women Mystics', in Abir Bazaz and Alexandra Verini, eds, *Gender and Medieval Mysticism from India to Europe* (London: Routledge, 2023), pp. 170–88.

46. Martin, 'Rajasthan: Mirabai and Her Poetry', pp. 242–3.

47. Alexandra Verini, 'Women's Mystical Friendships: Margery Kempe and Mirabai', in Kathryn Loveridge et al., eds, *Women's Literary Cultures in the Global Middle Ages: Speaking Internationally* (Cambridge: D.S. Brewer, 2023), pp. 43–59 (at p. 54).

48. See further Martin, 'Rajasthan: Mirabai and Her Poetry', p. 244.

49. Martin, 'Invoking Mirabai', p. 172. See also Ritu Varghese, 'Mirabai in Popular Imagination: Reading Bhakti Canon in Contemporary Context', *Artha Journal of Social Sciences* 19:2 (2020), 67–81; Ritu Varghese, 'Mirabai in Public Spheres', *Women's History Review* 32:5 (2023), 611–31; and Chloe Martinez, 'The Autobiographical Pose: Life Narrative and Religious Transformation in the Mirabai Tradition', *South Asia* 41:2 (2018), 418–34.

50. *Oxford English Dictionary*, 'bhakti', https://www.oed.com/dictionary/bhakti_n?tab=meaning_and_use#21532679 [accessed 16 December 2023].

51. *The Devotional Poems of Mīrābāī*, trans. A.J. Alston (Delhi: Motilal Banarsidass, 1980), p. 9. Permission to quote granted by Motilal Banarsidass Publishing House.

52. Martin, 'Invoking Mirabai', p. 176.

53. John Stratton Hawley, *A Storm of Songs: India and the Idea of the Bhakti Movement* (Cambridge, MA: Harvard University Press, 2015), p. 2.

54. See Holly Hillgardner, *Longing and Letting Go: Christian and Hindu Practices of Passionate Non-Attachment* (New York: Oxford University Press, 2016).

55. Verini, 'Women's Mystical Friendships'.

56. References are to *The Devotional Poems of Mīrābāī*, trans. Alston; page numbers are incorporated in the text.

57. On problems with translating these lines, see *The Devotional Poems of Mīrābāī*, trans. Alston, p. 130, n. 118.

58. See further V.K. Sethi, *Mira: The Divine Lover*, second edition (Dera Baba Jaimal Singh: Radha Soami Satsang Beas, 1988), p. 93.

Chapter 7: The Moon of Worlds and Tales: An Epilogue

1. On *The Marvels of the East* or *The Wonders of the East*, see further Asa Simon Mittman and Susan M. Kim, 'The Wonders of the East', in *Primary Sources on Monsters*, vol. 2 (Leeds: Arc Humanities Press, 2018), pp. 67–70. See also Greta

Austin, 'Marvellous People or Marvellous Races? Race and the Anglo-Saxon *Wonders of the East*', in Timothy S. Jones and David A. Sprunger, eds, *Marvels, Monsters and Miracles: Studies in the Medieval and Early Modern Imagination* (Kalamazoo, MI: Medieval Institute Publications, 2002), pp. 25–51; John Block Friedman, 'The Marvels-of-the-East Tradition in Anglo-Saxon Art', in Paul E. Szarmach, ed., *Sources of Anglo-Saxon Culture* (Kalamazoo, MI: Medieval Institute Publications, 1986), pp. 319–41; and Heide Estes, 'Wonders and Wisdom: Anglo-Saxons and the East', *English Studies* 91 (2010), 360–73 (at p. 361).

2. See further Ke Jeong-hee and Justin M. Byron-Davies, 'The Role of Kisaeng *Sijo* Poets in Medieval Korean Literature', in Loveridge et al., eds, *Women's Literary Cultures in the Global Middle Ages*, pp. 103–22 (at p. 104).

3. *Encounters with the Korean Lyrical Spirit: An Anthology of Sijoi*, trans. Ko Jeong-hee and Justin M. Byron Davies (Seoul: ASIA Publishers, 2019); page numbers included in the text.

4. *Encounters with the Korean Lyrical Spirit*, p. 133, n. 21.

5. For a discussion, see Jeong-hee and Byron-Davies, 'The Role of Kisaeng *Sijo* Poets', p. 108.

Appendix

1. Translation my own, based on the edition by Means, *Medieval Lunar Astrology*, pp. 245–52.

2. Translation my own, based on the edition by Means, *Medieval Lunar Astrology*, pp. 223–42.

3. Translation my own, based on the edition by Means, *Medieval Lunar Astrology*, pp. 205–8.

4. Translation my own, based on the edition by Means, *Medieval Lunar Astrology*, pp. 112–47.

5. Translation my own, based on the edition by Means, *Medieval Lunar Astrology*, pp. 95–104.

6. Translation my own, based on the edition by Means, *Medieval Lunar Astrology*, pp. 105–11.

7. Translation my own, based on the edition by Means, *Medieval Lunar Astrology*, pp. 201–2.

8. Translation my own, based on the transliterated edition of the Arabic in *Poesía Estrófica*, ed. Corriente, pp. 67–8.

9. Translation my own, based on the transliterated edition of the Arabic in *Poesía Estrófica*, ed. Corriente, p. 68.

10. Translation my own based on the edition in Sells, ed. and trans., *The Translator of Desires*, pp. 174–6.

BIBLIOGRAPHY

Primary Sources

Manuscripts and Prints

Aberdeen University Library MS 24
Almanach auf das Jahr (*Almanac of the Year*) (1484)
Codex Upsaliensis (DG 11)
Baltimore, Walters Art Museum, W.605
Baltimore, Walters Art Museum, W.622
Baltimore, Walters Art Museum, W.624
London, British Library, Cotton Nero A. X/2
London, British Library, MS Harley 2253
Musée Condé, Chantilly, France, MS 65 (lat. 1284)
Oxford, Bodleian Library, MS Ashmole 210
Oxford, Bodleian Library, MS Ashmole 370
Oxford, Bodleian Library, MS Ashmole 391(2)
Oxford, Bodleian Library, MS Bodley 266
Oxford, Bodleian Library, MS Bodley 614
Oxford, Bodleian Library, MS Canon Misc. 248
Oxford, Bodleian Library, MS Digby 48
Oxford, Bodleian Library, MS Douce 18
Oxford, Bodleian Library, MS Douce 49
Oxford, Bodleian Library, MS Rawlinson D. 939
Oxford, Bodleian Library, MS Selden Supra 90
Paris, Bibliothèque Nationale, lat. 7351

BIBLIOGRAPHY

Editions and Translations

Aberdeen Bestiary, https://www.abdn.ac.uk/bestiary/ms24/f12v.

Albert of Saxony, *Quæstiones in Aristotelis De cælo*, ed. Benoît Patar (Louvain-la-Neuve: Editions de l'Institut Supérieur de Philosophie, 2008).

Ælfric of Eynsham, *Ælfric's Catholic Homilies: The First Series*, ed. Peter Clemoes (Oxford: Oxford University Press, 1997).

Ancrene Wisse: A Corrected Edition of the Text in Cambridge, Corpus Christi College, MS 402 with Variants from other Manuscripts, ed. Bella Millett, 2 Vols, EETS O.S. 325 and 326 (London: Oxford University Press, 2005–2006).

Ancrene Wisse: Guide for Anchoresses: A Translation Based on Cambridge, Corpus Christi College, MS 402, trans. Bella Millett (Exeter: University of Exeter Press, 2009).

The Anglo-Saxon Missionaries in Germany, ed. C.H. Talbot (London: Sheed and Ward, 1954).

Anglo-Saxon Prognostics: An Edition and Translation of Texts from London, British Library, MS Cotton Tiberius A. iii, ed. R.M. Liuzza (Woodbridge: Boydell & Brewer, 2011).

Arderne, John, *Treatises of Fistula in Ano*, ed. D'Arcy Power (Oxford: Oxford University Press, 1910).

Ariosto, Lodovico, *Orlando furioso*, commentary by Emilio Bigi, ed. Cristina Zampese (Milan: Rizzoli, 2012).

Ariosto, Lodovico, *Orlando Furioso: A New Verse Translation*, trans. David R. Slavitt (Cambridge, MA: Harvard University Press, 2010).

Ariosto, Lodovico, *A Romantic Epic of Ludovico Ariosto: Orlando Furioso (The Frenzy of Orlando), Part Two*, trans. Barbara Reynolds (London: Penguin, 1991).

ʿAṭṭār of Nishapur, *The Conference of the Birds*, trans. Afkham Darbandi and Dick Davis (London: Penguin, 2011).

Bede, *Bedae Opera de temporibus*, ed. Charles W. Jones (Boston, MA: Medieval Academy of America, 1943).

Bede, *Bede: The Reckoning of Time*, trans. Faith Wallis (Liverpool: Liverpool University Press, 1999).

The Beowulf Manuscript: Complete Texts and the Fight at Finnsburg, ed. and trans. R.D. Fulk (Cambridge, MA: Harvard University Press, 2010).

Bernard of Clairvaux, *Sancti Bernardi Opera*, 8 vols, ed. J. Leclercq, C.H. Talbot, and H.M. Rochais (Rome: Editiones Cistercienses, 1957–77).

Bible (Douay-Rheims), www.drbo.org.

Biblia Latina cum Glossa Ordinaria: Facsimile Reprint of the Edito Princeps Adolph Rusch of Strassburg, 1480/1481, 4 vols (Brepols: Turnhout, 1992).

Bosworth-Toller's Anglo-Saxon Dictionary Online, https://bosworthtoller.com.

Calila e Dimna, ed. Juan Manuel Cacho Blecua and María Jesús Lacarra (Madrid: Clásicos Castalia, 1984).

Chaucer, Geoffrey, *The Canterbury Tales*, ed. Jill Mann (London: Penguin, 2005).

Chaucer, Geoffrey, *The Riverside Chaucer: Third Edition*, ed. Larry D. Benson and F.N. Robinson (Oxford: Oxford University Press, 2008).

Chaucer, Geoffrey, *Troilus and Criseyde, with Facing-Page Il Filostrato*, ed. and trans. Stephen A. Barney (New York: Norton, 2006).

A Choice of Anglo-Saxon Verse, ed. and trans. Richard Hamer (London: Faber & Faber, 2015).

Chrétien de Troyes, *Arthurian Romances*, trans. W.W. Kibler and C.W. Carroll (London: Penguin, 1991).

Classical Japanese Prose: An Anthology, ed. Helen Craig McCullough (Stanford, CA: Stanford University Press, 1990).

The Complete Harley 2253 Manuscript, vol. 3, ed. and trans. Susanna Greer Fein, David Raybin, and Jan Ziolkowski (Kalamazoo, MI: Medieval Institute Publications, 2015).

'Dafydd ap Gwilym', https://dafyddapgwilym.net/eng/3win.php (University of Swansea).

Dante Alighieri, *The Divine Comedy: Inferno, Purgatorio, Paradiso*, trans. Robin Kirkpatrick (London: Penguin, 2012).

'Dictionnaire Electronique de Chrétien de Troyes' (University of Ottawa), http://zeus.atilf.fr/dect.

'Digital Dante', https://digitaldante.columbia.edu (Columbia University Libraries).

The Early South English Legendary, or, Lives of Saints, ed. Carl Horstmann (London: N. Trübner & Co., 1887)

Encounters with the Korean Lyrical Spirit: An Anthology of Sijoi, trans. Ko Jeong-hee and Justin M. Byron Davies (Seoul: ASIA Publishers, 2019).

English Wycliffite Sermons, vol. 1, ed. Anne Hudson (Oxford: Oxford University Press, 2022).

The Exeter Book, ed. George Philip Krapp and Elliott Van Kirk Dobbie (New York: Columbia University Press, 1936).

Fête-Dieu (1246–1996), Vol II: Vie de Sainte Julienne de Cornillon, ed. Jean-Pierre Delville (Louvain-la-Neuve: Institut d'Etudes Médiévales, 1999).

Geoffrey of Monmouth, *The History of the Kings of Britain*, trans. Lewis Thorpe (Harmondsworth: Penguin, 1966).

Gervase of Canterbury, *Opera historica*, ed. W. Stubbs, 2 vols (London: Longman & Co., 1879).

Gregory the Great, *Moralia in Iob, Corpus Christianorum* (Turnhout: Brepols, 1953).

Gruffudd Gryg, 'The April Moon', in *Medieval Welsh Poems*, ed. Joseph P. Clancy (Dublin: Four Courts Press, 2003).

Guillaume de Lorris and Jean de Meun, *Le Roman de la Rose*, ed. and trans. Armand Strubel (Paris: Livre de Poche, 1992).

Guillaume de Lorris and Jean de Meun, *The Romance of the Rose*, trans. Frances Horgan (Oxford: Oxford University Press, 1994; repr. 2008).

Henryson, Robert, *The Complete Works*, ed. David J. Parkinson (Kalamazoo, MI: Medieval Institute Publications, 2010).

Hermits and Anchorites in England, 1200–1550, ed. E.A. Jones (Manchester: Manchester University Press, 2019).

Hispano-Arabic Poetry: A Student Anthology, ed. and trans. James T. Monroe (Piscataway, NJ: Gorgias Press, 2004)

Ibn al-Fāriḍ, ʿUmar, *Dīwān Ibn al-Fāriḍ: tahqīq wa-dirāsah naqdīyah*, ed. Abd al-Khāliq Mahmūd (al-Haram [Jīzah]: ʿAyn lil-Dirāsāt wa-al-Buḥūth al-Insānīyah wa-al-Ijtimāʿīyah, 1995).

Ibn al-Fāriḍ, ʿUmar, *The Mystical Poems of Ibn al-Fāriḍ: Edited in Transcription from the Oldest Extant Manuscript in the Chester Beatty Collection*, ed. A.J. Arberry (London: Emery Walker, 1952).

BIBLIOGRAPHY

Ibn al-Fāriḍ, ʿUmar, *Sufi Verse, Saintly Life*, trans. Th. Emil Homerin (Mahwah, NJ: Paulist Press, 2001).

Ibn ʿArabī, Muḥyddin, *The Bezels of Wisdom*, trans. R.W.J. Austin (Mahwah, NJ: Paulist Press, 1980).

Isidore of Seville, *Traité de la Nature* (Bordeaux: Féret et Fils, 1960).

Islamic Mystical Poetry: Sufi Verse from the Early Mystics to Rumi, ed. and trans. Mahmood Jamal (London: Penguin, 2009).

John of Sacrobosco, *The Sphere of Sacrobosco and Its Commentators*, ed. and trans. Lynn Thorndike (Chicago, IL: University of Chicago Press, 1949).

Kalīla and Dimna, trans. Wheeler Thackston (Indianapolis, IN: Hackett Publishing, 2019).

The Katherine Group MS Bodley 34, ed. Emily Rebekah Huber and Elizabeth Robertson (Kalamazoo, MI: Medieval Institute Publications, 2016).

Lanfranc, *Science of Cirurgie*, ed. Robert V. Fleischhacker (London: Kegan Paul, 1894).

'The Life of Juliana of Cornillon', trans. Barbara Newman, in *Living Saints of the Thirteenth Century: The Lives of Yvette, Anchoress of Huy; Juliana of Cornillon, Author of the Corpus Christi Feast; and Margaret the Lame, Anchoress of Magdeburg*, ed. Anneke B. Mulder-Bakker (Turnhout: Brepols, 2011).

Lucian of Samosata, *True Story; Lucius, or the Ass*, trans. Paul Turner (Richmond: Alma Classics, 2018).

Lydgate, John, *Reson and Sensuallytee: Edited from the Fairfax Ms. 16 (Bodleian) and the Additional Ms. 29,729 (Brit. Mus.)*, ed. Ernst Sieper (London: Kegan Paul, Trench, Trübner & Co., 1901).

Mandeville, John, *The Book of John Mandeville*, ed. Tamarah Kohanski and C. David Benson (Kalamazoo, MI: Medieval Institute Publications, 2007).

Medical Writings from Early Medieval England, ed. M.A. D'Aronco and John D. Niles (Cambridge, MA: Harvard University Press, 2023).

The Medieval Bestiary in English: Texts and Translations of the Old and Middle English Physiologus, ed. and trans. Megan Cavell (Peterborough: Broadview Press, 2022).

Medieval Lunar Astrology: A Collection of Representative Middle English Texts, ed. Laurel Means (Lewiston, NY: E. Mellen, 1993).

'Medieval Sourcebook: Innocent III (r. 1198–1216): Letters on Papal Policies', https://sourcebooks.fordham.edu/source/inniii-policies.asp.

Mīrābāī, *The Devotional Poems of Mīrābāī*, trans. A.J. Alston (Delhi: Motilal Banarsidass, 1980).

Nezāmi, *Layli and Majnun*, trans. Dick Davis (London: Penguin, 2021).

Nicholas of Lynn, *The Kalendarium of Nicholas of Lynn*, ed. Sigmund Eisner, trans. Gary Mac Eoin and Sigmund Eisner (Athens: University of Georgia Press, 1980).

The Old English Martyrology: Edition, Translation, and Commentary, ed. and trans. Christine Rauer (Woodbridge: Boydell & Brewer, 2013).

Old English Poems of Christ and His Saints, ed. and trans. Mary Clayton (Cambridge, MA: Harvard University Press, 2013).

Patrologiae cursus completus: series Latina, ed. J.P. Migne, 221 vols (Paris: Migne, 1844–55, 1862–5).

Pearl, in *The Poems of the Pearl Manuscript in Modern English Translation: Pearl, Cleanness, Patience, Sir Gawain and the Green Knight* (Exeter: Exeter University Press, 2008).

Pearl, ed. Sarah Stanbury (Kalamazoo, MI: Medieval Institute Publications, 2001).

The Penguin Anthology of Classical Arab Literature, ed. and trans. Robert Irwin (London: Penguin, 1999).

Peter of Abano (Pseudo-Hippocrates), *Libellus de medicorum astrologia*, trans. Petrus de Abano (Venice: Erhard Ratdolt, 1447–1527).

The Poetic Edda, trans. Carolyne Larrington (Oxford: Oxford University Press, 2014).

The Poetic Edda: A Dual-Language Edition, ed. and trans. Edward Pettit (Cambridge: Open Book Publishers, 2023).

Popol Vuh: The Definitive Edition of the Mayan Book of the Dawn of Life and the Glories of Gods and Kings, trans. Dennis Tedlock (New York: Touchstone, 1996).

The Qur'an, trans. Abdel Haleem (Oxford: Oxford University Press, 2008).

'The Riddle Ages', https://theriddleages.wordpress.com.

al-Shushtarī, Abū al-Ḥasan, *Poesía Estrófica (Cejeles Y/O Muwassahāt) Atribuida al Místico Granadino As-Sustarī Siglo XIII. d.C.*, ed. F. Corriente (Madrid: Consejo Superior de Investigaciones Cientificas, Instituto de Filologia, Departamento de Estudios Arabes, 1988).

al-Shushtarī, Abū al-Ḥasan, *Songs of Love and Devotion*, trans. Lourdes María Alvarez (Mahwah, NJ: Paulist Press, 2009).

Sir Gawain and the Green Knight, in *The Poems of the Pearl Manuscript in Modern English Translation: Pearl, Cleanness, Patience, Sir Gawain and the Green Knight* (Exeter: Exeter University Press, 2008).

Snorri Sturluson, *The Prose Edda*, trans. Jesse L. Byock (London: Penguin Classics, 2005).

Somer, John, *The Kalendarium of John Somer*, ed. Linne R. Mooney (Athens: University of Georgia Press, 1998).

To the Moon: An Anthology of Lunar Poems, ed. Carol Ann Duffy (London: Picador, 2009).

The Translator of Desires, ed. and trans. Michael Sells (Princeton, NJ: Princeton University Press, 2021).

The Wonders of the East, ed. Asa Simon Mittman and Susan M. Kim, in *Primary Sources on Monsters*, vol. 2 (Leeds: Arc Humanities Press, 2018), pp. 67–70.

Secondary Sources

Acker, Paul, 'Dwarf-Lore in *Alvíssmál*', in *The Poetic Edda: Essays on Old Norse Mythology* (New York: Routledge, 2002), pp. 213–27.

Adamson, Peter, *Al Kindi* (Oxford: Oxford University Press, 2007).

Adamson, Peter, and Richard C. Taylor, eds, *The Cambridge Companion to Arabic Philosophy* (Cambridge: Cambridge University Press, 2004).

Addas, Claude, *Quest for the Red Sulphur: The Life of Ibn ʿArabī*, trans. Peter Kingsley (Cambridge: Islamic Texts Society, 1993).

Agozzino, Maria Teresa, 'Dafydd ap Gwilym', in *The Oxford Dictionary of the Middle Ages*, ed. Robert E. Bjork (Oxford: Oxford University Press, 2010).

Akbari, Suzanne Conklin, 'The Persistence of Philology: Language and Connectivity in the Mediterranean', in *A Sea of Languages: Rethinking the Arabic Role in Medieval Literary History*, ed. Suzanne Conklin Akbari and Karla Mallette (Toronto: University of Toronto Press, 2013), pp. 3–22.

BIBLIOGRAPHY

Alamichel, Marie-Françoise, '"This Wyde World, Which That Men Seye Is Round": Movement and Meaning in *The Franklin's Tale*', *Etudes anglaises* 67:3 (2014), 259–73.

Alter, Joseph S., 'Heaps of Health, Metaphysical Fitness: Ayurveda and the Ontology of Good Health in Medical Anthropology', *Current Anthropology* 40:1 (1999), 43–66.

Alvarez, Lourdes María, '*Calila e Dimna*', in *The Oxford Dictionary of the Middle Ages*, ed. Robert E. Bjork (Oxford: Oxford University Press, 2010).

Andrén, Anders, 'Sun and Moon', in *The Pre-Christian Religions of the North: History and Structures*, ed. Jens Peter Schjødt, John Lindow, and Anders Andrén (Turnhout: Brepols, 2020), pp. 1465–80.

'Art of the Buddhist Relic Online Exhibition', https://exhibitions.library.vanderbilt. edu/hart3164w-art-budhist-relic.

Attlee, James, *Nocturne: A Journey in Search of Moonlight* (London: Hamish Hamilton, 2011).

Austin, Greta, 'Marvellous People or Marvellous Races? Race and the Anglo-Saxon *Wonders of the East*', in *Marvels, Monsters and Miracles: Studies in the Medieval and Early Modern Imagination*, ed. Timothy S. Jones and David A. Sprunger (Kalamazoo, MI: Medieval Institute Publications, 2002), pp. 25–51.

Barasch, Moshe, *Gestures of Despair in Medieval and Early Renaissance Art* (New York: New York University Press, 1976).

Baring-Gould, S., *Curious Myths of the Middle Ages* (London: Rivingtons, 1873).

Barker, Peter, 'John of Glogów', in *De sphaera of Johannes de Sacrobosco in the Early Modern Period: The Authors of the Commentaries*, ed. Matteo Valleriani (Cham: Springer Nature, 2020), pp. 137–60.

Bartoszewicz, Agnieszka, *Urban Literacy in Late Medieval Poland* (Turnhout: Brepols, 2017).

Bazaz, Abir, and Alexandra Verini, eds, *Gender and Medieval Mysticism from India to Europe* (London: Routledge, 2023).

Beckwith, John, *Early Medieval Art: Carolingian, Ottonian, Romanesque* (London: Thames & Hudson, 1964).

Belting, Hans, *Florence and Baghdad: Renaissance Art and Arab Science*, trans. Deborah Lucas Schneider (Cambridge, MA: Belknap Press, 2011).

Bermann, Sandra, and Catherine Porter, eds, *A Companion to Translation Studies* (Malden, MA: John Wiley & Sons, 2014).

Berti, Enrico, 'La classificazione aristotelica delle scienze in Pietro d'Abano', *Trans/Form/Ação* 37:3 (2014), 17–32.

Bitterli, Dieter, *Say What I Am Called: The Old English Riddles of the Exeter Book and the Anglo-Latin Riddle Tradition* (Toronto: University of Toronto Press, 2009).

Black, Deborah L., 'The "Imaginative Syllogism" in Arabic Philosophy: A Medieval Contribution to the Philosophical Study of Metaphor', *Mediaeval Studies* 51 (1989), 242–67.

Bloom, Harold, *How to Read and Why* (London: Fourth Estate, 2000).

Boehrer, Bruce, Molly Hand, and Brian Massumi, eds, *Animals, Animality, and Literature* (Cambridge: Cambridge University Press, 2018).

Bowers, John M., *An Introduction to the Gawain-Poet* (Gainesville: University Press of Florida, 2013).

Braswell, Laurel, 'The Moon and Medicine in Chaucer's Time', *Studies in the Age of Chaucer* 8 (1986), 145–56.

Bruhn, Mark, 'Art, Anxiety, & Alchemy in the *Canon's Yeoman's Tale*', *Chaucer Review* 33 (1999), 288–315.

Brunner, Bernard, *The Moon: A Brief History* (New Haven, CT: Yale University Press, 2010).

Bryan, Elizabeth J., 'Astronomy Translated: *Caput Draconis* and the Pendragon Star in Geoffrey of Monmouth, Wace, and Laȝamon', *Arthuriana* 26:1 (2016), 141–63.

Bryant, Edwin F., ed., *Krishna: A Sourcebook* (New York: Oxford University Press, 2007).

Burnett, Charles, 'Arabic into Latin', in *The Cambridge Companion to Arabic Philosophy*, ed. Peter Adamson and Richard C. Taylor (Cambridge: Cambridge University Press, 2004), pp. 370–404.

Burnett, Charles, 'The Coherence of the Arabic–Latin Translation Program in Toledo in the Twelfth Century', *Science in Context* 14:1–2 (2001), 249–88.

Busbee, Mark Bradshaw, 'A Paradise Full of Monsters: India in the Old English Imagination', *LATCH* I (2008), 51–72.

Campi, L., and S. Simonetta, eds, *Before and After Wyclif: Sources and Textual Influence* (Basel: Fédération Internationale des Instituts d'Etudes Médiévales, 2022).

Campion, Nicholas, *A History of Western Astrology*, vol. 2, *The Medieval and Modern Worlds* (London: Bloomsbury, 2013).

Cassell, Anthony, '"Luna est Ecclesia: Dante and the "Two Great Lights"', *Dante Society of America* 119 (2001), 1–26.

Cerulli, Anthony Michael, *Somatic Lessons: Narrating Patienthood and Illness in Indian Medical Literature* (Albany: State University of New York Press, 2012).

Cesario, Marilina, '*Fyrenne Dracan* in the *Anglo-Saxon Chronicle*', in *Textiles, Text, Intertext: Essays in Honour of Gale R. Owen-Crocker*, ed. Maren Clegg Hyer (Woodbridge: Boydell & Brewer, 2016), pp. 153–70.

Chang, Kang-I Sun, and Stephen Owen, eds, *The Cambridge History of Chinese Literature*, vol. 1, to 1375 (Cambridge: Cambridge University Press, 2010).

Chardonnens, László Sándor, *Anglo-Saxon Prognostics 900–1100: Study and Texts* (Leiden: Brill, 2007).

Coley, David, *Death and the Pearl-Maiden: Plague, Poetry England* (Columbus: Ohio State University Press, 2019).

Collette, Carolyn P., *Rethinking Chaucer's Legend of Good Women* (Woodbridge: Boydell & Brewer, 2014).

Conklin Akbari, Suzanne, and Karla Mallette, eds, *A Sea of Languages: Rethinking the Arabic Role in Medieval Literary History* (Toronto: University of Toronto Press, 2013).

Cowen, Janet M., 'Chaucer's *Legend of Good Women*: Structure and Tone', *Studies in Philology* 82:4 (1985), 416–36.

Cupane, Carolina, and Bettina Krönung, eds, *Fictional Storytelling in the Medieval Eastern Mediterranean and Beyond* (Leiden: Brill, 2016).

Dean, Ruth J., with Maureen B.M. Boulton, ed., *Anglo-Norman Literature: A Guide to Texts and Manuscripts* (London: Anglo-Norman Text Society, 1999).

Dmytryshyn, Basil, *Medieval Russia: A Source Book, 850–1700* (London: Harcourt Brace Jovanovich, 1991).

Elgood, Cyril, *A Medical History of Persia and the Eastern Caliphate: From the Earliest Times Until the Year AD 1932* (Cambridge: Cambridge University Press, 1951).

El-Zein, Amira, *Islam, Arabs, and the Intelligent World of the Jinn* (Syracuse, NY: Syracuse University Press, 2009).

Erler, Mary C., and Maryanne Kowaleski, eds, *Gendering the Master Narrative: Women and Power in the Middle Ages* (Ithaca, NY: Cornell University Press, 2003).

Estes, Heide, 'Wonders and Wisdom: Anglo-Saxons and the East', *English Studies* 91 (2010), 360–73.

Fabricius, Johannes, *Alchemy: The Medieval Alchemists and Their Royal Art* (Copenhagen: Rosenkilde and Bagger, 1976).

Friedman, John Block, 'The Marvels-of-the-East Tradition in Anglo-Saxon Art', in *Sources of Anglo-Saxon Culture*, ed. Paul E. Szarmach with the assistance of Virginia Darrow Oggins (Kalamazoo, MI: Medieval Institute Publications, 1986), pp. 319–41.

Fu, Rebecca Shuang, 'Women's Literary Practices in Late Medieval China (600–1000)' (unpublished dissertation, University of Pennsylvania, 2015).

Fulton, Helen, *Dafydd ap Gwilym and the European Context* (Cardiff: University of Wales Press, 1989).

Gao, Yugong, 'Cranes and People in China: Culture, Science, and Conservation' (unpublished dissertation, University of Texas at Austin, 2001).

Gasper, Giles E.M., and Brian K. Tanner, ' "The Moon Quivered like a Snake": A Medieval Chronicler, Lunar Explosions, and a Puzzle for Modern Interpretation', *Endeavour* 44:4 (2020), 1–9.

Ghazoul, Feria J., '*Majnun Layla:* Translation as Transposition', in *A Companion to Translation Studies*, ed. Sandra Bermann and Catherine Porter (Malden, MA: John Wiley & Sons, 2014), pp. 375–87.

Ghosh, Kantik, 'After Wyclif: Philosophy, Polemics and Translation in *The English Wycliffite Sermons*', in *Before and After Wyclif: Sources and Textual Influence*, ed. L. Campi and S. Simonetta (Basel: Fédération Internationale des Instituts d'Etudes Médiévales, 2022), pp. 167–86.

Gillespie, Vincent, '*Ethice Subponitur?* The Imaginative Syllogism and the Idea of the Poetic', in *Medieval Thought Experiments: Poetry, Hypothesis, and Experience in the European Middle Ages*, ed. Philip Knox, Jonathan Morton, and Daniel Reeve (Turnhout: Brepols, 2018), pp. 297–327.

Goldie, Peter, ed., *The Oxford Handbook of Philosophy of Emotion* (Oxford: Oxford University Press, 2010).

Goldstein, Bernard R., 'Colors of Eclipses in Medieval Hebrew Astronomical Tables', *Aelph* 5 (2005), 11–34.

Goodman, L.E., *Avicenna* (London: Routledge, 1992).

Gray, Douglas, ed., *The Oxford Companion to Chaucer* (Oxford: Oxford University Press, 2003; online 2005).

Green, Tamara M., *The City of the Moon God: Religious Traditions of Harran* (Leiden: Brill, 1992).

Gruber, Christiane, ed., *The Moon: A Voyage through Time* (Toronto: Aga Khan Museum, 2019).

Gruffydd, R. Geraint, 'Gruffudd Gryg', *Oxford Dictionary of National Biography*, Online, https://www.oxforddnb.com (2004).

Hammond, Marlé, *A Dictionary of Arabic Literary Terms and Devices* (Oxford: Oxford University Press, 2018).

Hansen, Kelli, 'Johannes de Sacrobosco and the Sphere of the Universe', https://library.missouri.edu/news/special-collections/johannes-de-sacrobosco (University of Missouri Library, 2014).

Harlan-Haughey, Sarah, 'The Circle, The Maze, and the Echo: Sublunary Recurrence and Performance in Chaucer's *Legend of Ariadne*', *Chaucer Review* 52:3 (2017), 341–60.

Hatt, Cecilia A., *God and the Gawain-Poet: Theology and Genre in Pearl, Cleanness, Patience, and Sir Gawain and the Green Knight* (Cambridge: D.S. Brewer, 2015).

Hawley, John Stratton, *A Storm of Songs: India and the Idea of the Bhakti Movement* (Cambridge, MA: Harvard University Press, 2015).

Heng, Geraldine, 'A Global Middle Ages', in *A Handbook of Middle English Studies*, ed. Marion Turner (Hoboken, NJ: John Wiley & Sons, 2013), pp. 413–29.

Heng, Geraldine, *The Global Middle Ages: An Introduction* (Cambridge: Cambridge University Press, 2021).

Herschel, William, 'The Discovery of Uranus', https://www.rmg.co.uk/stories/blog/astronomy/discovery-uranus.

Hikuroa, Daniel, 'Mātauranga Māori: The ūkaipō of Knowledge in New Zealand', *Journal of the Royal Society of New Zealand* 47:1 (2017), 5–10.

Hillgardner, Holly, *Longing and Letting Go: Christian and Hindu Practices of Passionate Non-Attachment* (New York: Oxford University Press, 2016).

Hornbeck, J. Patrick, and Michael van Dussen, eds, *Europe after Wyclif* (New York: Fordham University Press, 2016).

Hsy, Jonathan, *Antiracist Medievalisms: From 'Yellow Peril' to Black Lives Matter* (Leeds: Arc Humanities Press, 2021).

Hyer, Maren Clegg, ed., *Textiles, Text, Intertext: Essays in Honour of Gale R. Owen-Crocker* (Woodbridge: Boydell & Brewer, 2016), pp. 153–70.

Idel, Moshe, and Bernard McGinn, eds, *Mystical Union in Judaism, Christianity, and Islam: An Ecumenical Dialogue* (1996; repr. London: Bloomsbury, 2016).

Illig, Jennifer, 'Preparing for Easter: Sermons on the Eucharist in English Wycliffite Sermons', in *Europe after Wyclif*, ed. J. Patrick Hornbeck and Michael van Dussen (New York: Fordham University Press, 2016), pp. 247–64.

Irwin, Robert, ed., *The New Cambridge History of Islam*, vol. 4, *Islamic Cultures and Societies to the Eighteenth Century* (Cambridge: Cambridge University Press, 2010).

Isaacson, Nathaniel, 'Locating Kexue Xiangsheng (Science Crosstalk) in Relation to the Selective Tradition of Chinese Science Fiction', *Osiris* 34:1 (2019), 139–57.

Jagot, Shazia, 'Averroes, Islam, and Heterodoxy in the Spanish Chapel "Triumph of St Thomas Aquinas"', *Interfaces: A Journal of Medieval European Literature* 6 (2019), 7–32.

Jagot, Shazia, 'Chaucer and Ibn al-Haytham (Alhacen): *Perspectiva*, Arabic Mathematics, and the Acts of Looking', *Studies in the Age of Chaucer* 44 (2022), 27–61.

Jeong-hee, Ke, and Justin M. Byron-Davies, 'The Role of Kisaeng *Sijo* Poets in Medieval Korean Literature', in *Women's Literary Cultures in the Global Middle Ages: Speaking Internationally*, ed. Kathryn Loveridge, Liz Herbert McAvoy, Sue Niebrzydowski, and Vicki Kay Price (Cambridge: D.S. Brewer, 2023), pp. 103–22.

Johnson, David, and Elaine Treharne, eds, *Readings in Medieval Texts: Interpreting Old and Middle English Literature* (Oxford: Oxford University Press, 2005).

Jones, E.A., 'Ceremonies of Enclosure: Rite, Rhetoric and Reality', in *Rhetoric of the Anchorhold: Space, Place and Body within the Discourses of Enclosure*, ed. Liz Herbert McAvoy (Cardiff: University of Wales Press, 2008), pp. 34–49.

Jones, Sarah Rees, ed., *Learning and Literacy in Medieval England and Abroad* (Turnhout: Brepols, 2003).

Jones, Timothy S., and David A. Sprunger, eds, *Marvels, Monsters and Miracles: Studies in the Medieval and Early Modern Imagination* (Kalamazoo, MI: Medieval Institute Publications, 2002).

Jorgensen, Alice, Frances McCormack, and Jonathan Wilcox, eds, *Anglo-Saxon Emotions: Reading the Heart in Old English Language, Literature, and Culture* (Farnham: Ashgate, 2015).

Juste, David, Benno van Dalen, Dag Nikolaus Hasse, and Charles Burnett, eds, *Ptolemy's Science of the Stars in the Middle Ages* (Turnhout: Brepols, 2020).

Kalin, Ibrahim, ed., *The Oxford Encyclopedia of Philosophy, Science, and Technology in Islam* (Oxford: Oxford University Press, 2014).

al-Karaki, Balqis, 'Dissimilar Premises, Similar Conclusions: On the Partial Rationality of Metaphor – A Comparative Study', *Journal of Near Eastern Studies* 70:1 (2011), 81–100.

Karateke, Hakan T., H. Erdem Çipa, and Helga Anetshofer, eds, *Disliking Others: Loathing, Hostility, and Distrust in Premodern Ottoman Lands* (Boston, MA: Academic Studies Press, 2018).

Kay, Sarah, *Animal Skins and the Reading Self in Medieval Latin and French Bestiaries* (Chicago, IL: University of Chicago Press, 2017).

Keene, Donald, 'The Tale of the Bamboo Cutter', *Monumenta Nipponica* 11:4 (1956), 329–55.

Kesling, Emily, *Medical Texts in Anglo-Saxon Literary Culture* (Cambridge: D.S. Brewer, 2020).

Khalaf, Omar, 'The Old English *Alexander's Letter to Aristotle*: Monsters and Hybrids in the Service of Exemplarity', *English Studies* (2013), 659–67.

Kim, Susan M., '"If One Who Is Loved Is Not Present, a Letter May Be Embraced Instead": Death and the *Letter of Alexander to Aristotle*', *Journal of English and Germanic Philology* 109 (2010), 33–51.

King, Peter, 'Emotions in Medieval Thought', in *The Oxford Handbook of Philosophy of Emotion*, ed. Peter Goldie (Oxford: Oxford University Press, 2010), pp. 167–87.

Klein-Franke, Felix, *Iatromathematics in Islam: A Study on Yuhanna Ibn aṣ-Ṣalt's Book on Astrological Medicine: Edited for the First Time* (Hildesheim: Georg Olms Verlag, 1984).

Knox, Philip, Jonathan Morton, and Daniel Reeve, eds, *Medieval Thought Experiments: Poetry, Hypothesis, and Experience in the European Middle Ages* (Turnhout: Brepols, 2018).

Knysh, Alexander, *Islamic Mysticism: A Short History* (Leiden: Brill, 2000).

Knysh, Alexander, 'Sufism', in *The New Cambridge History of Islam*, vol. 4, *Islamic Cultures and Societies to the Eighteenth Century*, ed. Robert Irwin (Cambridge: Cambridge University Press, 2010), pp. 60–104.

Knysh, Alexander, 'Waḥdat al-Wujūd', in *The Oxford Encyclopedia of Philosophy, Science, and Technology in Islam*, ed. Ibrahim Kalin (Oxford: Oxford University Press, 2014).

Kren, Claudia, 'The Medieval Man in the Moon', *Mediaevalia* 7 (1981), 221–38.

Krönung, Bettina, 'The Wisdom of the Beasts: The Arabic Book of Kalīla and Dimna and the Byzantine Book of Stephanites and Ichnelates', trans. Angela Kinney, in *Fictional Storytelling in the Medieval Eastern Mediterranean and Beyond*, ed. Carolina Cupane and Bettina Krönung (Leiden: Brill, 2016), pp. 427–60.

Lacy, Norris J., and Joan T. Grimbert, eds, *A Companion to Chrétien de Troyes* (Cambridge: D.S. Brewer, 2005).

Laffin, Christina, 'Medieval Women's Diaries', in *The Cambridge History of Japanese Literature*, ed. Haruo Shirane and Tomi Suzuki with David Lurie (Cambridge: Cambridge University Press, 2016), pp. 268–79.

Laffin, Christina, *Rewriting Medieval Japanese Women: Politics, Personality and Literary Production in the Life of Nun Abutsu* (Honolulu: University of Hawai'i Press).

Lambert, Ladina Bezzola, *Imagining the Unimaginable: The Poetics of Early Modern Astronomy* (Leiden: Brill, 2022).

Lavinsky, David, 'Knowynge Cristes Speche: Gender and Interpretive Authority in the Wycliffite Sermon Cycle', *Journal of Medieval Religious Cultures* 38:1 (2012), 60–83.

Lazikani, A.S., 'The Broken Moon: Lunar Semiotics in *Ancrene Wisse* and *Pearl*', *Chaucer Review* (forthcoming).

Lazikani, A.S., *Emotion in Christian and Islamic Contemplative Texts: Cry of the Turtledove* (New York: Palgrave Macmillan, 2021).

Lazikani, A.S., 'The Man in the Moon, An Anonymous Medieval Lyric', https://www.english.ox.ac.uk/article/the-moon-an-anonymous-medieval-lyric.

Le Goff, Jacques, with Jean-Maurice de Montremy, *My Quest for the Middle Ages*, trans. Richard Veasey (Edinburgh: Edinburgh University Press, 2003).

Leeming, David, *A Dictionary of Asian Mythology* (Oxford: Oxford University Press, 2002).

Legge, Dominica M., *Anglo-Norman Literature and Its Background* (Oxford: Clarendon Press, 1963).

Leisawitz, Daniel, 'Ironic Geography in Ariosto's *Orlando furioso*', *Renaissance Quarterly* 75:2 (2022), 367–402.

Lewis, C.S., *The Discarded Image: An Introduction to Medieval and Renaissance Literature* (1964; repr. Cambridge: Cambridge University Press, 2012).

Lindow, John, 'Poetry, Dwarfs, and Gods: Understanding *Alvíssmál*', in *Learning and Understanding in the Old Norse World: Essays in Honour of Margaret Clunies Ross*, ed. Judy Quinn, Kate Heslop, and Tarrin Wills (Turnhout: Brepols, 2007), pp. 285–303.

Liuzza, Roy Michael, 'Anglo-Saxon Prognostics in Context: A Survey and Handlist of Manuscripts', *Anglo-Saxon England* 30 (2001), 181–230.

Louth, Andrew, ed., *The Oxford Dictionary of the Christian Church* (Oxford: Oxford University Press, 2022).

Loveridge, Kathryn, Liz Herbert McAvoy, Sue Niebrzydowski, and Vicki Kay Price, eds, *Women's Literary Cultures in the Global Middle Ages: Speaking Internationally* (Cambridge: D.S. Brewer, 2023).

Lucas, Angela, 'Astronomy, Astrology and Magic in Chaucer's *Franklin's Tale*', *Maynooth Review* 8 (1983), 5–16.

Mac Carthy, Ita, 'Ariosto the Lunar Traveller', *Modern Language Review* 104:1 (2009), 71–82.

McAvoy, Liz Herbert, ed., *Anchoritic Traditions of Medieval Europe* (Woodbridge: Boydell, 2010).

McAvoy, Liz Herbert, ed., *Rhetoric of the Anchorhold: Space, Place and Body within the Discourses of Enclosure* (Cardiff: University of Wales Press, 2008).

McAvoy, Liz Herbert, and Sue Niebrzydowski, 'Introduction: Medieval Women's Literary Cultures and Thinking beyond the Local', in *Women's Literary Cultures in the Global Middle Ages: Speaking Internationally*, ed. Kathryn Loveridge, Liz Herbert McAvoy, Sue Niebrzydowski, and Vicki Kay Price (Cambridge: D.S. Brewer, 2023), pp. 1–20.

McCormack, Frances, 'Those Bloody Trees: The Affectivity of *Christ*', in *Anglo-Saxon Emotions: Reading the Heart in Old English Language, Literature, and Culture*, ed. Alice Jorgensen, Frances McCormack, and Jonathan Wilcox (Farnham: Ashgate, 2015), pp. 143–61.

McCormick, Betsy, Leah Schwebel, and Lynn Shutters, 'Introduction: Looking Forward, Looking Back on the *Legend of Good Women*', *Chaucer Review* 52:1 (2017), 3–11.

McCrae, Niall, *The Moon and Madness* (Exeter: Imprint Academic, 2011).

McDonald, Craig, 'The Perversion of Law in Robert Henryson's Fable of the *Fox, The Wolf, and the Husbandman*', *Medium Ævum* 49:2 (1980), 244–53.

McFadden, Brian, 'The Social Context of Narrative Disruption in *The Letter of Alexander to Aristotle*', *Anglo-Saxon England* 30 (2001), 91–114.

McGrath, William A., 'Vessel Examination in the Medicine of the Moon King', in *Buddhism and Medicine: An Anthology of Premodern Sources*, ed. C. Pierce Salguero (New York: Columbia University Press, 2017), pp. 501–13.

Mallette, Karla, *European Modernity and the Arab Mediterranean: Toward a New Philology and a Counter-Orientalism* (Philadelphia: University of Pennsylvania Press, 2010).

Mallette, Karla, *Lives of the Great Languages: Arabic and Latin in the Medieval Mediterranean* (Chicago, IL: University of Chicago Press, 2022).

Marroun, Marianne, '*Kalila Wa Dimna*: Inception, Appropriation, and Transmimesis', *Comparative Literature Studies* 48:4 (2011), 512–40.

Marshall, Anne, 'Medieval Wall Painting in the English Parish Church', https://reeddesign.co.uk/paintedchurch/index.htm.

Martin, Janet, *Medieval Russia, 980–1584* (Cambridge: Cambridge University Press, 2007).

Martin, Nancy M., 'Invoking Mirabai: Elision and Illumination in the Global Study of Women Mystics', in *Gender and Medieval Mysticism from India to Europe*, ed. Abir Bazaz and Alexandra Verini (London: Routledge, 2023), pp. 170–88.

Martin, Nancy M., 'Rajasthan: Mirabai and Her Poetry', in *Krishna: A Sourcebook*, ed. Edwin F. Bryant (New York: Oxford University Press, 2007), pp. 241–54.

Martinez, Chloe, 'The Autobiographical Pose: Life Narrative and Religious Transformation in the Mirabai Tradition', *South Asia* 41:2 (2018), 418–34.

Martins, Roberto de Andrade, 'André do Avelar and the Teaching of Sacrobosco's *Sphaera* at the University of Coimbra', in *De sphaera of Johannes de Sacrobosco in the Early Modern Period: The Authors of the Commentaries*, ed. Matteo Valleriani (Cham: Springer Nature, 2020), pp. 313–58.

'Medieval Manuscripts in Oxford Libraries', https://medieval.bodleian.ox.ac.uk.

'Medieval Disability Glossary', https://medievaldisabilityglossary.hcommons.org.

Menocal, María Rosa, *The Arabic Role in Medieval Literature: A Forgotten Heritage* (Philadelphia: University of Pennsylvania Press, 2004).

Menocal, María Rosa, Raymond P. Scheindlin, and Michael Anthony Sells, eds, *The Literature of Al-Andalus* (Cambridge: Cambridge University Press, 2000).

Mogford, Neville, 'Moon and Tide: A New Interpretation of Exeter Riddle 22 Based on the Medieval Science of Computus', *Review of English Studies* 73 (2022), 201–18.

Montgomery, Scott L., *The Moon and the Western Imagination* (Tucson: University of Arizona Press, 1999).

Moor, Bilha, 'The Jew, the Orthodox Christian, and the European in Ottoman Eyes, ca. 1550–1700', in *Disliking Others: Loathing, Hostility, and Distrust in Premodern Ottoman Lands*, ed. Hakan T. Karateke, H. Erdem Çipa, and Helga Anetshofer (Boston, MA: Academic Studies Press, 2018), pp. 75–106.

Morrison, Elizabeth, and Larisa Grollemond, *Book of Beasts: The Bestiary in the Medieval World* (Los Angeles: J. Paul Getty Museum, 2019).

Mostow, Joshua S., 'Early Heian Court Tales', in *The Cambridge History of Japanese Literature*, ed. Haruo Shirane and Tomi Suzuki with David Lurie (Cambridge: Cambridge University Press, 2016), pp. 121–8.

Mulder-Bakker, Anneke B., *Lives of the Anchoresses: The Rise of the Urban Recluse in Medieval Europe*, trans. Myra Heerspink Scholz (Philadelphia: University of Pennsylvania Press, 2005).

Mulder-Bakker, Anneke B., *Living Saints of the Thirteenth Century: The Lives of Yvette, Anchoress of Huy; Juliana of Cornillon, Author of the Corpus Christi Feast; and Margaret the Lame, Anchoress of Magdeburg* (Turnhout: Brepols, 2011).

Murphy, Patrick J., *Unriddling the Exeter Riddles* (University Park, PA: Penn State University Press, 2011).

Navarro, Tayra M.C. Lanunza, 'Pedro Sánchez Ciruelo. A Commentary on Sacrobosco's *Tractatus de sphaera with a Defense of Astrology*', in *De sphaera of Johannes de Sacrobosco in the Early Modern Period: The Authors of the Commentaries*, ed. Matteo Valleriani (Cham: Springer Nature, 2020), pp. 53–89.

Nedkvitne, Arnved, *The Social Consequences of Literacy in Medieval Scandinavia* (Turnhout: Brepols, 2004).

Nenci, E., 'Francesco Capuano di Manfredonia', in *De sphaera of Johannes de Sacrobosco in the Early Modern Period: The Authors of the Commentaries*, ed. Matteo Valleriani (Cham: Springer Nature, 2020), pp. 91–100.

Netton, Richard, *Islam, Christianity, and the Realms of the Miraculous* (Edinburgh: Edinburgh University Press, 2018).

ní Mheallaigh, Karen, *The Moon in the Greek and Roman Imagination: Myth, Literature, Science and Philosophy* (Cambridge: Cambridge University Press, 2020).

ní Mheallaigh, Karen, *Reading Fiction with Lucian: Fakes, Freaks, and Hyperreality* (Cambridge: Cambridge University Press, 2014).

Nuttall, Jennifer, *Troilus and Criseyde: A Reader's Guide* (Cambridge: Cambridge University Press, 2012).

O'Boyle, Cornelius, 'Astrology and Medicine in Later Medieval England: The Calendars of John Somer and Nicholas of Lynn', *Sudhoffs Archiv* 89:1 (2005), 1–22.

O'Desky, Leona, 'Chaucer's *Troilus and Criseyde*: Astrology and the Transference of Power' (unpublished dissertation, Rutgers University, 1974).

Okada, H. Richard, *Figures of Resistance: Language, Poetry, and Narrating in the Tale of the Genji and Other Mid-Heian Texts* (Durham, NC: Duke University Press, 1991).

O'Keeffe, Katherine O'Brien, *Stealing Obedience: Narratives of Agency and Identity in Later Anglo-Saxon England* (Toronto: University of Toronto Press, 2012).

Owen, Stephen, 'The Cultural Tang (650–1020)', in *The Cambridge History of Chinese Literature*, vol. 1, to 1375, ed. Kang-I Sun Chang and Stephen Owen (Cambridge: Cambridge University Press, 2010), pp. 286–380.

Pan, Yanlin, 'Paradigm Shifts, Iconographic Changes: The Moon Goddess Chang'e and Other Beauties in Paintings of the Mid Ming' (unpublished dissertation, University of California Davis, 2013).

Pang, Hannah, *The Moon* (London: 360 Degrees, 2018).

Paper, Jordan, *Through the Earth Darkly: Female Spirituality in Comparative Perspective* (London: Bloomsbury, 2018).

Parker, Robert, 'Selene', in *Oxford Classical Dictionary* (Oxford: Oxford University Press, 2024).

Partridge, Esmé L.K., 'The Celestial "Polished Mirror": The Mystical Dimension of the Moon According to Muḥyddin Ibn ʿArabī', *Journal of the Muḥyddin Ibn ʿArabī Society* 68 (2020), 103–16.

Pearn, John, 'Master John of Arderne (1307–1380): A Founder of Modern Surgery', *ANZ Journal of Surgery* 82:1–2 (2012), 46–51.

Perillo, Kate, 'The Limits of *Ongietenisse*: Translating Global Imagination in the Old English *Letter of Alexander to Aristotle*', *Parergon* 35:2 (2018), 67–89.

Pormann, Peter, and Emilie Savage-Smith, *Medieval Islamic Medicine* (Edinburgh: Edinburgh University Press, 2022).

Porta, Miquel, and John M. Last, eds, *A Dictionary of Public Health* (Oxford: Oxford University Press, 2018).

Préaux, Claire, *La Lune dans la pensée grecque* (Brussels: Palais des Académies, 1973).

Putter, Ad, *An Introduction to the Gawain-Poet* (London: Longman, 1996).

Reischauer, Edwin O., 'The Izayoi Nikki (1277–1280)', *Harvard Journal of Asiatic Studies* 10:3–4 (1947), 255–387.

Richardson, Kristina, *Roma in the Medieval Islamic World: Literacy, Culture and Migration* (London: I.B. Tauris, 2021).

Ridgeon, Lloyd, ed., *The Cambridge Companion to Sufism* (Cambridge: Cambridge University Press, 2014).

Ridgeon, Lloyd, 'Mysticism in Medieval Sufism', in *The Cambridge Companion to Sufism*, ed. Lloyd Ridgeon (Cambridge: Cambridge University Press, 2014), pp. 125–49.

Rissanen, Matti, 'Colloquial and Comic Elements in "The Man in the Moon"', *Neuphilologische Mitteilungen* 81:1 (1980), 42–6.

Riva, M.A., L. Tremolizzo, M. Spicci, C. Ferrarese, G. De Vito, G.C. Cesana, and V.A. Sironi, 'The Disease of the Moon: The Linguistic and Pathological Evolution of the English Term "Lunatic"', *Journal of the History of the Neurosciences* 20:1 (2011), 65–73.

Roberts, Mere, Frank Weko, and Liliana Clarke, 'Maramataka: The Maori Moon Calendar', *AERU*, Research Report no. 238 (Canterbury: Lincoln University, 2006).

Ross, Ellen M., *The Grief of God: Images of the Suffering Jesus in Late Medieval England* (Oxford: Oxford University Press, 1997).

Rubin, Miri, *Corpus Christi: The Eucharist in Late Medieval Culture* (Cambridge: Cambridge University Press, 1991).

Rudd, Gillian, 'Lions, Mice, and Learning from Animals in Henryson's *Fables*', in *Animals, Animality, and Literature*, ed. Bruce Boehrer, Molly Hand, and Brian Massumi (Cambridge: Cambridge University Press, 2018).

Safi, Omid, '"The Real Intention Was My Beloved": The Moon in Persian Sufi Poetry', in *The Moon: A Voyage through Time*, ed. Christiane Gruber (Toronto: Aga Khan Museum, 2019), pp. 35–44.

Saif, Liana, 'Homocentric Science in a Heliocentric Universe', in *Astrology in Time and Place: Cross-Cultural Questions in the History of Astrology*, ed. Nicholas Campion and Dorian Gieseler Greenbaum (Newcastle-upon-Tyne: Cambridge Scholars Publishing, 2015).

Salguero, C. Pierce, ed., *Buddhism and Medicine: An Anthology of Premodern Sources* (New York: Columbia University Press, 2017).

Saparmin, Norzakiah binti, 'History of Astrology and Astronomy in Islamic Medicine', *International Journal of Academic Research in Business and Social Sciences* 9:9 (2019), 282–96.

Schimmel, Annemarie, *And Muhammad Is His Messenger: The Veneration of the Prophet in Islamic Piety* (Chapel Hill: University of North Carolina Press, 1985).

Schjødt, Jens Peter, John Lindow, and Anders Andrén, eds, *The Pre-Christian Religions of the North: History and Structures* (Turnhout: Brepols, 2020).

Schnapp, Jeffrey T., 'The Chatter of People and Things', *Modern Language Quarterly* 72:3 (2011), 319–39.

Schove, Justin D., *Chronology of Eclipses and Comets, AD 1–1000* (Woodbridge: Boydell Press, 1984).

Schreiber, Mordecai, *The Shengold Jewish Encyclopedia* (Rockville, MD: Schreiber Publishing, 2007).

Schuurman, Anne, 'Pity and Poetics in Chaucer's *Legend of Good Women*', *PMLA* 130:5 (2015), 1302–17.

Sells, Michael, 'Bewildered Tongue: The Semantics of Mystical Union in Islam', in *Mystical Union in Judaism, Christianity, and Islam: An Ecumenical Dialogue*, ed. Moshe Idel and Bernard McGinn (1996; repr. London: Bloomsbury, 2016), pp. 87–124.

Sethi, V.K., *Mira: The Divine Lover*, second edition (Dera Baba Jaimal Singh: Radha Soami Satsang Beas, 1988).

Shirane, Haruo, and Tomi Suzuki with David Lurie, eds, *The Cambridge History of Japanese Literature* (Cambridge: Cambridge University Press, 2016).

Silverblatt, Irene, *Moon, Sun, Witches* (Princeton, NJ: Princeton University Press, 1987).

Smith, William H., 'John of Sacrobosco', in *The Oxford Dictionary of the Middle Ages*, ed. Robert E. Bjork (Oxford: Oxford University Press, 2010).

Soper, Harriet, *The Life Course in Old English Poetry* (Cambridge: Cambridge University Press, 2023).

Stephenson, F.R., L.V. Morrison, and C.Y. Hohenkerk, 'Measurement of the Earth's Rotation: 720 BC to AD 2015', *Proceedings: Mathematical, Physical and Engineering Sciences* 472:2196 (2016), 1–26.

Stephenson, F.R., and Said S. Said, 'Records of Lunar Eclipses in Medieval Arabic Chronicles', *Bulletin of the School of Oriental and African Studies, University of London* 60:1 (1997), 1–34.

Stockdale, Jonathan, *Imagining Exile in Heian Japan: Banishment in Law, Literature, and Cult* (Honolulu: University of Hawai'i Press, 2015).

Stokes, M., 'The Moon in Leo in Book V of *Troilus and Criseyde*', *Chaucer Review* 17:2 (1982), 116–29.

Strickland, Debra Higgs, ed., *The Mark of the Beast: The Medieval Bestiary in Art, Life, and Literature* (New York: Garland, 1999).

Strickland, Debra Higgs, *Medieval Bestiaries: Text, Image, Ideology* (Cambridge: Cambridge University Press, 1995).

Szarmach, Paul E., with the assistance of Virginia Darrow Oggins, eds, *Sources of Anglo-Saxon Culture* (Kalamazoo, MI: Medieval Institute Publications, 1986).

Taavitsainen, Irma, *Middle English Lunaries: A Study of the Genre* (Helsinki: Société Néophilologique, 1988).

Talattof, Kamran, *Nezami Ganjavi and Classical Persian Literature: Demystifying the Mystic* (Cham: Palgrave Macmillan, 2022).

Talattof, Kamran, and Jerome W. Clinton, eds, *The Poetry of Nizam Ganjavi: Knowledge, Love, and Rhetoric* (New York: Palgrave, 2000).

Thorndike, Lynn, *A History of Magic and Experimental Science* (New York: Columbia University Press, 1923).

Treharne, Elaine, 'The Context of Medieval Literature', in *Readings in Medieval Texts: Interpreting Old and Middle English Literature*, ed. David Johnson and Elaine Treharne (Oxford: Oxford University Press, 2005), pp. 7–14.

Turner, Marion, 'Illness Narratives in the Later Middle Ages: Arderne, Chaucer, and Hoccleve', *Journal of Medieval and Early Modern Studies* 46 (2016), 61–87.

Twitchett, Denis C., ed., *The Cambridge History of China*, vol. 3, *Sui and T'ang China, 589–906 AD, Part One* (Cambridge: Cambridge University Press, 1979).

Ullmann, Manfred, *Islamic Medicine* (Edinburgh: Edinburgh University Press, 2008).

Uri, John, '175 Years Ago: Astronomers Discover Neptune, the Eighth Planet', https://www.nasa.gov/history/175-years-ago-astronomers-discover-neptune-the-eighth-planet/#:~:text=On%20the%20night%20of%20Sept,orbit%20of%20the%20planet%20Uranus.

Usó, María José Martínez, and Francisco J. Marco Castillo, 'Occultation of Planets by the Moon in European Narrative Medieval Sources', *Journal for the History of Astronomy* 50:2 (2019), 192–220.

Valleriani, Matteo, ed., *De sphaera of Johannes de Sacrobosco in the Early Modern Period: The Authors of the Commentaries* (Cham: Springer Nature, 2020).

Varghese, Ritu, 'Mirabai in Popular Imagination: Reading Bhakti Canon in Contemporary Context', *Artha Journal of Social Sciences* 19:2 (2020), 67–81.

Varghese, Ritu, 'Mirabai in Public Spheres', *Women's History Review* 32:5 (2023), 611–31.

Verini, Alexandra, 'Women's Mystical Friendships: Margery Kempe and Mirabai', in *Women's Literary Cultures in the Global Middle Ages: Speaking Internationally*, ed. Kathryn Loveridge, Liz Herbert McAvoy, Sue Niebrzydowski, and Vicki Kay Price (Cambridge: D.S. Brewer, 2023), pp. 43–59.

Wada, Yoko, ed., *A Companion to Ancrene Wisse* (Cambridge: D.S. Brewer, 2003).

Wallis, Faith, *Medieval Medicine: A Reader* (Toronto: University of Toronto Press, 2010).

Wang, Eugene Y., 'Mirror, Moon, and Memory in Eighth-Century China: From Dragon Pond to Lunar Palace', *Cleveland Studies in the History of Art* 9 (2005), 42–67.

Warbrick, Isaac Rereata Makiha, Deborah Heke, Daniel Hikuroa, Shaun Awatere, and Valance Smith, 'Te Maramataka: An Indigenous System of Attuning with the Environment, and Its Role in Modern Health and Well-Being', *International Journal of Environmental Research and Public Health* 20:3 (2023), 1–12.

Warren, Ann. K., *Anchorites and Their Patrons in Medieval England* (Berkeley: University of California Press, 1985).

Watson, Nicholas, '"With the Heat of the Hungry Heart": Empowerment and *Ancrene Wisse*', in *Gendering the Master Narrative: Women and Power in the Middle Ages*, ed. Mary C. Erler and Maryanne Kowaleski (Ithaca, NY: Cornell University Press, 2003), pp. 52–70.

Weever, Jacqueline de, 'Chaucer's Moon: Cinthia, Diana, Latona, Lucina, Proserpina', *Names* 34:2 (1986), 154–74.

White, David Gordon, *The Alchemical Body: Siddha Traditions in Medieval India* (Chicago, IL: University of Chicago Press, 2012).

Wilcox, Andrew, 'The Dual Mystical Concepts of Fana' and Baqa' in Early Sufism', *British Journal of Middle Eastern Studies* 38:1 (2011), 95–118.

Wilcox, Jonathan, '"Tell Me What I Am": The Old English Riddles', in *Readings in Medieval Texts: Interpreting Old and Middle English Literature*, ed. David Johnson and Elaine Treharne (Oxford: Oxford University Press, 2005), pp. 46–59.

Williams, Edgar, *Moon: Nature and Culture* (London: Reaktion Books, 2014).

Williams, Madi, *Polynesia, 900–1600* (Leeds: Arc Humanities Press, 2021).

Williams, Mark, *Fiery Shapes: Celestial Portents and Astrology in Ireland and Wales, 700–1700* (Oxford: Oxford University Press, 2010).

Windeatt, Barry, *Oxford Guides to Chaucer: Troilus and Criseyde* (Oxford: Oxford University Press, 2005).

Wood, Chauncy, *Chaucer and the Country of the Stars: Poetic Uses of Astrological Imagery* (Princeton, NJ: Princeton University Press, 1970; repr. 2015).

Wren, James A., 'Salty Seaweed, Absent Women, and Song: Authorizing the Female as Poet in the *Izayoi nikki*', *Criticism* 39:2 (1997), 185–204.

Yamomoto, Dorothy, *The Boundaries of the Human in Medieval English Literature* (Oxford: Oxford University Press, 2000).

Ye, Shuxian, *A Mythological Approach to Exploring the Origins of Chinese Civilization* (Singapore: Springer, 2002).

Yoeli-Tlalim, Ronit, 'Re-visiting "Galen in Tibet"', *Medical History* 56:3 (2012), 355–65.

• • •
PLATES

1. Scholars studying the moon and the sun (England, twelfth century): Oxford, Bodleian Library, MS Bodley 614, fol. 2r; codex; parchment; 15.24 × 10.8 cm. Digital Bodleian.
2. 'Scholar Gazing at the Moon' (China, fifteenth–sixteenth century), unknown artist in the tradition of Ma Yuan: ink and colour on silk; overall dimensions 297 × 130.1 cm. Seattle Art Museum, Eugene Fuller Memorial Collection. Accession number 36.12. Photographer: Susan Dirk.
3. Bowl showing the 'planets', including the moon, surrounding the sun (central or northern Iran, late twelfth/early thirteenth century): ceramic; stonepaste; polychrome inglaze and overglaze painted and gilded on opaque monochrome glaze (mina'i); 9.5 × 18.7 cm. Metropolitan Museum of Art, New York. Purchase, Rogers Fund, and Gift of The Schiff Foundation, 1957. Object number 57.36.4.
4. Fan showing the Chinese moon goddess, Chang'e (China, 1350–1400): ink and colours on silk; 25.5 × 26.1 cm. Art Institute of Chicago, Samuel M. Nickerson Collection. Reference number 1947.534.
5. *The Frenzy of Orlando*: St John and Astolfo travel to the moon (France, c. 1878): black-and-white engraving by Gustave Doré (1832–1883). Bibliothèque nationale de France, Paris. GRANGER – Historical Picture Archive / Alamy.
6. Illustration of *The Tale of the Bamboo Cutter*, showing the baby moon-princess cared for by her adoptive earthly parents (Japan, late seventeenth century): hand-illustrated set of three volumes; ink, colour, gold, and silver on paper; 23.2 × 16.7 cm. Metropolitan Museum of Art, New York, Rogers Fund 1921. Object number 21.174.1a-c.

7. The Angel Israfil holds a full moon (sixteenth century): Zakariyyā al-Qazwīnī's/Qazvini's *The Wonders of Creatures and the Marvels of Existence*: ink and opaque watercolours on paper; 20 × 29.9 cm. Photograph © Museum of Fine Arts, Boston. Museum purchase with funds from the Francis Bartlett Donation of 1912 and by contribution. 14.599a–b (recto side).

8. Descent from the Cross showing the moon and the sun in a medieval psalter (Flanders, thirteenth century): Oxford, Bodleian Library, MS Douce 49, fol. 123v; codex; parchment; 136 × 93 mm. Digital Bodleian.

9. Wall painting depicting the Crucifixion; Christ is between Mary and John the Evangelist, with the sun and the moon above (fourteenth century, restored nineteenth century): east wall of the People's Chapel in Dorchester Abbey in Dorchester-on-Thames, Oxfordshire. © Michael Garlick (cc-by-sa/2.0) geograph.org.uk/p/4969876 Dorchester Abbey: Crucifixion wall painting in the People's Chapel, taken Friday, 27 May, 2016.

10. A 'zodiac man', showing which star sign impacts which part of the body (England, *c.* 1424): Oxford, Bodleian Library, MS Ashmole 370, fol. 27v; codex; parchment; 19.1cm × 24.1 cm. Digital Bodleian.

11. Francisco de Zurbarán (1598–1664), *Immaculate Conception* (Spain, early 1660s): oil on canvas, 166 × 108 cm. National Gallery of Ireland, Dublin. National Gallery of Ireland Collection NGI.273.

12. After Luca della Robbia (*c.* 1399–1482), *The Virgin and Child on a Crescent Moon* (Tuscany, mid-fifteenth century): sculpture; polychromed cartapesta; relief, 32 × 19.7 cm. Ashmolean Museum, Oxford. Asset ID: 4590. CMS Object ID: 351406. Accession Number: WA1941.12. © Ashmolean Museum.

13. Footed bowl (*tazza*) with eagle emblem, inscribed with *naskh* script speaking of the moon (Syria, thirteenth century): glass; dip-moulded; blown; enamelled; gilded; 18.3 × 20.3 × 12.7 cm. Metropolitan Museum of Art, New York, Edward C. Moore Collection, Bequest of Edward C. Moore, 1891. Object number 91.1.1538.

14. Illustration of Layla and Majnun falling in love at school (Iran, 1529): Walters manuscript W.622, folio 123a; paper; 16.5 cm × 27 cm. The Walters Art Museum, Baltimore.

15. The Land of the Sun and the Land of the Moon (England, twelfth century): Oxford, Bodleian Library, Bodley MS 614, fol. 42r; codex; parchment; 15.24 × 10.8 cm. Digital Bodleian.

16. Painting in the parecclesion of the Kariye Camii, detail of angel rolling up the scroll of heaven with the moon, sun, and stars (Istanbul, *c.* 1320–1): fresco; diameter of unfurled scroll 86 m; width of scroll in hands of angel 75 m. akg-images / Album / Prisma: AKG1919717.

INDEX

Page numbers in italic text indicate an entry in the Appendix.

INDEX

Xuanzong, Emperor, 35

Yamomoto, Dorothy, 118
Yoeli-Tlalim, Ronit, 101
Yuan dynasty, 6
Yun Seon-do 164

Zacut, Abraham, 113–14
zajal, 147
Zakariyyā al-Qazwīnī *see* Qazvini
Zodiac Man, 89–91
Zurbarán, Francisco de, 132